An Introduction

An Introduction to Business and Industry

John Old and Tony Shafto

PITMAN PUBLISHING
128 Long Acre, London WC2E 9AN

A Division of Longman Group UK Limited

© John Old and Tony Shafto, 1987

First published in Great Britain 1987
Reprinted 1989

British Library Cataloguing in Publication Data
Shafto, T. A. C.
  An introduction to business & industry.
  1. Business enterprises
  I. Title   II. Old, John
  338.7'024658   HD2731

ISBN 0–273–02281–4

Printed and bound in Singapore

Contents

Preface   vii

Acknowledgements   viii

1   The business of production   1

What business is about · some basics of production · the
organisation of business · some business decisions

2   Business in private ownership   16

Non-corporate organisations · companies · companies in practice ·
the growth of companies · other business structures

3   The non-profit-seeking societies and public ownership   35

The Co-operative Movement · the building societies · worker co-
operatives · the nationalised industries · government services ·
interdependence of the private and public sectors

4   The business environment   53

Government influence on business · business in the world
economy · the International Monetary Fund · social attitudes to
business

5   The production process   73

Business functions · production systems · business organisations

6   Marketing and distribution   95

Assessing the market · promoting sales · analysing the market ·
distribution · exporting

7   The firm and the customer   114

The need for consumer protection · consumer protection laws ·
consumer credit · the institutions of consumer protection · the
business firm and the consumer

8 The firm and its suppliers 132

The purchasing function · purchasing organisation and procedures · stock control · modern technology and purchasing

9 Finance and the firm 148

The need for and sources of short-term finance · the need for and sources of long-term and permanent capital · the capital market · the finance of overseas trade

10 The costs of production 168

Types of cost · falling and rising costs · cost and price · further aspects of costs

11 People at work I 184

The employment contract · payment for work · training for work

12 People at work II 201

Trade unions · employer organisations · the management of people · case study

13 Management and integration 225

Managing people · the personnel side of the modern firm · structure and management of the firm · more about efficiency and objectives

14 Business communications 237

The importance of communications · communications in practice · methods of communication · barriers to communication

15 Statistical interpretation and presentation 265

Handling numbers · presenting data visually · misleading and deceptive presentation · presenting and using accounts · calculating trends

16 Information processing and technology 293

Business records · electronic publishing · electronic shopping

17 Business in a changing world 304

Facing the inevitability of change · types of change · the electronic revolution · changing technology and the structure of business 317

Role playing 317

Comprehensive exercises 323

Index 333

Preface

The teaching of Business Studies in schools and colleges of further education has been developing steadily for a number of years but the subject has sometimes been distorted by the influence of the long Commerce and Accounting traditions to the neglect of other important managerial disciplines such as purchasing, marketing and management communications. Teachers have also been hampered by the lack of a single comprehensive textbook to cover the many aspects of the subject.

We believe that this book will fill that gap and help the further development of the subject.

We have assumed that the reader is coming to the study of business with no previous knowledge and while parallel study of related subjects such as accounting and economics will always be helpful we have also assumed no knowledge of these.

Our approach has been essentially practical. We have constantly used practical examples and from the first few pages we have encouraged the student to 'think like a business person' and to learn how to solve real business problems. We make no apologies for our underlying assumption that the purpose of the business organisation is to produce goods and services that people want and are prepared to pay for so that the owners can make profits and the workers pursue satisfying and rewarding careers.

The book is in four main parts. It starts by outlining the nature of business and production, the structure of production organisations and the environment in which they operate. It then goes on to examine the business processes of production, marketing, customer relations and purchasing. In the third part we examine the essential business resources of finance and people. At the end of this part there is a case study based on our own experiences to emphasise how all these various strands are integrated in the actual problems faced by business management. The final part lays further stress on this integration and on the skills of communication, statistical interpretation and information technology which are of enormous importance to business in a changing world.

Within each chapter there are Rapid Review questions and sugges-

tions for project type work are given at the end of chapters. Relevant
questions from actual examination papers are given after Chapters
4, 8, and 12 and there are many further questions of all kinds at the
end of the book. There are also a number of role playing exercises.
Most of these have been tested in the classroom. It is our hope that
this book will help still further to close the narrowing gap between
the classroom and the workplace and to assist more and more young
people to accept with confidence the challenge of business life in today's
rapidly changing world.

Acknowledgements

The authors wish to express their grateful thanks to the following organisations for suppling information and giving permission to reproduce
material: British Telecom, Canon (UK) Ltd, the Coventry Co-operative
Society and the Co-operative Union Ltd, the Forward Trust Group
HMSO, ICFC Birmingham, IBM Birmingham, the Office of Fair Trading, and Unilever PLC.

We are grateful to the Associated Examining Board for permission
to reproduce questions from past examination papers.

We also wish to thank Desmond Evans, author of *People and Communication* (Pitman Publishing) for permission to use a number of his
useful diagrams.

We are especially indebted to Steve Bowyer, Head of Business Studies
at the Aldridge Comprehensive School, Walsall, for allowing us to test
the book with his students during its preparation. His constructive
comments and willingness to use the material in its 'raw' state were
a great help.

1 The business of production

What business is about

Producing for a market

Reduced to basics, all business is about producing something that some-body else wants and is prepared to pay for. In a modern, developed and complex country like Britain, people may work in an enormous range of occupations. Some work with their hands, some mind machines, some drive vehicles. Some process information, some super-vise the work of others in large organisations. Some work in firms owned by other people and others work for government organisations.

What all of these occupations have in common is that people are making a living by doing work and producing things that other people are prepared to pay for. When pop singers become 'overnight sensa-tions', what has happened is that people are now prepared to pay large amounts of money to hear them perform. Not much, if anything, has changed in terms of what they do or how they do it. The important change has been in the **market** for their singing.

Similarly there is little point, at least in business terms, in putting lots of effort, time, and money into doing or making something that nobody wants.

So every business has to **serve a market** and every job involves doing something that is valuable to other people. Many fortunes have been made from a simple idea that has met a widely felt need. The invention of the 'cat's eye' for marking roads is an example.

Using technology

Of course there is little point in knowing what people would like if there is no way of making it. For centuries people have tried in vain to invent perpetual motion machines, which would keep running with-out fuel. Business, however, does often succeed by finding new or improved ways of making existing products or of meeting a particular need. For example, the need to have a simple and rapid aid to calculation has been met at different times by the abacus log, tables, the slide rule, the mechanical calculating machine and now by the electronic pocket calculator.

Successful business, then, involves **satisfying a market**. It also involves the efficient use of whatever resources in the form of materials and knowledge are available. The ability to meet a need is as important as recognising that need. It is not enough to know what people want. You have to be able to make or do something to satisfy that want.

In the same way it is not always obvious how to use new technology. In the 1960s there were several competing views about the airlines of the future: whether, for example, to carry approximately the same number of people but at much higher speeds – in the Concorde – or to carry many more people at roughly the same speed as previously, in Jumbo jets. Today there is little doubt which choice was commercially correct.

This book looks at both of these aspects of business. We look at the various ways production and productive resources are organised but we must never lose sight of the fact that a business will not be successful, however technically efficient it may be, if it fails to satisfy the wants of the market.

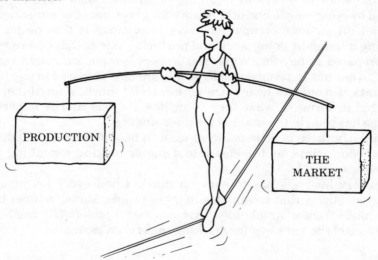

Fig 1.1 Business is a sort of balancing act between the market and production

Rapid review

State two basic requirements for a successful business.

Some basics of production

From what we have already said it should be clear that **production** is not just about 'making things'. There is an old joke which looks at the total population, subtracts all those unemployed or too old or too young to work, then subtracts all those not physically working with their hands and goes on in similar vein until concluding that there are only two people working – 'and I'm sick of doing your share!' Of course this is not serious but one assumption that is made here, and which is a very common fallacy, is that the only really productive work involves people making things. A famous commentator once remarked that a certain part of America was full of people doing 'unproductive' things such as making films and television programmes. But without these people who would want to buy the things, the television sets, for example, that are made by other people?

Similarly, in a car manufacturing company only a fraction of the workforce physically 'make' cars. With the increasing application of robotics this fraction may well fall further, perhaps even to zero. The work of the car makers, however, would be useless without the work of others such as the designers, production engineers, salespeople, transport drivers and so on.

Production for the whole economy

Production, therefore, involves both making things and providing services. In fact, in today's economy the provision of services is becoming more and more important.

It is customary to distinguish between primary, secondary and tertiary production.

Primary activities involve extracting natural resources from the environment, e.g. farming, mining, fishing, forestry and drilling for oil.

Secondary activities involve the manufacture, processing and assembly of physical goods, e.g. car production and oil refining.

Tertiary activities involve the provision of services either to members of the public, e.g. tourism or the health services, or to other industries, e.g. transport, banking and insurance.

As we have seen, there appears to be a long-term trend towards the production of services rather than goods. One reason for this may be that, as incomes have risen over time, people have wanted to buy more services rather than goods. At the same time improved technology has made it possible to produce the same amount of goods or more goods for a smaller expenditure of effort and resources. This can be seen in industries as apparently different as farming and computers.

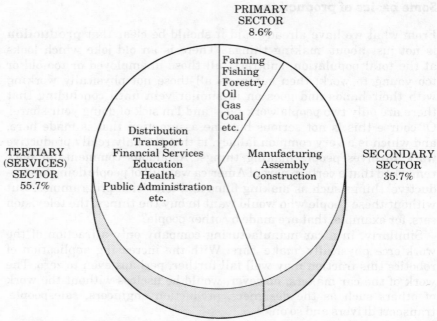

Fig 1.2   Services accounted for more than half of all economic activity in Britain in 1984

Specialisation

From what we have just seen it is clear that one feature of modern business is **specialisation.** Different firms pursue different activities, make different goods and provide different services. Within firms there are departments specialising in different activities, and people specialising in different skills.

Many of the advantages of specialisation are the result of the **division of labour** whereby total production is divided amongst a number of workers, who each concentrate on a limited number of tasks. This allows efficiency to be improved and production to be increased in a number of different ways.

1   People can use their skills to the full. Rather than waste their time on things that others can do better they can concentrate all their time and effort where these can be most productive.
2   People learn to do things better if they can practise them over a period of time. Even if they have no skills to begin with they can acquire them through specialisation.

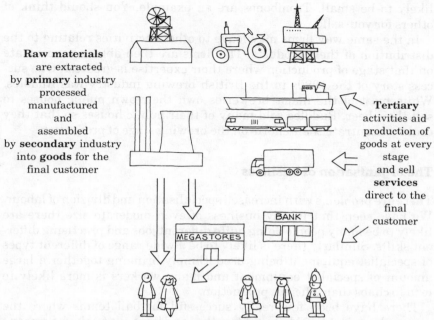

Raw materials
are extracted
by **primary** industry
processed
manufactured
and
assembled
by **secondary** industry
into **goods** for the
final customer

Tertiary
activities aid
production of
goods at every
stage
and sell
services
direct to the
final
customer

Fig 1.3   In a modern economy, the complex stages of production support one another, and all serve the final customer

Even where there is no question of exploiting or acquiring skills the division of labour can get work done more efficiently. This can be seen very clearly when a bucket chain is formed to fight a fire. No one in the chain is using any special skill, nor is there time to develop skills, but this is a much more efficient way to fight a fire than to leave it to uncoordinated individual efforts. The advantages of this sort of organisation are used in the assembly line of a modern factory.

The division of labour also operates between firms. Many large firms still find it to their advantage to buy goods and services from specialist suppliers rather than try to do everything themselves. For example, General Motors, the world's largest motor manufacturer, has made a point of buying in many, in some cases over 60 per cent, of the components for its cars.

Many of the specialist suppliers to large firms are **small firms**. One of the principal reasons for the survival and success of small firms has been the demand for specialised goods and services from large organisations. The total demand for some products may be fairly small so that the firms that specialise in producing them will also be small. There are also some goods and services which are sold to the general public where demand is rather limited. The firms producing these are likely to be small. Trombones are an example. You should think of others for yourself.

In the same way firms may leave to others activities relating to the distribution of their products. The firms are then able to concentrate on that stage of production where their expertise is greatest. One success story of the 1980s in the British brewing industry was Ruddles. While most of the major breweries own their own public houses to sell their beer, Ruddles sold many of their public houses so that they could concentrate their efforts on the brewing stage of production.

The organisation of business

There are problems with increased specialisation and division of labour. We have seen that in any business of even moderate size there are likely to be many people doing quite different jobs and practising different skills. Similarly there is likely to be a wide range of different types of specialist equipment being used. Simply bringing together a large amount of specialist equipment and many workers is more likely to lead to chaos than efficient production.

There have been few really successful football teams where the players have just been brought together and 'sent out to play'. Someone must pick the team, decide who plays where and organise tactics. Similarly, someone in a business enterprise has to ensure that what each specialist worker, department and piece of equipment is doing fits in with what is being done by everybody else. This is the work of that part of the business which is called, in general terms, **management**. Management is as essential to the success of the business, and as productive, as any other type of work.

The work of management

Planning what is to be produced, how it is to be produced, how marketed and so on.

Forecasting business trends, including such things as future requirements of customers and price movements.

Co-ordinating the different parts, activities and members of the business for maximum efficiency.

Controlling the business – which includes having a clear plan and targets, checking actual performance against these and taking any necessary corrective action.

Motivating the people in the business because success can only be achieved by the people involved and a well motivated workforce performs more effectively.

This list gives a brief summary of the activities of every successful business person whether or not he or she has ever sat down and thought about them in this way. It is interesting that the reaction of many successful managers to this list is that it is 'stating the obvious', while the less successful often allege that this is all very well in theory but in practice they must concentrate on some of these aspects and leave the rest to others.

Some problems of size

One noticeable feature of the British economy has been the growth of large firms. Some of the reasons for this will become clearer later in this book when, for example, we explain the attraction of **economies of scale**, which mean that things can be produced at lower cost in large numbers. But the greater the number of people and activities organised in one firm the greater the need for good management.

For example, assembly lines may lead to cheaper and faster production but they are vulnerable to stoppages and breakdowns. If one worker stops, all must stop. This kind of stoppage is more likely if working on an assembly line leads to boredom and lack of motivation, so good management is essential.

Similarly, having a large number of specialists and specialised departments in a firm can bring a number of benefits. At the same time, the need for skilful co-ordination is increased if disruption and breakdowns are to be avoided.

Problems of small firms

A small firm is likely to suffer from a number of disadvantages. These can be summarised as:

1   The inability to benefit from economies of scale, i.e. those cost savings which are the direct result of operating on a large scale. These are explained more fully in a later chapter.

2   The inability to employ people with very specialist skills, unless the market for these skills is itself very small. The lack of specialist managers in such areas as finance and marketing is often a serious disadvantage for the small firm which may produce a good product but lack the skills to obtain the money needed to produce it at low cost or to sell it in large quantities. Of course if the firm *is* able to obtain these skills it is likely to grow large!

3   It can be prone to accident or misfortune. The small firm may be dependent on very few people and if these fall ill or suffer an accident then the firm can quickly collapse.

4   The firm is often tied to a particular locality or activity and cannot always adapt easily to change. An extreme example is a small shop which loses trade because of the imposition of some traffic regulation that makes it less convenient for passing customers. A large retail chain is constantly relocating its stores as local conditions change.

The survival of the small firm

It would be wrong, however, to take too gloomy a view of the future of small scale enterprise. Indeed, small firms now receive considerable government help and encouragement. The Government may guarantee bank loans under certain conditions, so banks can lend in the knowledge that the loan will be repaid, if necessary, from taxpayers' money. People who risk their money to assist new business enterprise may receive tax concessions under the Business Expansion Scheme.

In many activities, especially those depending on local, personal service, and on people rather than machines, there are no very great economies of scale. In some, new forms of co-operative enterprise have developed to take advantage of some marketing benefits of size while retaining the advantages of independent, local enterprise. The retail trade, for example, has developed the **voluntary chain** (e.g. Spar and Mace) where traders concentrate their buying from an agreed wholesale member, enjoy reduced administrative costs and have a national brand image. Retailing has also seen an extension of **franchising** where small independent traders operate under the guidance and limited control of a large organisation.

Small firms are sometimes more flexible in adapting to change and the economic 'bad times'. The owner of the small firm has to find something to make or sell to survive because the business is the only source of income. In similar conditions a branch of a large company would simply be closed.

Moreover there will always be small firms because there are always people of independent minds who much prefer to work for themselves rather than for a large organisation.

Rapid review

1   What is involved in modern production in addition to actually 'making things'?
2   How does specialisation improve efficiency and increase production?
3   How has specialisation assisted many small firms to survive?
4   State five aspects of the 'work of management'.
5   Why is good management essential for a large organisation?
6   State the possible disadvantages likely to be suffered by a small firm.

7 **State two ways in which small firms may survive in spite of the problems of small scale operation.**

Some business decisions

Business objectives

For any business to flourish there needs to be an idea of what it is trying to achieve. If you do not know where you want to go you are unlikely to arrive.

Profits

For many businesses it may seem clear that the object is to 'make profits' or 'to be profitable'. Certainly this must be true to some extent of any business. We have to remember that business involves using resources and technology to try to satisfy the needs and wants of customers. If we compare:

VALUE OF OUTPUT with VALUE OF RESOURCES USED

then the value of output will be greater than, equal to or less than the value of resources used. If we put a monetary value on these amounts and ignore the possibility that they exactly balance then the business will be either making a profit, or using up more value than it is producing, i.e. suffering a loss. This is a waste of resources and likely to lead to eventual business failure.

Other business objectives

Profit, however, is not the only business objective, or even the main one. Making profits may be an indication of efficiency, but equally it may not. A firm holding an exclusive patent might have a 'licence to print money' and its profits could not be used to compare its efficiency with that of other firms faced with intense competition.

It is all very well to have 'profit' as an objective but this does not necessarily give a clear idea of what the firm should be doing on either a long- or short-term basis. Many people who run businesses may have in mind that as long as the firm makes some satisfactory level of profit, it is more important to pursue other objectives such as making good quality products or achieving business expansion.

Among the other objectives that have been suggested as being important to business organisations and the people who run them, are:

Survival of the firm in the long run even if this means sacrificing some lucrative but risky short-term opportunities

Growth of the firm in terms of the number of people employed, the number of customers served, or the range of goods and services produced

Higher sales or **increased share** and domination of the market. This may involve taking over other firms.

Public sector objectives

The British economy is often described as a **mixed economy** because it is a mixture of the **private sector**, in which production is organised by people who either work for themselves or who combine together for their own profit, and of the **public sector**, that part of the economy directly controlled by the Government.

Figure 1.4 gives some idea of the importance of this public sector. In the United Kingdom in 1984 it accounted for nearly a quarter of total expenditure and provided employment for around 28 per cent of the workforce. The sector includes services ranging from the police and the health service to railways and electricity generation. It is usually thought that making profits is not the only objective for these

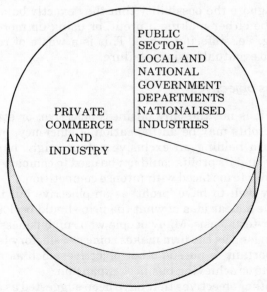

Fig 1.4   Private and public sector shares in the British economy

activities. Other important objectives might include fairness and equality of treatment for all, maintaining and improving the general standard of living and so on.

The trouble with objectives like these is that, while it is generally agreed that they are desirable, it is often difficult to make them meaningful in practice. What, for example, does 'equality of treatment' really mean?

For this reason public sector organisations are often set more concrete targets such as maintaining a particular level of output while remaining inside some definite monetary budget. This is easiest in the **nationalised industries** such as coal mining and gas supply, where output and input can be readily measured. It is much more difficult for services such as the fire brigades or schools.

Choices in production

Decisions need to be taken about how to organise production. There is rarely only one way to make something or to provide a service. You may be aware of the difference between **intensive** and **extensive** farming. Food can be produced intensively from a small amount of land, using high concentrations of labour, machinery, fertilisers and so on, or, extensively, from a larger tract of land, using fewer of the other resources.

The assembly industry in West Africa employs large numbers of people working with fairly simple tools. In Europe or Japan the same product is likely to be produced using relatively few workers but much machinery. The same technology is available to the industries in all these areas but the methods employed are different. Why?

The reason lies in the **relative cost** of labour, machinery and land. If land is scarce it is likely to be expensive in relation to labour and machinery. It makes sense to spend more on labour or machinery and economise on land. Similarly, if labour commands comparatively high wages it can best be put to use in combination with a lot of machinery. On the other hand, if labour of the same quality is cheaper then it makes sense to economise on machines and employ more workers.

Land, labour and **capital** (capital meaning plant, machinery, buildings and so on) are sometimes referred to as the **factors of production**. Today this is an arbitrary term (see the note at the end of this chapter) and it gives rise to some rather academic arguments such as 'should management be seen as a special feature of labour or as a separate factor of production?'. However, it is useful to think in terms of separate factors of production because it reminds you that there is more than one way to do something. One factor can always be substituted for another. Whether or not this is efficient is not just a matter of technology but also of relative costs.

The location decision

This sort of thinking also applies to the question of where to locate the business or its different parts. For example, it may be cheaper to produce goods in one part of the country, while the people most likely to buy them may live in another. It is then necessary to compare the cost savings achieved by location in the cheaper production area with the additional costs of transporting the goods to the customer.

It is sometimes suggested that certain industries are 'tied' to certain areas because the goods could not possibly be produced elsewhere. This is not strictly true. A change in technology or of prices could make it worthwhile to move to another location. For example, geologists had been aware of the likely presence of deep sea oil deposits for many years before improved technology and higher oil prices made development of these oil fields profitable.

As technology and the demands of customers have changed, so, too, has the pattern of industrial location. Several hundred years ago production and population were concentrated in the South and West of England. The Industrial Revolution of the last century, with its dependence on deposits of coal and iron, brought a shift to the North. In this century, the decline of older manufacturing industries and the reduced dependence on coal and home-produced iron have helped to cause a return towards the South.

Individual businesses may feel these effects as well. Better communications, including improved roads and telecommunications, may make them question whether they should build new production facilities in areas where there is more space or where land costs are lower.

Many activities rely for their success on the presence of relatively few highly skilled people. If these people are found in a particular locality or if they prefer to live in a particular region these preferences can be a major influence on location. We can take examples from old and new industries. The production of high quality pottery depends on some very skilled artists and designers. For historical reasons these tend to be found in North Staffordshire which still remains the home of the leading pottery manufacturers. The computer industry depends on some extremely skilled people who, in England, prefer to work in the southern half of the country, close to a major university where they can maintain contact with the leaders in their particular fields of knowledge. The new 'knowledge-based' industries are thus to be found in the Thames Valley and in the Cambridge Science Park area.

Once an industry is established in a particular area it becomes a source of activity for a range of other industries and services such as building, retailing, banking, insurance and the growing leisure industry. If the central or core industry then declines these other satellite activities, and eventually the whole area, face decline. A startling illustration of the importance of a dominant firm in an area was seen in 1971 when fear that Rolls Royce was going to collapse caused people to queue at the offices of the Derby Building Society to withdraw their money. There was a local rumour that the building society would not survive the large-scale selling of houses as Rolls Royce workers moved away. South Wales has seen the drastic effect of the decline of coal mining in the area.

Note on factors of production

The distinction between land, labour and capital was made in the 18th century and reflected what were then thought to be the three great classes of European society: the landowners, labourers and capitalists. Today, if we were drawing up a list of 'factors of production', i.e. the ingredients essential for production to take place, we would probably use a different set of categories.

If you have studied any commerce or economics you may have read textbooks that include **enterprise** or **organisation** as a fourth factor of production on the basis that someone has to combine land, labour and capital, and the reward for those who do so successfully is profit. In fact the inclusion of enterprise as a separate factor does raise a number of difficulties and, at this stage of study, we prefer to omit it and concentrate instead on the various aspects of management which contribute to successful business organisation.

Rapid review

1   What is profit?
2   State three possible business objectives other than profit.
3   What is meant by the term a 'mixed economy'?
4   State a possible objective for a major nationalised industry.
5   What is the difference between 'intensive' and 'extensive' farming?
6   What is the term to describe land, labour and capital usually used in production?
7   State two influences on the location of modern industry.

Exercises

1   Make a short list of innovations or improvements to existing products that you would like to see in the future. Do this *now* before reading on.

When you have made your list ask yourself:
To what extent is my list influenced by what is technically feasible rather than by what I would really like to see? For example, if you have mentioned safety devices on cars have you thought about a car programmed to avoid accidents altogether? This, in fact, may already be a technical, if not a commercial, possibility.

Now go through your list and see if it can be revised if you ignore the technical limitations of the present time.

2   Draw up a similar list of new ways that the present level of technology could be used. For example, a 'sun ray lamp' that could be used for horticulture, or a fridge and a cooker combined.

As you draw up this list try not to think of what people might want but concentrate on what might be feasible.

You may find that one item on your first list matches one from the second. If it does, you could be on your way to making a fortune! However, even if you do not have a match you are engaged in the sort of thinking that countless successful business people have experienced, consciously or unconsciously. They have worked out new ways of satisfying people's wants and new ways of using the resources available to them.

3   Make a list of four primary activities, five secondary and five tertiary. Do this now.

After you have made your list, for each primary activity try to think of one secondary and one tertiary activity without which it would be difficult or impossible to operate.

For example, modern dairy farming (primary) requires milking machinery (secondary) and the inspection and testing of cattle as well as the transport and marketing of milk (tertiary).

Do the same with your secondary and tertiary activities.

You should now see how each stage of production is dependent on other stages. No industry is self-sufficient. In a modern economy each activity is very dependent upon a range of other activities.

4   Choose an apparently straightforward type of business, a retail grocery business, for example, and list the different kinds of work activity it involves.

Make sure that you have included the 'behind the scenes activities' such as secretarial work and wage calculation.

To what extent is it feasible to have all these different jobs carried out by different people? You should be able to see how greater size enables greater division of labour and specialisation, and smallness of size means that people must 'double up' on the jobs they do.

5   What do you think are the drawbacks of having a very large organisation?

6   Some activities such as window cleaning are often literally 'one-person businesses'. Identify one similar type of business. What do you think makes these activities specially suitable for smaller firms?

7   There are management tasks to be performed even in the 'one-person firms'. Try to identify those tasks which would fall under the headings given on page 6.
8   Many firms publish extracts from their annual reports in the national press. Use one or more of these reports to try to identify the company's objectives.
9   Very often the reports stress rising sales (favourably) or declining sales (unfavourably). Critically examine 'increased sales' as an objective. What are the benefits of increased sales and who receives the benefits – shareholders, managers, workers or customers? Are there any circumstances in which increased sales would not necessarily be in the interests of any or all of these groups?
10   Try writing out an objective, or list of objectives, for a public sector organisation (e.g. a school might have objectives related to examination passes).
   When you feel that your list is complete try to identify the advantages and drawbacks of each objective (e.g. an objective framed in terms of percentages of examination passes might encourage efficient teaching but also discourage teachers from entering students who might pass but could fail.)
11 *a* Why are the centres of many cities full of skyscraper blocks rather than low-rise buildings?
b Why have many bus companies switched to 'driver-only operation'? Why have road hauliers been keen to see an increase in the permitted size of juggernaut lorries?
c Do your answers to these questions have anything in common?

2 Business in private ownership

In Chapter 1 we have seen how the industrial system co-ordinates the valuable resources of the country to produce the vast range of goods and services used in a modern community. The actual business of production takes place in a number of different types of organisation, from small one-person stores and workshops to countrywide chains and giant manufacturing firms. In the United Kingdom around 70 per cent of these business organisations are owned in one form or another by private people or groups of people. These organisations together form what is known as the private sector of the economy. In this chapter we examine the legal framework within which they operate and the different ways in which they are owned and run.

1 Non-corporate organisations

Two types of non-corporate organisation are normally recognised: sole proprietorships, also known as sole traders, and partnerships. The non-corporate organisation exists only as long as its owner(s) agree to keep it in being; it is not legally distinct from the individuals who own it.

Sole proprietors

The legal framework

Many people have an ambition to run their own business and to 'be their own boss'. Some have acquired skills by working in someone else's business. Others may want to market what they think is a bright and profitable idea. For many a business grows out of a hobby, a part-time special interest which becomes a full-time occupation.

Imagine, for example, some people who collect old coins for a hobby. In the course of time their knowledge increases. They learn how to value coins, where to contact other collectors and so on. Sometimes they sell coins to other collectors and sometimes buy from them. At this stage coin collecting is still a part-time interest and is treated as such in the eyes of the law. The legal position is important. It affects the coin collectors' responsibility to pay tax on any gains they make from dealing and it also affects their responsibility towards the people they deal with. Individuals who occasionally buy and sell coins must not indulge in dishonest practices, nor deliberately misdescribe or tell lies about the coins, for example. However, they do not have as many legal responsibilities as a full-time self-employed dealer or trader who is liable to:

1 Register for Value Added Tax if total sales are above a limit set (and altered from time to time) by the law.
2 Pay income tax and National Insurance contributions on earnings.
3 Incur special legal obligations for care and accuracy in describing and selling stock. These responsibilities have been established by various Acts of Parliament including the Trades Descriptions Acts, the Sale of Goods Act 1979 (which brought together a great deal of earlier law) and the Supply of Goods and Services Act 1982. These and other laws are examined in Chapter 7. At this stage it is only necessary for you to realise that setting up a regular business involves responsibilities greater than those which apply to a person carrying on a hobby. Notice also that the customer has more protection from the law when buying from a business as opposed to dealing with a genuine private seller.

There need be no definite point at which the coin collectors actually decide that they are setting up a business. Rather there comes a point at which so much dealing is done that legally they become subject to the law as it relates to a business rather than that relating to a private individual. This can occur while the collector is still employed in another paid occupation. This simple form of business is known as a **sole proprietorship**.

Features of sole proprietorships

Sole proprietorships are the most numerous form of business in the United Kingdom, although, because they tend to be on a very small scale, they account for only a relatively small part of total business activity. A hundred small shops, for example, sell less than one large chain of shops owned by a single organisation. There are over half a million sole proprietorships paying Value Added Tax and probably half that number again whose total sales are below the legal minimum for VAT registration.

Sole proprietors can be found in primary industry as many farmers and fishermen still operate on this basis and in the secondary sector where there are small manufacturing, building and construction businesses. They are probably most abundant, however, in the tertiary sector of the economy. Here much of the work is performed by people rather than by machines. Personal services can often be offered at lower cost on a small scale, by small local organisations, than on a large scale. The conditions thus favour the small business whose success depends on the personal involvement and commitment of the owner and where enterprise and willingness to work hard without watching the clock count for more than the amount and value of machines owned. The continued growth of services of all kinds, including an increasingly important group of sports and leisure services can be expected to provide conditions favourable for the small scale business.

Advantages of sole proprietorship

It is the simplest form of business organisation. No or very few formalities are necessary when it is set up. It is subject only to the laws, such as those relating to consumer protection, payment of taxes and employment of workers, that apply to all businesses. In some activities, such as operating hire vehicles for carrying passengers, or practising law or medicine, the owner may have to have a licence or possess certain approved qualifications – but these also apply to all forms of organisation. Nevertheless this simplicity and ease of entry to the business world does bring some possible dangers.

Limitations of the sole proprietor

Sole proprietors depend for their success on their own abilities, their own effort and money (although money may be put into the business by family or friends). Even if they employ other people the sole proprietors have the final responsibility for making decisions. They are responsible for the financial commitments undertaken by their organisation.

This last point is very important. If the business fails the proprietor cannot simply shut up shop and renounce all debts and obligations such as the money owed to suppliers or the promises made to customers. In the eyes of the law there is no distinction between business and personal responsibilities. If the business-person or private individual, owes more than she or he can pay – taking account of all that they own – then they stand the risk of being made bankrupt. In this case they have **unlimited liability** for their own business debts. The business creditors (the people to whom the business owes money) could force the sole proprietor into personal bankruptcy, possibly losing his or her house and possessions.

Sole proprietorship

Owned by	one person
Run by	owner
Financed by	retained earnings and owner's personal borrowings
Limited liability	no
Legal regulation	general law relating to business operations

Partnerships

Instead of taking on the entire responsibility of running a business alone an individual might share this with another person and so form a partnership.

Features of partnerships

People can 'drift into' a partnership arrangement just as they can a sole proprietorship. A group of musicians might form a pop group for their own pleasure and to entertain friends. If they were good enough they could be asked to play at local dances and parties and start to earn money which they could share. At some stage, as with the coin collector, this activity could reach the stage where it would be considered in law to be a business partnership even if all the members continued with other paid occupations.

Partnerships, such as medical or legal practices or building firms, are often formed by two or more people with similar skills and abilities to share the workload. Often, however, people with different skills or resources may come together to combine their different contributions and so strengthen the organisation. For example one person might contribute a large share of the finance used to form the business but leave its management to another who had the necessary 'knowhow'. One who takes no active part in managing the enterprise, but who simply contributes money, is often known as a **sleeping partner**.

Partnerships are subject to the normal laws applying to all business ventures and to any special laws relating to particular activities. In addition they are governed by a body of partnership law which has been built up from a series of Acts of Parliament, starting with the Partnerships Act of 1890 and including various, more recent, Companies Acts, modified by decisions made in the higher courts of law.

The most important feature of partnership law that you should understand is that all partners, including 'sleeping' partners, unless protected under the provisions of the Limited Partnership Act (examined below) have to accept **unlimited personal liability** for the debts and obligations of the business.

This is important for creditors and others with a claim on the business. They can pursue a legal claim against the partner they think most likely to be rich enough to pay their claim and not the one whose error, dishonesty or lack of skill caused the claim. No matter what agreement the partners had made between themselves as to how business losses and profits should be shared and regardless of the amount of finance each has contributed or agreed to contribute to the firm, each one has this full personal liability. Entering a partnership is indeed a risk and no one should do so without realising the possible results. It is often desirable to seek advice from a lawyer and/or an accountant before doing so. A partner's liability, of course, applies only to business debts and not to the purely private actions of fellow partners.

In the interests of the partners and of the people with whom they deal, the law limits the number of people permitted to trade as a partnership in most activities to a maximum of 20. This limit does not apply to solicitors, accountants, members of a recognised stock exchange or to other groups specifically exempted by the Department of Trade and Industry.

Partnership agreements

It is not legally necessary but often desirable for the members to draw up a partnership agreement among themselves. This agreement would clarify certain matters likely to cause disputes such as:

1 Establishing that a relationship is that of a partnership and not of employer and employee. This can have important legal and taxation consequences.
2 Setting out what should happen to business assets, such as machinery and unsold stock, should the firm cease to function.
3 Establishing the length of time the partnership is expected to last or under what circumstances one partner could be removed by the others.
4 Clarifying how profits and losses should be shared. This agreement would not affect the rights of people outside the firm to sue any individual partner.

Limited partnerships

The only qualification to this right would occur when the partnership is limited under the provisions of the Limited Partnerships Act of 1907.

A limited partnership can be formed in which some partners invest money but agree not to take any active part in the business – if they do become involved in its management they lose their limited status. Limited partners can lose the money they have agreed to invest but no more. There must, however, be at least one general partner whose liability is unlimited and creditors may sue any of the general partners. This has not been found to be a very satisfactory form of business organisation and there are very few limited partnerships.

Partnerships in practice

After sole proprietorships, partnerships are among the most common forms of business in Britain, where there are over 300 000 partnerships. Many of these partnerships are run by members of the professions, such as architects, solicitors and accountants. Many others are found in a wide variety of business activities from service engineering to entertainment.

Limited partnership status can be useful when a partner wishes to withdraw or retire from active management in the business but does not wish to withdraw his or her capital. In general, however, the practical advantages of limited partnerships can be achieved more satisfactorily by setting up a limited company as explained later in this chapter.

Advantages of partnerships

As we have seen, setting up a partnership can be a fairly informal process: the legal restrictions are few. The participation of more people means that more skills and finance can be brought into the business and the benefits of division of labour can be exploited. Moreover, the wellbeing of the firm is not necessarily dependent on one person.

Even the unlimited liability provision can be useful in some activities because it may increase the confidence of those who deal with the organisation. For example, in many professions the rules of the professional association or the law itself may require the practitioners to accept unlimited liability. This is because it is felt that certain professional people, such as doctors, solicitors and accountants, should be seen to be committing their full resources to their clients and demonstrating that they themselves have the fullest confidence in the service they are providing.

Limitations of partnerships

Although a partnership can clearly be larger than a sole proprietorship there are still limits to its size, quite apart from the legal restriction on the maximum number of partners. Unlimited liability is a major factor in that:

1   It will deter some people from investing in the business.
2   Partners are assumed to be acting on behalf of the partnership in 'utmost good faith'. Among other things this means that they must declare to the other partners any benefits they are receiving from the partnership and they must not compete with it. In addition, the actions of any one of them will be binding on the others. All this requires a great deal of trust and this may not be forthcoming against a background of unlimited liability!

Partnerships

Owned by	usually 2–20 people
Run by	owners
Financed by	retained earnings and owners' personal borrowings
Limited liability	usually no
Legal regulation	general law relating to business operations, Partnership Act 1890 and Limited Partnership Act 1907

Rapid review

1   What are non-corporate organisations?
2   State three differences between the legal responsibilities of a private and a full-time trader.
3   State the main features and limitations of a sole proprietorship.
4   What is a partnership?
5   Does a sleeping partner always enjoy limited liability?
6   State 4 matters that you would expect to find mentioned in a partnership agreement.
7   State the main advantages and limitations of partnerships.

Companies

The legal framework of companies

Companies are the most important type of 'bodies corporate' to operate in the British business system. A **body corporate** is an organisation which has a legal identity quite separate from those of its members. This means, for example, that it can own property in its own right, employ people, including members, in its own right and sue and be sued for breach of contract.

Perhaps you belong to another type of body corporate – a society. If so, you know that the society has assets which belong to it and not to its members. The same applies to companies, even to a small one that may be chiefly owned and run by one person. Unlike the case of the sole proprietorship the law will make a distinction between the owner and the firm when this is a company. People have been convicted and imprisoned for, in effect, stealing money from companies of which they have virtually been the sole owners.

One effect of this distinction between owners and their companies is that these organisations may be registered as **limited liability companies**. Companies have their own debts and liabilities and the effect of limited liability is to separate the owners from these debts. The owners will either have paid some money into the company or given some finite financial guarantee to be called upon in the event of the company running into trouble – a point to which we return later in the chapter. They cannot be called upon to pay any further money to meet the company's debts and they certainly cannot be forced into personal bankruptcy like sole proprietors or partners. It may even be that the company might owe them money and, as creditors, they can sue the company. If injured while working for the company they may even have a legal claim to recover financial loss – a useful right when, in practice, the loss will be met by the company's insurance office.

Limited liability is a major privilege and like all privileges it can be abused. Some unscrupulous people have been known to start up companies, run them recklessly or dishonestly, liquidate them (one of the terms used to describe the termination of a company) with insufficient funds left to meet their debts and not too long afterwards start the whole process again. We return to this situation later in the chapter and we shall see that the Government is at present considering proposals to reform the law.

Whatever changes are made in the law it is certain that the formation and operation of companies must be subject to more regulation and more detailed laws than non-corporate organisations.

Registration

Companies have to be registered with the Registrar of Companies. Documents that must be submitted with the application for registration are described in Fig 2. 1. Registered companies must meet a number of legal obligations. For example, annual accounts must be submitted to the Registrar and anybody can see a copy of these accounts on payment of a small fee – in 1982 there were 1 800 000 such 'searches'. In addition the directors of companies have certain legal obligations. Directors are the people selected by the members to control and operate the company. If the directors neglect their duties and damage the company it can use its separate legal identity to sue them.

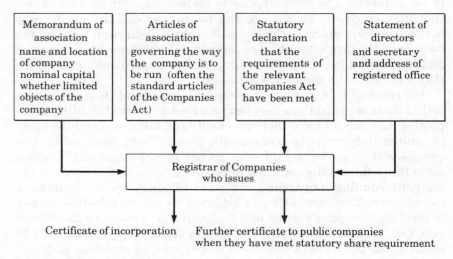

Fig 2.1   Setting up a company

The Department of Trade and Industry monitors the conduct of companies and company directors. In 1982 it conducted over 1000 prosecutions of companies and directors for offences which included not keeping proper accounts, non-submission of the annual returns required by company law and improper winding up (another form of termination) of companies.

Types of company

Public companies are those that may sell their shares and debentures (forms of loan described in Chapter 9) to the public. They must have a total financial capital authorised by the memorandum of association – the document which establishes the identity, basic structure and objectives of the company – of £50 000. The form of Memorandum which was prescribed by Regulations in 1984 is reproduced in Figs 2.2 and 2.3.

Note the clear statement in Fig 2.2 that the company is public. At least 25 per cent of the minimum authorised capital, i.e. £12 500 must

A PUBLIC COMPANY LIMITED BY SHARES
Memorandum of Association

1.   The company's name is Western Electronics Public Limited Company.

2.   The company is to be a public company.

3.   The company's registered office is to be situated in England and Wales.

4.   The company's objects are the manufacture and development of such descriptions of electronic equipment, instruments and appliances as the company may from time to time determine, and the doing of all such other things as are incidental or conducive to the attainment of that object.

5.   The liability of the members is limited.

6.   The company's share capital is £5 000 000 divided into 5 000 000 shares of £1 each.

We, the subscribers to this memorandum of association, wish to be formed into a company pursuant to this memorandum; and we agree to take the number of shares shown opposite our respective names.

Names and addresses of subscribers	Number of shares taken by each subscriber
1. James White, 12 Broadmead, Birmingham.	1
2. Patrick Smith, 145A Huntley House, London Wall, London EC2.	1
Total shares taken	2

Dated   19 .

Witness to the above signatures,
Anne Brown, 13 Hute Street, London WC2.

Fig. 2.2   Specimen Memorandum from Table F, The Companies (alteration of Table A etc.) Regulations 1984

be fully paid into the company by the members when it is first set up. The title of a public company must contain the words public limited company or the abbreviation PLC or, if it wishes, the equivalent in Welsh if its registered office is in Wales. Companies which do not meet the requirements of the 1980 Companies Act (later incorporated in the Companies Act 1985) for registration as public companies are private companies and it is a criminal offence to offer the shares or debentures of a private company for sale publicly. All companies must have at least two members (subscribers) but there is no longer any upper limit on numbers for private companies.

A PRIVATE COMPANY LIMITED BY SHARES
Memorandum of Association

1.   The company's name is The South Wales Motor Transport Company cyfyngedig.

2.   The company's registered office is to be situated in Wales.

3.   The company's objects are the carriage of passengers and goods in motor vehicles between such places as the company may from time to time determine and the doing of all such other things as are incidental or conducive to the attainment of that object.

4.   The liability of the members is limited.

5.   The company's share capital is £50 000 divided into 50 000 shares of £1 each.

We, the subscribers to this memorandum of association, wish to be formed into a company pursuant to this memorandum; and we agree to take the number of shares shown opposite our respective names.

Names and addresses of subscribers	Number of shares taken by each subscriber
1. Thomas Jones, 138 Mountfield Street, Tredegar.	1
2. Mary Evans, 19 Merthyr Road, Aberystwyth.	1
Total shares taken	2

Dated   19 .

Witness to the above signatures,
Jane Moore, Woodlands, Fieldside Road, Bryn Mawr.
Fig 2.3   Specimen Memorandum from Table B, The Companies (alteration of Table A etc.) Regulations 1984

Most companies will divide their financial capital or funds used to form the organisation, into shares. The £50 000, for instance, could be divided into 50 000 shares each of £1. People subscribing to the company by the purchase of shares are, therefore, normally known as shareholders. Shares are described more fully in Chapter 9.

In 1982 there were 5324 public companies in the United Kingdom and 807 817 private companies. Many private companies remain in formal existence even though they may not be actively trading so that, in practice, it is unlikely that there are more of these than sole proprietorships actually in business. The great majority of companies are limited liability companies but there are some unlimited companies whose shareholders do not have the privilege of limited liability. On the other hand these companies do not have to lodge copies of their accounts with the Registrar so that they can keep their affairs more private.

Although most companies are limited by share, with the shareholders risking only the money they have paid or agreed to pay for their shares, there are some that are limited by guarantee. A number of these are financial institutions such as banks, operating in the City of London. Members of companies limited in this way undertake to pay an agreed amount of money into the firm when and if required to do so. This type of company is appropriate where the organisation could incur large financial debts or liabilities but does not actually require much financial capital for its normal operations.

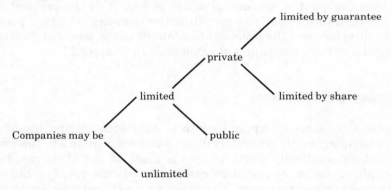

Fig 2.4

Note The public company must not be confused with the quite separate state owned and controlled public corporation examined in Chapter 3.

Companies in practice

We have already seen that companies are very numerous and they can vary enormously in size from very small family operations which are often sole proprietorships, to the giant manufacturing and multi-national groups producing a wide range of goods and services in many nations.

Limited company status is suited to any type of operation in which the owners wish to limit the amount of money they are putting at risk in a business enterprise. Small businesses may be converted from sole proprietorships to public companies with, perhaps a husband and wife as the two member-shareholders required by law. Family firms are often private companies with members of the family holding all or most of the shares. By forming a company or by buying an inactive company and starting it trading again, the owners of a business organisation can participate in the venture and share in its profits or losses without running the risk of personal ruin. The knowledge that they are protected by limited liability can mean that shareholders of a small business are freed from the feeling that they must take an active interest in it to protect themselves. This is all the more true for large public companies. It would be impossible for the thousands of shareholders in such a company to have and active voice in its management even if they so wished. Accordingly the shareholders elect directors to operate the company on their behalf. As each share normally carries the right to have one vote those members who have the largest number of shares, and thus the greatest amount of money at risk, have the greatest say in electing directors and so controlling the company. The part played by the directors and the practical limitations to the power of directors in the case of large companies are explained in Chapter 13.

Advantages of companies

Because it is a body corporate, with a legal identity and life of its own, a company exists separately from its owners. Unlike a partnership it is not automatically dissolved by the death of one of its members although, of course, its operation can be severely disrupted on the loss of the main owner–manager. The company itself, however, could survive under new ownership. Some companies are now so long established that they have long outlived their original owners. This legal immortality can provide a valuable element of stability and continuity for the business.

A great attraction, as we have seen, is limited liability. It is sometimes said that it reduces the risks of business activity but this is not strictly true. What it does do is to transfer to customers and suppliers some of the financial risks that in non-corporate organisations would be carried by the proprietors or partners. In 1982 3745 companies were compulsorily wound up in circumstances that left creditors with unpaid debts and nearly 16 000 were liquidated (terminated usually at the request of their owners), many in similar circumstances. This has been criticised as offering opportunities to the unscrupulous.

In view of the unfairness of a system that allows owners of a business to pass some of their risks to other people, we have to ask whether it offers advantages sufficient to compensate for this heavy social price. It is usually argued that society does benefit in a number of ways:

1 Limited liability encourages many more people to put their money into business ventures than would otherwise do so. This means that the economic system is able to tap a greater reserve of valuable financial resources than would otherwise be the case.

2 The system permits a special form of specialisation. The ownership of financial capital is separated from its control, particularly in large-scale business operated through giant public companies. Shareholders need take no active part in the business. At the same time, because shareholders provide the finance, those who direct and manage the company do not need to have any financial resources of their own. Companies can recruit the best managerial talent without asking for any financial contribution and able young people can study 'business studies' and enter a managerial career regardless of their own lack of money!

3 Limited liability encourages business firms to undertake riskier ventures. This means that the economic system is able to produce a richer variety of products and technological innovations. Customers benefit from greater choice and suppliers from having more business ventures to supply.

Limitations of companies

Because of the privileges granted to companies they and their directors are subject to official scrutiny and to legal restrictions on their activities. In 1984 the British Government published a White Paper (policy statement) on Insolvency (inability to pay debts). This proposed that the law relating to people who run limited companies which fail and leave unpaid debts should be strengthened. For example, it was proposed that the courts should have the power to disqualify such people from holding subsequent directorships for 15 years and that, if a company has compulsorily been terminated, they should automatically be disqualified for 3 years. It was also proposed to introduce a new civil offence of 'wrongful trading' so that the directors of companies that have been mismanaged could be sued by the liquidators, without the protection of limited liability.

This White Paper was the basis of a subsequent Insolvency Bill which was extensively amended and 'watered down' in its passage through Parliament, so that many of the safeguards proposed in the White Paper are still not in operation.

Part of the price that companies have to pay for their privileged status is some loss of confidentiality in financial matters. Profitable companies may be exposed to the risks of takeover as there are always people on the look out for rewarding investments and many of these have the knowledge and resources to search the records kept at the Companies Registry. In some businesses the loss of financial confidentiality is so serious that they cannot consider becoming limited companies.

Private Limited Companies

Owned by	any number of shareholders
Run by	directors, usually major shareholders, elected by the shareholders
Financed by	share capital, firms' own retained earnings and firms' own borrowings
Limited liability	yes
Legal regulation	general law relating to business operations Companies Acts publication of accounts supervision by Dept of Trade obligations on directors shares may not be sold to the general public

---

Public Limited Companies

Owned by	any number of shareholders
Run by	directors, elected by shareholders. Directors often have only a small shareholding, and ownership may be very diffuse
Financed by	share capital, including sale to the general public. Firms' own retained profit and borrowings.
Limited liability	yes
Legal regulation	as for private limited companies firms must have issued at least £12 500 of original share capital

Rapid review

1 What is meant by limited liability and why is it a privilege?
2 State two essential features of a public company.
3 State two ways in which a private limited company is different from a public limited company?
4 Who runs a large company on behalf of the shareholders?
5 List three ways in which a limited company is different from a partnership.
6 Can a private limited company keep its accounts completely secret?

The growth of companies

One important feature of the company structure is that it provides a kind of short cut to business growth. One company, the parent, can own the shares of another company. Thus, if the company owns enough shares it can control that other. To have full legal control the controlling company should own or control at least 51 per cent of the voting (usually the ordinary) shares of what then becomes the **subsidiary company**. Sometimes companies own less than 51 per cent but have enough to achieve effective control (because small shareholders rarely group together or even take much interest in the company as long as satisfactory dividends are paid) or extensive influence. The company subject to this controlling influence is then said to be an **associated company**.

A successful company may, therefore, grow in two ways. It may simply increase sales, extend its markets and product range, employ more people and acquire more equipment. This is known as **internal growth**.

Alternatively it can purchase the voting shares of other companies and so grow by what is known as a process of **merger** or **take-over**. Strictly a merger takes place when two companies come together to form a new, expanded company and take-over when one is bought and 'swallowed up' by the other. In practice there is little difference as there is almost always one dominant firm taking over control of the other so the terms are virtually interchangeable.

Mergers or take-overs can be **vertical, horizontal** or **lateral**

Vertical take-over takes place when a company buys another in the same industry but at a different stage in the chain of production. For example, a manufacturer may take over a mining company. As mining is at an earlier production stage than manufacturing this is known as a **backwards take-over** or sometimes as **backwards integration. Forward integration** takes place when the taken over organisation is at a later production stage, for example when a manufacturer takes over a chain of retail stores.

Horizontal take-over takes place when the two firms operate at the same stage of production in the same industry, e.g. two engineering manufacturers and **lateral take-over** when the production stages are the same but the industries are different. This is also sometimes referred to as **conglomerate** merger. A company is often called a conglomerate when it owns subsidiaries in several different industries.

There can be a number of possible motives for company growth by merger or take-over. The importance of growth as a business objective has already been recognised, and growth by take-over is quicker than internal expansion. The parent company may also gain some additions to its management team from the new subsidiary. Horizontal take-over may be a means of reducing the extent of market competition and gaining greater market power to control production, prices and profits. Vertical take-over can help to secure supplies of essential materials or components, and deny them or raise their cost to competitors, or ensure reliable distribution outlets for the company's products. At one time growth was thought to be to the benefit of the community because large companies were assumed to be more efficient (through economies of scale) than small ones. This is no longer so readily assumed. Small companies have frequently been shown to be more efficient, flexible and profitable. After a period of 'merger mania' in the 1960s and early 70s it became clear that not all of these were successful in improving efficiency and profitability and the difficult economic conditions of the early 1980s led to a number of 'de-mergers'. In some cases subsidiary companies were encouraged to become independent through 'management buy-outs' in which the existing team of senior managers buy sufficient shares in the subsidiary to gain control and freedom from membership of the larger company group.

The effect on the employees of a company when it is taken over can be very great indeed, as the subsidiary now becomes subordinate to the interests of the parent. Some production plants may be closed and some activities stopped. The company may, of course, be required to undertake new activities and processes. Often it will be expected to conform to procedures established by the parent. Some cost reductions may depend on adopting common practices over such matters as accounting and office administration.

These changes may give new and wider opportunities to some people but be very disturbing to others, especially managers who have been secure in their business worlds for a long time. Such managers may face the choice of re-training, relocating their families and generally starting many things again, or accepting redundancy. This can be harsh, but adapting to a changing environment is a necessary process in a dynamic industrial community.

Other business structures

Different forms of business are suited to different circumstances, industries, ownership needs and stages of development. This chapter has not covered all possible types of business organisation. There are, for example, a number of societies which are subject to special laws and regulations. The most important of these, the building societies and the co-operative societies, are examined in Chapter 3.

Rapid review

1 List the main types of merger/take-over.
2 State two important motives for take-over.
3 Why do the senior managers of a company subject to a take-over bid often try to resist take-over?

Exercises

1 Setting up a sole proprietorship may be relatively straightforward but still involves a number of business decisions. Draw a simple flow chart to show the main decisions that have to be made in the process of establishing this type of business. Consult your teacher if you are not sure how to draw a flow chart.
2 Barristers are obliged to practice as sole proprietors. Suggest possible reasons for this.
3 Some partnerships have claims in their literature and advertising such as 'Established 1880'. As this would mean that all the original partners were dead what can such a claim mean and why does the firm make it?
4 If you were forming a partnership would you want to draw up a partnership contract? If not, why not? If you would, explain why. What sort of matters would you want the contract to specify?
5 Suppose you were forming a partnership and wished to trade under a different name. Find out from the Companies Act 1985 what action you would have to take.
6 From the advertising pages of your local newspaper make a list of the firms which you think are sole proprietorships or partnerships. List the activities of these firms and discuss your results.
7 In Question 4 you were asked to imagine yourself setting up a partnership, and whether you would want a partnership contract. Suppose your partnership had operated successfully for several years. Now list the pros and cons of turning the same partnership into a private limited company.
8 'Limited liability is vitally important for modern business.' 'Limited liability is a privilege which is much too open to abuse.' Discuss these apparently conflicting statements.

9   Write to a large public limited company to obtain a copy of its Annual Report and Accounts. Use these to identify:
a the major activities of the firm;
b what seem to be the objectives of the firm;
c the number of shares issued and the number held by directors. Comment on your findings.
10   Explain clearly the differences between business organisations which are legally 'corporations' and those that are 'non-corporate'.
11   The following activity is suitable for a team of students.

The 'Yellow Pages' telephone directory lists local firms specialising in particular trades and activities. Use these lists to identify the types of business organisations that seem to be most numerous in the different activities. Discuss your findings and compare them with the results of the local newspaper search (Question 6). Suggest possible reasons for any differences you may notice.
12   Few months pass without press reports of a take-over battle in which two or more large companies struggle for control of another. With the help of your teacher locate one such battle. Collect as many press reports as you can about it and write a report in which you attempt to show:

Why the company is being taken over or threatened with take-over.

Why the company or companies seeking to gain control wish to achieve the take-over.

What will be the effects of the take-over on competition and services to consumers.

3 The non-profit-seeking societies and public ownership

The Co-operative Movement

Aims and organisation of the Movement

All the business organisations examined in Chapter 2 had one common feature: even if profit was not the only aim it was certainly an important motivation for owners and senior managers. There are, however, a number of organisations that do not exist to make profits for their owners. Indeed, they do not have owners in the normal sense at all. They are societies or groups of people who originally came together to provide for their members benefits that, at the time, were not available anywhere else.

Among the most important of these are the co-operative societies. The Co-operative Movement in Great Britain owes its origins to the efforts of working people in mid-nineteenth century Britain to provide themselves with honest and efficient retail shops. At that time these were not widely available.

The basic principles of the Movement's organisation, as established by the original group of Rochdale Pioneers, are well known. They are shown in Fig 3.1. Any customer over a minimum age – usually sixteen – may become a shareholder-member. In 1984 there were over eight and a half million members on the books though by no means all were regular shoppers and there was no certainty that all were still alive! Those shareholders who attend members' meetings are able to elect management committees which appoint specialist full-time managers to run the shops and other business units within the society's area. Each local retail society is independent, but is linked to other societies within the Movement through membership of the Co-operative Union and participation in the affairs of the Co-operative Wholesale Society or, in Scotland, of the Scottish CWS. The retail societies are the shareholders of the wholesale societies. In principle, therefore, the customers own the retail societies which own the wholesale societies. Business profits move in the reverse direction, from the wholesale to the retail societies and thence to the customer shareholders.

The Movement has long been strongly linked to the wider Labour

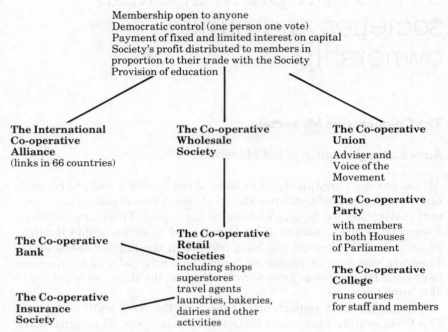

Some of the Rochdale Principles

Membership open to anyone
Democratic control (one person one vote)
Payment of fixed and limited interest on capital
Society's profit distributed to members in proportion to their trade with the Society
Provision of education

The International Co-operative Alliance
(links in 66 countries)

The Co-operative Wholesale Society

The Co-operative Union
Adviser and Voice of the Movement

The Co-operative Party
with members in both Houses of Parliament

The Co-operative Bank

The Co-operative Retail Societies
including shops superstores travel agents laundries, bakeries, dairies and other activities

The Co-operative College
runs courses for staff and members

The Co-operative Insurance Society

Fig 3.1   The Co-operative Movement

movement and its belief in democratic control is enshrined in the 'one member, one vote' principle at shareholders' meetings, regardless of the size of the member's shareholding.

Modern problems of the co-operatives

The practical reality of today is rather different. It is difficult to identify a service offered by any section of the Movement which is not provided to a higher standard and at a lower cost by other retail and service organisations. Lacking an aim relevant to modern social conditions the societies have either clung to past traditions under the domination of ageing members, many of whom are former employees, or sought to mirror the more vigorous multiple stores to pursue profit and turnover to the offence of those members who believe that the Movement is something more than a commercial enterprise.

The societies face many dilemmas. Successful modern business requires firm, determined professional management able to make swift decisions. Such management is not likely to develop under the domination of the old traditionalists. The Movement has broad social ideals which are often opposed to modern commercialism but without commercial success it has no money to give practical effect to these ideals.

The main source of managerial skill in the Movement lies in the wholesale societies which, by and large, are still successful in commercial terms. Not surprisingly they have come to dominate the retail societies but this has been frequently resented by societies which have ignored advice and warnings from the professional managers until faced by financial collapse. The CWS was largely instrumental in setting up a national retail organisation: Co-operative Retail Services, which has taken over many failed local societies and activities – so many, in fact, that by 1984 it was faced with major problems, and it was declining to absorb any more. Consequently the Wholesale Society was developing fresh retail services and by 1984 had taken over responsibility for retail operations in a number of major areas, including Belfast and London.

The need to improve general management standards and reduce the number of independent societies has been a constant theme of discussion since the mid-1950s, but in 1984 there were still 115, although the official policy was to bring this number down to around 25.

Trading policies vary greatly from one society to another. Some are seeking to attract finance from the public – a matter of some importance in view of the very low value of the average shareholding – around £9 or less in many societies. Methods of returning profits (where made) to members also vary. They include the familiar Co-op trading stamp, the traditional dividend based on value of purchases, still retained in some areas and experiments in using profits to finance cash discounts and 'special offers'.

It is very difficult to make general statements to give an accurate picture of such a diverse Movement. Fig 3.2 indicates that it is still a significant, though declining, force in distribution. Its shops include 60 superstores. In 1982 the ratio found by dividing total turnover by stocks held at the end of the year was 11.7, compared with 9.8 for other large multiples. This relatively high rate of stock turnover may be the result of the Co-ops' strength in food sales. Their profit margin on turnover was 21.8 per cent compared with 26.9 per cent for the retail trade as a whole, and for large multiples.

Rapid review

1   State two important principles adopted by co-operative societies.
2   State the main problems faced by co-operative societies today.

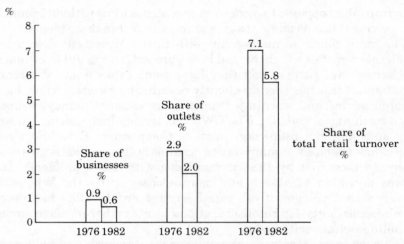

Fig 3.2 The decline of the co-ops. Sources: British Business HMSO 20 July 1985, Annual Abstract of Statistics HMSO 1983 Edit.

The building societies

Something of the same conflict between social ideals and the demands of commercial efficiency can be seen in the development of the modern building societies. In their case, however, the conflict seems to be more generally weighted in favour of commercial success with earlier social ideals more readily sacrificed. It is perhaps significant that the former Co-operative Building Society broke many of its links with the Co-operative Movement and became the Nationwide Building Society.

The early building societies also arose during the mid-nineteenth century and were formed literally to help members to build their own homes. When the last member had secured a home the society was terminated. Later, however, 'permanent' societies were established and these became financial agents to enable the savings of their investing members to be used to buy homes for their borrowing members.

Building societies have no owners in the normal sense and they do not exist to pursue profits. Directors are appointed by those investing members who attend meetings. In fact very few do attend and vote so that, in practice, the established directors are able to remain in office for long periods and to appoint whoever they wish to fill vacancies. It is extremely difficult to challenge the domination of the established directors.

It is possible for one society to purchase another, and take-overs of this kind have reduced the number, but produced some very large, independent societies.

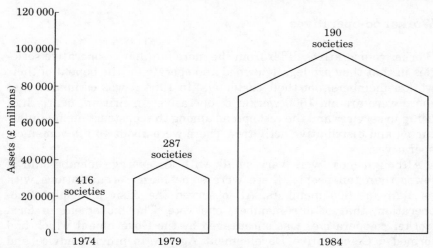

Fig 3.3 Building societies – the falling number of societies and the rising value of assets (Incidentally, what are the merits and drawbacks of showing information in this type of 'pictorial' form? See Chapter 15)

Fig 3.3 illustrates this growth and the importance of the societies as channels for personal savings. With growth has come a desire on the part of some managements to extend the range of their financial interests. By 1984 many were encouraging their investing members to treat building society deposit accounts as ordinary bank accounts, making frequent deposits and withdrawals. Some were even offering cheque book services. In that year the Government announced its intention to introduce legislation that would permit building societies to undertake a wider range of financial services and to increase their ability to compete with the banks. The Government proposed to bring the societies more firmly into the commercial banking system under the general control of the Bank of England.

In view of the changing role of building societies it seems desirable that they should be allowed to change their structure to become more like ordinary commercial public limited companies. It is possible that this may be allowed for some of the larger organisations, especially those wishing to operate in other countries of the European Community.

Rapid review

1 Why are building societies so called?
2 State two directions in which building societies seek to expand their services.

Worker co-operatives

Worker co-operatives differ from the more familiar co-operative societies in that they are legally owned and operate for the benefit of their
worker-members, not their customers. In 1984 it was estimated that
there were around 1000 worker co-operatives in Britain, nearly half
being in services and the rest spread among the construction, manufacturing and distributive activities. There were about 40 all-women co-
operatives.

Although most were very small, with an average membership of
fewer than ten people, there were some larger organisations with
as many as 600 members. All observed the basic principle of co-
operation, that of one member, one vote. The movement to form
worker co-operatives was encouraged by the Government which had
formed a Co-operative Development Agency to provide advice and
support.

One of the problems faced by any worker co-operative is the need
to balance the desire of members to share profits in the form of income
with the need to plough back profits to build up the business and acquire
up-to-date machines, technical and management skills. Swift and deci-
sive management might be difficult to obtain as a co-operative grew
and increased the number of members. This type of organisation has
tended to have difficulty in surviving in manufacturing but it may
well be suitable to the expanding service sector which is a feature
of the modern economy.

Rapid review

1 How does a worker co-operative differ from a retail co-operative society?
2 Suggest one major problem likely to be faced by a worker co-operative.

The nationalised industries

Nationalised industry is the term commonly used to describe an
industry in which the major production organisations are owned and
controlled by the State on behalf of the community as a whole. Some
industries, such as coal extraction, have just one dominant organisation
– British Coal – others, such as electricity supply have several: the
Central Electricity Generating Board and the area boards which distribute the power supply.

The public corporation

The form of organisation normally employed to operate within a nationalised industry is the public corporation. This is modelled on (but must not be confused with) the public company of the private sector, but it does not have shareholders. Its capital is provided by the government and is increased by additional loans authorised by the Government and by its own accumulated revenue which is surplus to costs. Commercial control and management of the corporation is in the hands of a chairman and board of directors chosen by the Government. The board is responsible to a Government Minister, who in turn is responsible to Parliament for the general policy of the corporation but not for its commercial management, which is supposed to be independent of government and political control. The early ideal of the public corporation was that it would enjoy the independence of the public company in its day-to-day business affairs but be accountable through Parliament to the public in whose interests it would function.

Problems of the public corporations

Critics of the nationalised industries suggest that the public corporations do not enjoy genuine independence in business decision-making, yet neither are they effectively accountable to Parliament and the community as a whole. Governments do influence a wide range of management decisions, especially where their political interests are involved. For instance, loss making production establishments in sensitive political areas have been kept open. In addition to political control there are difficulties resulting from the size and nature of some of the nationalised bodies. Both the railways and electricity supply suffer from what is known as 'peak loading'. This means that they have to have sufficient resources to meet peak or maximum possible demand at any one time. The product supplied, such as rail travel and electric power, cannot be effectively stored. The rail service has to carry all those passengers who wish to travel in, say, June at times of the day when those travelling on business are mingling with British holiday makers and foreign tourists. The capacity for generating electricity has to meet demand at, say, early evening or late afternoon on a very cold winter's day when the factories are all working, street lights are coming on and people at home are switching on fires and starting to cook evening meals. If the boards have the capacity to meet these peak demands then much of their equipment is going to be underused for much of the year. It is difficult to see how this problem can be avoided completely although moves can be made to reduce its scale. The railways, for example, can encourage travel at off-peak times by offering special fares.

The electricity boards can develop links with other countries so that power can be imported and exported at different times and the total supply capacity can be safely reduced.

Some of the public corporations are very large organisations and suffer from problems of effective management. Similar problems involving poor communications, slow decision-making and missed commercial opportunities are found in other very large companies in the private sector of the economy. On the other hand companies in the normal commercial private sector can be reorganised and, if necessary, split into smaller units more easily than can public corporations, which can only be changed significantly by a special Act of Parliament. Securing a new statute is likely to raise public controversy in which political stands are taken and opposition expressed, embarrassing the Government rather than securing a more efficient public service.

A number of the corporations are monopolies in that they are the sole suppliers of particular products or services such as coal and rail travel. The early supporters of nationalisation argued that a monopoly owned by the community and existing to serve the community would not behave in the same way as a monopoly which existed to make profits for private owners. It was not expected that the public monopoly would raise prices, restrict output and give poor-quality service because this behaviour was clearly not in the public interest.

It now seems more likely that monopolies behave as monopolies however they are owned. It is freedom from the fear of losing business to competitors – and hence of losing employment to other organisations – that causes the deterioration in efficiency and quality of service that is so often associated with monopolies. Independent enquiries have found many instances of abuse of monopoly power from public corporations. These include the use of misleading advertising, unjustified price rises, poor-quality service to customers and failure to make use of available technology.

Objectives of public corporations

An underlying difficulty with nationalised industries has been the failure to set clear objectives. The rather vague aim of operating in the public interest which seems to have been the only one envisaged in the early days of nationalisation was soon found to be hopelessly inadequate. This was inevitable because no one can really say definitely what the public interest is in any given set of circumstances. For example, should the electricity boards make profits, produce as much electricity as possible, charge low prices, operate at lowest possible cost or provide as much employment as possible? A case can be made for each single one of these possible objectives. High electricity board profits reduce the burden of taxation. An abundance of cheap power gives advantages to business firms in competition with other countries and reduces home living expenses. Keeping costs low is a form of efficiency though it could also mean paying very low wages and making workers redundant. Providing employment would reduce the social and human waste of unemployment and the cost of social welfare but would increase costs. Any one of these objectives could be pursued but not all at once. There is not just one public interest but many conflicting and incompatible interests.

Successive governments have sought to grapple with this difficulty and to set clearer objectives. White Papers (policy statements) were issued in 1961, 1967 and 1978. Each of these tended to strengthen the financial obligations of the corporations and to establish firmer financial objectives. The 1978 White Paper set a general obligation to achieve a 5 per cent real rate of return on capital investment. This meant that the return in the form of surplus revenue over costs should be 5 per cent higher than the current rate of price increases. If prices were increasing by 5 per cent a year then capital invested in the nationalised industries should earn a surplus revenue of 10 per cent a year. This White Paper also recognised the difficulties of political intervention and proposed that this should be written and subject to scrutiny by Parliament. A Bill to give effect to this proposal failed to go through Parliament before the 1979 General Election.

Following the election the Government sought to gain greater control over spending by the nationalised industries as part of its policy to limit the expansion of money in the economy. The public corporations were set cash limits for their spending. This forced them to reduce investment and delayed a certain amount of modernisation and new development. Further modification of objectives became subordinated to the Government's aims for de-nationalising, or privatising, selected public corporations.

The privatisation issue

Students of state-owned industries usually point out that there is no consistency from one country to another concerning the precise division between the State-owned and controlled public sector and the privately owned and operated private sector. Nor is there much consistency in the pattern of nationalisation within the United Kingdom. The rail and bus services have been nationalised but most of the rest of the commercial road services have remained in private hands. Coal and steel production have been nationalised but oil extraction and refining have been mostly in the hands of privately owned companies, though with the Government as a major shareholder in one large oil company. British Coal has never seriously entered the market as a distributor of coal and coal appliances but the area gas and electricity boards operate what are effectively chains of retail stores. The standard textbook attempts to present the economic explanation for the pattern of nationalisation in the UK have mostly been attempts to rationalise a situation which owes much more to political than to economic or commercial forces. Few of these rationalisations survive close and critical scrutiny.

The case for privatisation

It is against this rather confused background that we must now examine the modern controversy surrounding privatisation. The case for privatisation can be based on the following main arguments:

1   The corporations are freed from political control and intervention and can pursue entirely economic and commercial objectives.
2   They will gain access to the commercial capital and finance markets, and the ability to obtain additional investment capital will depend on economic and commercial judgements in these markets – not on political considerations.
3   The need to satisfy investment managers and financiers that past performance has been satisfactory before future investment finance can be obtained will encourage much improved standards of business efficiency.
4   Capital provision for privatised corporations will not form part of the Government's Public Sector Borrowing Requirement so that the Government's share of total borrowing in the economy will fall.
5   Exposure to the market forces of supply and demand in the private sector will weaken the power of trade unions to continue to secure rising pay regardless of the efficiency of the organisation.
6   It is argued that public ownership by selling shares to large numbers of individual shareholders is a truer form of public ownership and accountability to the community than state control where the public has no really effective voice.

The case against privatisation

Apart from conflicts of political dogma in which the forces of socialism are opposed to those of liberal capitalism, the economic argument against privatisation is based on the view that the 'privatisers' are confusing questions of resource ownership and control with those of market power. Many of those who recognise the problems and inefficiencies of some public corporations believe that these are linked to size and monopoly power rather than to public ownership as such. They fear that privatisation will do little to solve the basic problems and point out that the privatised British Telecom has retained most of its control over telecommunication services, and that when faced with a choice between privatising British Airways and improving the ability of the independent air lines to compete with it over the more profitable air routes, the Government favoured privatisation.

In addition to this major worry over the ownership/monopoly issue the following doubts can be raised:

1 No major industry is really free from political intervention. The public sector, in one form or another, is likely to remain a major customer or supplier of the privatised undertakings and be able to exert influence 'behind the scenes'. In some cases, including British Aerospace, Cable and Wireless, Britoil and Associated British Ports, the Government remains by far the largest and most influential shareholder. In these cases transfer to the private sector could be seen as little more than a legal technicality. Effective back door state control remains in practice.

2 Only the most profitable of the corporations are acceptable to private financiers and investment managers. The Government is likely to be left to control a hard core of unprofitable and increasingly troublesome organisations, most probably those in the declining 'smoke stack' industries such as coal and steel. If the Government enjoys short-term success in passing a fundamentally unprofitable corporation to the private sector, subsequent losses and distrust could make it difficult for the private finance markets to co-operate with future governments.

3 The removal of some organisations from the Public Sector Borrowing Requirement does not change the total borrowing nor the total supply of finance in the country and by making the PSBR look smaller may encourage central government to borrow more rather than less.

4 Trade union power arises from economic rather than just political causes. Union power is strongest in monopolies and weakest in competitive industries. By preserving monopoly in order to ease the path of privatisation the Government is actually helping to preserve union power. If it is thought that unions hinder economic progress and growth by out of date attitudes and restrictive practices, privatisation, resting on the preservation of monopoly, will do little to change this condition.

There are clearly many aspects to privatisation and this is likely to remain a controversial issue for some years. It must also be remembered that even after extensive privatisation there remains a substantial

public sector and we should not be so concerned with the de-
nationalisation issue that we entirely neglect the need to bring the
remaining nationalised industries closer to the original ideal of
business independence combined with public accountability and service
to the community as a whole.

Sale of shares to the public. Public Corporations become Public Companies	Sale of Council Houses	Contracting-out work in the Public Sector	Increase in competition in the Public Sector
Some share sales 1979–1985 British Petroleum ICL Ferranti British Aerospace British Sugar Cable and Wireless Amersham International National Freight Consortium Britoil Associated British Ports British Rail Hotels Jaguar British Telecom	Houses sold to tenants at favourable prices	e.g. Street cleaning School and hospital cleaning services	e.g. Some contract mail Private open-cast coal mining Some bus services Cable TV

Fig 3.4   The privatisation programme

Rapid review

1   **What is a nationalised industry?**
2   **State one way in which a public corporation is different from a public company and one way in which they are similar.**
3   **State two difficulties faced by public corporations.**
4   **Why is there a problem in setting an objective for a public corporation and what efforts have been made to overcome this?**
5   **State six *economic* arguments in favour of the case for the privatisation of nationalised industries.**
6   **State four *economic* arguments against privatisation.**

Government services

Central government

There are two sectors of the elected government in the United Kingdom,
the central government and local authorities. The central government
is formed by the political party which enjoys the support of a majority

in the House of Commons. The actual administration of government is in the hands of the civil service which is traditionally non-political and has a duty to serve any ruling party impartially.

Nevertheless the operation of any service provided by central government is ultimately subject to political control and this makes it very difficult to run directly any business organisation. Not only are political and commercial aims likely to be in constant conflict but there is also the need for any government organisation to operate strictly within the limits of powers granted and supervised by Parliament. The British Parliament is very jealous of its right to call to account any Government Minister to make sure he or she is not abusing his or her power. This right, essential to the preservation of political freedom, can make it almost impossible to run a business organisation. Business managers must be free to act quickly in response to changing market conditions without the fear of being called to account for each and every decision made.

On the other hand the central government, often in co-operation with local authorities, does provide many services which relate to business. Some of these regulate business activities in the interests of the community as a whole. Well-known examples include the testing of motor vehicle drivers, the inspection of food premises and slaughter houses, of factories and shops and the testing of weighing and measuring equipment in business premises.

The Departments of Trade and Industry are closely concerned with business affairs of all kinds. The Department of Trade is responsible for ensuring that company law is preserved and for protecting the community against business and financial fraud. It has traditionally been closely involved with supervision of the insurance industry. Another important traditional function has been that of upholding maritime law and administering the many measures designed to increase the safety of ships at sea and to ensure that ships are operated by competent officers.

The Department of Industry grew out of the tendency for governments in the second half of this century to become closely involved with a range of subsidies and licensing measures designed to influence business activities and decisions. These have included efforts to influence business location and to promote investment, especially investment in modern technology. The Department has also been involved in the administration of measures to encourage small-scale business enterprise.

In matters which are politically non-controversial governments have tended to distance themselves from direct regulation and control and have sought to hand over actual administration to semi-independent bodies – the Quasi Autonomous National Governmental Organisations (quangos). These include bodies such as the Monopolies and Mergers Commission, the Manpower Services Commission, the Business and Technology Education Council and many others. Some of these institutions are examined more closely in the next chapter.

The major spending departments of government can exercise considerable influence on business precisely through their spending. The Department of Education, for example, gave a significant degree of support to British computer manufacturers through its decision to subsidise the purchase by schools and colleges of selected microcomputers in the early 1980s. Some industries are very heavily dependent on the government as customer. The aerospace manufacturers rely on defence contracts to provide revenue for research and a very high proportion of all the research conducted by some of the major electronics manufacturers is financed out of the Government's defence budget.

Local authorities

The British local authorities are mostly controlled by the political party which, as a result of local elections, is able to obtain the support of a majority of the elected local representatives. Different areas are controlled by different parties and some of the largest authorities are likely to be controlled by political leaders hostile to the central government. The attitudes of local councillors towards business and towards the involvement of government in business may be very different from those of ministers of the central government.

The administration of local authority work is carried out by full-time non-elected employees who are also supposed to be politically impartial. In practice there is rather less impartiality in local than in national government administration.

Local authority activities are financed partly by revenues from the sale of services and from local taxation (property taxes known as rates) but also to a great degree by grants from general taxation controlled by the central government. Given the political differences between local and central government the opportunities for conflict are considerable and these are frequently the subject of public controversy. The nature and minimum level of many local authority duties, such as the provision of primary, secondary and tertiary education, of health care and social welfare, are determined by Parliamentary statutes. Each local authority can only act legally within powers granted to it by Parliament – often these are contained in a special statute relating to the particular authority – but it generally has considerable scope in extending its functions, in going beyond minimum legal standards, and in the inter-

SERVICES PROVIDED BY BOROUGH COUNCIL

A wide range of services is provided and some of them are shown below. The list is not exhaustive but it demonstrates the range.

Leisure & Recreation
Sports Halls (4)
Swimming Pool
Football Stadium
All-weather Sports Surface
Recreation Centre

Housing
Council Housing
Homelessness
House Renovation Grants
Home Insulation Grants
Rent Allowances

Other Services
Market
Street Naming & Numbering
Some Street Lighting
Industrial Units (leased)
Concessionary Bus Passes
Registration of Electors

Environmental Health
Pest Control
Cesspool Emptying
Refuse Collection
Litter Clearance
Smoke Control
Meat Inspection
Shops Hygiene

Planning
Planning Permissions
Building Regulations Control

COST IN 1985/86 OF SERVICES PROVIDED BY THE BOROUGH COUNCIL

Service	Gross Expenditure	%	Gross Income	Net Rate Poundage	%
	£		£	p	
Refuse Collection	577090	13.9	36910	6.39	18.0
Street Lighting	79060	1.9	–	0.93	2.6
Other Environmental Health Services	412220	9.9	195350	2.56	7.2
Leisure & Recreation	853660	20.5	292220	6.64	18.7
Housing:					
Contribution to Revenue A/c	283440	6.8	–	3.35	9.5
Renovation Grants	362540	8.7	291360	0.84	2.4
Insulation Grants	25950	0.6	18800	0.08	0.2
Rent Allowances	21200	0.5	–	0.25	0.7
Other Housing	34930	0.8	14730	0.24	0.7
Town & County Planning	395520	9.5	185050	2.49	7.0
Concessionary Fares	101380	2.4	9650	1.08	3.0
Public Offices	43470	1.1	8310	0.41	1.2
Administration & Depots	638780	15.3	59190	6.86	19.3
Cost of Rate Collection	254560	6.1	–	3.01	8.5
Other Services	82580	2.0	50710	0.37	1.0
	4166380	100	1162280	35.50	100

Fig 3.5

pretation of how its legal duties should be carried out.

Many services essential to the day-to-day conduct of business life and the ordinary life of the community are carried out by the local authorities. They include repair, maintenance and improvement of local roads, provision of street lights, disposal of waste and sewerage. In addition some authorities have powers to provide financial assistance to local business enterprises in the hope that these will provide improved local employment opportunities.

Modern authorities have been less ready than their nineteenth-century predecessors to become actively involved in providing services on a commercial basis. There are many reasons for this. Some of the most essential communication and 'civil protection' services such as telecommunications and the fire services are provided on a national scale or have, like water and hospital provisions, been transferred to separate regional authorities directly answerable to the central government. There is a reluctance to use taxpayers' money to subsidise business organisations which compete with businesses run by the payers of taxes and in any event most modern businesses are too specialised and complex to be run by authorities that are subject to political chance and change. Nevertheless many authorities have been prominent in providing sports and leisure facilities and these are rapidly becoming increasingly important as economic activities and sources of employment.

Rapid review

1   What are the two sectors of elected government in the United Kingdom?
2   What is a 'quango'?
3   List four services carried out by local authorities.
4   What objection might be raised to the running of a business corporation directly by a local authority?

Interdependence of the private and public sectors

Although we generally look upon the private and the public sectors of the economy separately it is essential to remember that they are very closely linked in practice. Many privately produced activities depend on the public services and many public services depend on private production. If, for example, firms use less electricity or if major users of electricity move their locations then the Central Electricity Generating Board has to change its production accordingly. Privately owned haulage contractors depend on the public roads, and their fortunes are dependent on the amount of tax they must pay in licence fees, in return for the use they make of the roads and the other public services, such as police and accident services.

At the same time the scale of many public sector activities is a major influence on some important private industries. When educational spending is reduced, for example, there is a fall in work on school and college buildings and equipment. Educational publishing contracts severely.

The term 'nationalised industry' is misleading. All the so-called nationalised industries contain a substantial element of privately owned enterprise. Even the coal industry relies on private firms for fuel distribution. Electricity power stations and coal mines make use of many specialised firms to manufacture and maintain their equipment.

This interdependence affects the results of government policies. A government wishing to reduce the percentage of the economy in the public sector may reduce spending, only to find that this reduction is causing such large cutbacks among privately-owned firms that there is very little change in the percentage shares of the two sectors.

Rapid review

1 What is meant when we say that the public and the private sectors of the economy are interdependent?
2 Why may a government trying to reduce the proportion of the economy in the public sector find that it has increased?

Exercises

1 Write a report on one of the Co-operative Movement's non-commercial activities, such as the Woodcraft Folk or the Guilds. You should be able to obtain initial information from the education/training officer of your local society.
2 Write a report comparing your local co-operative store or stores with one of the leading supermarket or superstore multiples. Your comparison should take into account such issues as prices, cleanliness of store, range of goods sold, attitude of assistants, waiting time at check-outs and any other aspect that influences a consumer's decision to support one store rather than another.
3 Obtain and study the rule book of one of the large national building societies and list the action that an individual investor or small group of investing members would have to take if they wished to secure the election of a director in opposition to the existing directors. What difficulties and costs would they have to face?

4　With the help of leaflets and information obtained from a local building society branch show to what extent this society is competing with the large High Street banks.

5　List the ways in which a worker co-operative differs from a small private company. Discuss the advantages and possible disadvantages to a worker of being a member of this type of co-operative.

6　List three major departments of central government which you think are able to influence the level and direction of business activity and outline the main ways in which that influence is exercised.

7　Many local authorities describe their services and show the proportions of the rates spent on them either on their rates notices or in leaflets issued with rates demands. Obtain one or more of these notices or leaflets and use it/them to describe and comment on the work of your local authority.

8　Write an essay in which you either support or oppose the view that local authorities should provide non-profit making, comprehensive, low-priced local bus services.

9　Choose one British nationalised industry and argue the case either for or against privatising this industry.

10　Choose one present or former public corporation which still retains a substantial degree of monopoly power and suggest ways in which the amount of competition which this organisation faces could be increased.

11　With the help of published reports and accounts choose one privatised former public corporation and compare its business performance before and after privatisation. How far do you believe this is typical of other privatised bodies?

4 The business environment

Government influence on business

Problems of the economy

Chapter 3 examined some of the ways in which the Government, either directly or through local authorities and the nationalised industries, is a supplier of goods and services. Government, however, has a much wider influence. Government policy is one element of the environment within which business organisations have to operate and many government decisions have important consequences for business activities.

Internal and external factors

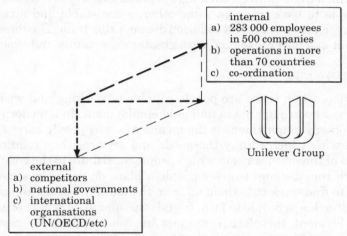

internal
a) 283 000 employees in 500 companies
b) operations in more than 70 countries
c) co-ordination

Unilever Group

external
a) competitors
b) national governments
c) international organisations (UN/OECD/etc)

Fig 4.1   Some of the internal and external factors which affect the modern business. Note the inclusion of governments and international bodies. Reproduced from 'Unilever's management and organisation' by courtesy of Unilever plc

A modern government is expected to exercise some control over the national economy and to try and create conditions under which the majority of people are able to enjoy improved living standards. An economy is said to be successful when general living standards are rising, and to be failing if general living standards are falling or lagging behind those in other comparable countries. The general improvement that is desired may appear to be hindered by several identifiable economic problems. The most common of these are outlined below.

Failure to achieve economic growth

Economic growth is the term used to describe the capacity of the economy to produce an increasing total supply of goods and services. Failure to achieve this makes it very difficult to raise general living standards because these require improvements in such areas as housing, transport, health care and education. General improvements in all the desired goods and services can only be achieved if total supply rises.

Inflation

This is the term used to describe the economic condition in which prices keep rising. In severe inflation price rises take place at an increasing rate. This condition makes it very difficult for governments, business firms and individuals to plan ahead. In very severe inflation the nation's money itself becomes worthless and trade has to revert to a system of barter in which there is direct exchange of goods and services. Sometimes it is possible to base trade on some other, more stable and acceptable, currency. Even the severest inflation does not stop trade. Business keeps going but at a lower level and with greater uncertainty and expense.

Unemployment

This exists when there are people capable of working and wishing to work but who are unable to find paid employment. In a modern industrial economy employment is the means whereby people earn a money income with which to buy the goods and services they require. It is also one of the main ways in which people contribute to the community to which they belong. It gives people a place or status in society and failure to find work cuts them off from the main life of the community. Work often helps people to form friendships and to form part of a group. Unemployment, therefore, is not just an economic problem, representing a waste of human resources which could be used to produce more goods and services. It is a serious social and human problem. The unemployed person has to live on a low income, loses social status and is more likely than the working person to suffer mental illness.

Regional unemployment

If unemployment is heavily concentrated in certain regions this causes severe social and political problems. Prosperity is relative rather than absolute. People see themselves as well or badly off in comparison with how they see others rather than by some definite standard of comfort or well being. Employment is essential to prosperity in a modern economy and a government is expected to avoid large differences in regional employment levels.

National balance of payments difficulties

The balance of payments is the term given to a country's financial accounts with the rest of the world. If a country finds itself paying more for its total imports of goods and services than it is able to earn through its exports abroad, then it is likely to find itself having balance of payments difficulties. Nations, like people, generally have to pay their way in the world. Nations, like people, who get badly into debt, may find that they lose some of their freedom and have to allow others to manage their financial affairs to some extent. This is humiliating for a nation whose people are likely to suffer reduced living standards during the period when its affairs are being controlled for the benefit of those to whom it owes money.

Policies open to governments

This is not the place to attempt to analyse the causes of these economic problems nor to explain the theories underlying the corrective measures likely to be taken by governments. Nevertheless, in order to understand how government action affects business firms it is necessary to recognise the main techniques of economic control which modern governments possess.

Direct controls

Assuming that the Government is able to control the country's legislature or law-making body (Parliament in the United Kingdom), it can make laws which give it the power to control important elements in the economy. For example, from time to time between 1966 and 1979 the British Government had powers to control price increases and sometimes it had considerable power over wage increases to employees and dividend payments made by companies to their shareholders. For a short time in 1966 all price and wage increases were forbidden.

In the past the British Government has controlled the export of money and dealings in gold. There were some years when British people travelling abroad could take with them no more than £50 without special permission from the Bank of England. Many other countries still have strict controls over exports of currency.

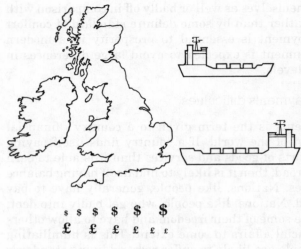

If the UK pays more for imports than she receives from exports there is a **balance of payments deficit.**

A persistent balance of payments deficit leads to a shrinking £ when exchanged for foreign currencies, i.e. a **falling exchange rate** for the £, people withdraw money from the UK.

Cost of living up

Wage claims from unions

Raw material costs up

A falling £ reduces export price but also **raises prices of imports** including food and basic materials.

To check the falling £ the Government may have to **raise interest rates** to stop money from leaving Britain.

Business costs rise!

Prices rise!

Fig 4.2   The balance of payments and business

There can also be controls on the amounts people are permitted to borrow and on the terms under which money can be borrowed. Britain introduced emergency regulations during the Second World War to regulate hire purchase and similar instalment credit agreements and credit regulations remained in force until the late 1970s and were sometimes tightened or relaxed as part of government economic management.

Controls have formed part of British Government regional policies. At one time strict controls were imposed on office building in London and some other large cities. In some areas until 1982 business development above a certain floor area required an Industrial Development Certificate (IDC) from the Department of Trade and Industry.

Local authorities exercise planning controls under the Town and Country Planning laws but these are mainly used to defend the rural *greenbelts* from business and private housing development. In areas where there is no objection to business the local authorities are actively competing with each other to attract firms from all over the world.

Taxation

When the famous eighteenth-century economist Adam Smith put forward his fundamental 'canons of taxation' one of his beliefs was that taxation should be levied in such a way that it should interfere as little as possible with the normal operations of business. In his view the only purpose of taxation was to collect revenue for the essential work of government. By the middle of the twentieth century, however, taxation had become an accepted way to achieve some redistribution of income and wealth from the wealthier to the poorer sections of the community and the great Cambridge economist Keynes and his followers had convinced governments that taxes could be used as a means of managing the economy, of intervening to influence market forces, especially total demand for goods and services. This view, of course, is the reverse of that held by Adam Smith.

Taxes are usually classified into two main groups, *direct* and *indirect*. Direct taxes are imposed directly on wealth and income and are payable by those who create the wealth and earn the income. Income tax is the best known direct tax. Indirect taxes are levied on economic activities and can be imposed at various stages of the production process, e.g. on entry to the country (import or customs duties), on manufacturer (excise duties on alcohol), on sale from one firm to another or to the final customer (value added tax). Whereas income taxes affect the net incomes actually received by people and, therefore, the amount of money available for spending, indirect taxes affect the final prices of goods and services and, therefore, the quantity that can be bought for any given level of spending.

Money

Money is an aid to trade and the exchange of goods and services. It provides a means of measuring and comparing values. It is a standard for measuring and recording delayed payments and obligations and a means whereby purchasing power can be stored for future use. Money can only carry out these functions effectively if it is acceptable throughout the community. Governments have used their authority to try and ensure this acceptability throughout the long history of money.

The Tools of Government
Policy – Effects on Business Firms

Measures	*Possible Effects on*
Controls	prices
	wages
	location
	movement of money
Taxation	prices
	incomes (wage claims)
	demand for business products
Money	ability to borrow
	interest rates
	credit available for buying goods and services
Incentives	favour certain activities such as exports
	location in areas of high unemployment
	small business expansion

The monarch's head on British coins is a symbol of this authority as was Caesar's head on ancient Roman coins.

All governments have been expected to take responsibility for the stability and acceptability of the national money. In Britain the issue of bank notes and coins is controlled by the Bank of England operating under the authority of and subject to regulations made by Parliament. Today, however, the most important form of money is bank credit. Apart from the day-to-day shopping transactions most payments are made by transferring credit from one bank account to another. The effective amount of money that I can spend at any given time is really the amount that my bank is prepared to allow me to spend. This can be more than the amount standing to my credit in my personal account at the bank. In addition, the bank may be prepared to allow me to *overdraw*, i.e. make payments in excess of the balance of my account, up to an agreed amount and make further purchases through the use of a *credit card*, again up to a stated amount.

If my bank agrees to raise my overdraft limit by, say, £1000 then it effectively increases my spending ability by £1000. In a very real sense banks are able to create money in this way. If the amount of money created by the banking system grows much faster than the total of goods and services in the country then the money available for buying these goods may be much greater than the quantity that can be bought at prevailing prices. These prices are then likely to rise. As governments

are expected to discourage constant price rises it is no great surprise
to find that from time to time governments have tried to control money
by limiting lending by the banks and by making it more expensive
to borrow money, i.e. by forcing up interest rates charged by banks
to their borrowers.

Incentives

Incentives take several forms, including relief from taxation, grants
from public funds, loans at favourable rates of interest and guarantees
of loan repayment to enable banks to lend money more cheaply and
freely.

In the United Kingdom these are most commonly applied to problems
such as high unemployment, especially where this is heavily concentrated in certain areas or industries. The Government may offer financial help to firms prepared to create jobs in these areas and industries.
Incentives and controls are also sometimes applied to foreign trade.

Regional incentives and controls have been much reduced since 1980
and in 1985 there were four main types of assisted area: Northern
Ireland; 'development areas'; 'intermediate areas'; and 'enterprise
zones'.

Northern Ireland has its own set of incentives but, unfortunately
it also has its own special political and economic problems and solution
of these is necessary before any conventional regional incentives can
be applied with much confidence.

Development areas cover 15 per cent of the working population, and
are entitled to the most assistance. Firms willing to invest in development areas may qualify for automatic assistance, selective assistance
given to a limited amount in return for the creation of genuine new
jobs, as well as help through the European Regional Development Fund.

Intermediate areas cover a further 20 per cent of the working population, including Birmingham, a former growth area, and firms in these
can qualify for selective (job creating) assistance and help through the
European Regional Development Fund.

Enterprise zones are smaller areas, selected on the basis of their
potentiality for growth; they are not necessarily in areas which otherwise qualify for assistance. Firms do not receive any taxpayers' money
but they may obtain relief from local taxes (rates) for a period and
are relieved of some of the unwieldy local authority planning controls.

A further development has been the formation of a number of *freeports*. These are situated close to sea or airports and access to them
is controlled by the Customs and Excise. Within the freeport area firms
can import and work on goods free of any import taxes. Taxes are paid
only when the goods leave the freeport for distribution within the

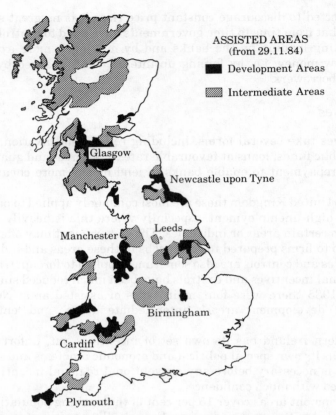

ASSISTED AREAS
(from 29.11.84)

■ Development Areas

▨ Intermediate Areas

Glasgow

Newcastle upon Tyne

Leeds

Manchester

Birmingham

Cardiff

Plymouth

Fig 4.3   The development and intermediate areas in the UK

United Kingdom. If goods are re-exported no duty is payable. This reduces manufacturing costs.

Export incentives are limited by international trade agreements but most countries have organisations similar to the British Export Credits Guarantee Department which provides insurance for risks of non-payment for exports and guarantees that bank loans will be repaid.

A similar bank loan repayment guarantee scheme, on a limited scale, has been made available for small firms.

The effect of policy changes on business

Any changes in government economic policy will affect the conditions under which business firms operate.

Controls on prices and incomes

During the period of prices and incomes controls firms had to work within the rules governing price and wage rises. This could cause problems when managements found themselves facing pressure from unions to raise wages – and pressure from the Government not to do so. Both employers and worker representatives sometimes felt that general rules were not suited to their own particular circumstances. The longer controls lasted the more difficulties they caused. In time firms became skilled at finding ways to overcome the controls which became less and less effective.

One industry with a long history of government regulation of prices is farming. British farm price controls date from the Second World War but since Britain's entry to the European Community the United Kingdom's farm policies have had to conform to the Community's Common Agricultural Policy (CAP) and to regulations designed for countries where the proportion of people directly employed in farming is much greater than in Britain. The Community's CAP has generally encouraged a high level of production and has set prices that have usually been high by world market standards. Imports of food from outside the Community have been discouraged and even penalised by special import taxes. The effect has been to set much of the Community's agriculture rather apart from world food markets.

Another result of the policy has been to create stores of surplus production that cannot be sold within the Community at the prices charged. These have become notorious as butter and beef mountains, and milk and wine lakes. Taxpayers in Europe have had to pay the costs of this over-production and growing resistance to such a wasteful system has forced some sudden changes in policy. Dairy farmers, for example, have suddenly had to face milk quotas and reductions in price. Farmers who have borrowed large amounts of money to modernise their milk production and who cannot readily adapt their land to other types of farming have faced very severe problems and some have had to go out of business.

Taxes

Tax changes can also affect business. An increase in income tax, for example, reduces net incomes that can be used to purchase goods and services so people will have to buy less. However, this reduced buying power is not evenly spread through all industries. There is often little scope for reducing some purchases; for example, people who have to travel to work may not be able to reduce spending on transport. On the other hand if large numbers of households decide to abandon or postpone purchases of furniture or foreign holidays then suppliers of these can face severe problems.

Indirect tax changes can also have an impact on particular trades and industries. Increases in taxes on particular products such as petrol or whisky are likely to reduce spending on these products and their suppliers suffer directly. However, as we have just seen, many people will not be able to reduce spending on basic goods such as petrol. Instead they may have to cut down their spending on some other goods or services such as foreign holidays. Some industries are much more vulnerable than others to taxation changes.

Money

We would expect controls over the expansion of money to reduce the amount of money and credit available for spending and thus to reduce demand for many products – often the same ones likely to suffer from increases in taxes. However, the consequences may go even further. One way in which a government might try to restrict growth of money is to encourage general interest rates to rise. Interest is the payment which a borrower of money pays to the lender in return for the use of the money borrowed. If the amount of the interest charge rises then fewer people will wish to borrow money. A reduction in borrowing by individuals will cause a reduction in demand for consumer goods and services. Firms are also large-scale borrowers from banks; they borrow in order to acquire machines, extend their premises and generally expand their operations. If the cost of borrowing rises, firms will borrow less. There will be a drop in demand for goods such as machines and vehicles normally made for industry. There will also be a failure on the part of firms to increase their ability to produce goods more competitively.

Incentives also create the eventual problem that they become difficult to remove even when they are no longer needed. Pressure groups are formed to persuade the Government how disastrous it would be to remove any of the help that has formerly been given.

Rapid review

1 State the five main problems likely to be faced by a modern industrial economy.
2 List four ways in which a government can try to exercise some degree of control over a modern economy.
3 Give one example of a direct tax and two examples of an indirect tax.
4 Explain the following: development area, intermediate area, enterprise zone, freeport.

5   List two ways in which the Export Credits Guarantee Department helps
    exporters.
6   State one problem resulting from the Common Agricultural Policy of
    guaranteed farm prices.
7   Why could some business firms suffer problems after an increase in income
    tax?
8   Would you expect unemployment to rise or fall after a large general
    increase in Value Added Tax?
9   Why might a business firm decide not to extend a factory after a rise in
    bank interest rates?

Business in the world economy

Few nations can isolate themselves from the wider world economy.
About a third of all business activity in Britain is directly related to
foreign trade. If imports rise faster and more consistently than exports
both industry and individuals will soon feel the consequences. What
these consequences are will depend to a large extent on the policies
adopted by government in the face of a *balance of payments deficit*.
This is the term used to described the condition where total import
values exceed total export values.

Reduction in total demand

If the Government takes the view that the cause of the problem is
that total demand in the economy for goods and services is greater
than can be supplied from the home production system without relying
on excessive imports then it may try to reduce this total demand. It
may do this by reducing its own spending, e.g. on roads, education,
health and social services and other elements of public sector services,
by increasing taxes, as outlined earlier in this chapter, or by putting
pressure on the banks to reduce the scale of their lending and by forcing
up interest rates.

Most of the possible effects of these actions on business firms have
already been indicated. It will be more difficult and expensive to borrow
money. People will buy fewer foreign produced goods and services but
they are also likely to reduce their purchases of many home produced
products as well. Many business firms will suffer and may be beyond
recovery when the balance of payments deficit has been closed and
demand is allowed to expand once more.

Changes in currency values

If the Government were to take no action then there would almost certainly be a change in the value of the nation's currency in comparison with other currencies used in world trade. Importers usually have to pay their suppliers either in the currency used in the supplying country or in the world's main trading currency, United States dollars ($US). Suppose, for simplicity, all payments to importers have to be paid in $US whereas British firms selling exports to foreign countries wish to be paid in British pounds (£). If a British balance of payments deficit persists then British importers are selling more pounds to obtain the $US they need than are being bought by foreign firms buying British produced goods and services. In any market when the supply of a commodity is greater than the demand, sellers have to bring their prices down. This is true of currencies when they are traded in the world foreign exchange markets. As the exchange value of the £ falls, sellers of the £ obtain fewer $US in exchange. When a country has a serious trade problem its currency is likely to fall in value, i.e. depreciate in relation to most of the other main world currencies such as the German mark, the Swiss and French francs and the Japanese yen.

The effect of this change in currency values is different for different people. The British person on holiday in France finds that pounds exchange for fewer francs and there is less money to spend. On the other hand the American tourist in Britain can buy more pounds and everything becomes cheaper in terms of dollars exchanged.

Similarly those British manufacturing firms which are selling their goods in foreign countries can reduce the prices marked in foreign currencies. Exporters and firms which sell to foreign tourists are usually pleased when the national currency depreciates because their goods and services become more attractive to foreign buyers and they hope to sell more. On the other hand importers and people going abroad find that everything costs more pounds and they tend to buy less.

You may think that this encouragement to exports and discouragement to imports is bound to cure the balance of payments deficit but unfortunately it is not quite as simple as this, particularly for the United Kingdom which borrows substantial amounts of money from foreign countries. The exchange value of the pound depends on a number of other influences, including the price of oil and the general level of interest rates, as well as the flow of imports and exports. However, the tendencies outlined in this section normally hold good. A falling pound helps exporters and is welcomed by visitors to Britain, but is disliked by importers and British people travelling abroad. A rising pound is not welcome to exporters and foreign tourists in Britain but is liked by British importers and British tourists abroad.

Controls on trade and exchange

Some countries, faced by balance of payments problems and often by large debts to foreign countries, feel that they have to put restrictions on imports of foreign-produced goods and services and on purchases of foreign currencies. These countries are also likely to forbid or strictly control the export of money of any kind to other countries.

Trade restrictions may be either open (overt) or hidden. Hidden restrictions take the form of barriers claimed to be necessary for other reasons, e.g. safety regulations that require expensive and time-consuming inspection or administrative controls that involve costly licences or detailed documents that require lengthy checking and which can be used to block entry if the slightest error is found.

Open controls usually take one of the following forms:

a *Tariffs* (*import duties*) These are taxes imposed on goods entering the country. They raise the price of imports and discourage demand in favour of home-produced goods. In practice home producers may simply raise prices and increase profits or simply become less efficient. Foreign suppliers, on the other hand may be able to reduce prices and become more efficient and still compete effectively.

b *Quotas* These are set limits to the quantity of imports allowed for stated goods or for goods from specific countries. The UK has voluntary quota arrangements for some Japanese goods, including cars and some electronic equipment. There are often disputes concerning the precise details of quota agreements and traders tend to become experts at evasion, e.g. by changing the product or by routeing goods through a non-restricted country. Traders seem to regard barriers such as quotas as a challenge to their ingenuity!

c *Payment restrictions* Importers may be forbidden to obtain the foreign currency necessary to pay for foreign goods or be forced to obtain it through government-controlled banks at unrealistic rates of exchange that force up the prices of foreign goods.

We cannot here discuss the very complex economic issues raised by these restrictions which are common in developing countries. Most countries, including the United Kingdom and the USA have applied some of them at various times. By 1985 pressure was building up in the USA to limit what American producers were calling 'unfair trade'. We can see, however, that any restriction on trade or the movement of money must tend to reduce the total volume of trade in the world and probably the total volume of world production. Nevertheless trade and financial restrictions are a very real problem in the modern world and they have to be faced by firms engaged in international trade. They also encourage corruption, as great power is placed in the hands of officials who inspect goods and issue licences. Producers who are sheltered behind a 'wall' of trade protection usually become inefficient and unable to face strong competition.

The International Monetary Fund

We have seen that business managers and owners are likely to find themselves having to cope with sudden changes caused by shifts in the policies of governments or trading blocs such as the European Community. On the other hand business firms can themselves try to influence the policies of these sources of power. They can at least seek the support of political leaders if they suffer losses caused by restrictions such as the CAP's milk quotas of 1984. However, if a country's government gets into such economic trouble that it cannot honour basic international obligations such as the repayment of money owed then it can expect to find itself under intense pressure to pursue policies that are acceptable or believed to be essential by its creditors.

One of the most important creditors to a country in such a position is likely to be the International Monetary Fund. This is an international financial body set up in the mid-1940s for the purpose of helping nations which have temporary trade and balance of payments problems. It was hoped that if such countries could be provided with sufficient funds and supplies of acceptable trading currencies they would be able to restore their trade balances without having to resort to measures such as import controls and exchange rate changes that damaged world trade. The IMF has constantly pursued the broad aim of promoting world trade and maintaining stability in world trade.

Most nations outside the Soviet trade bloc belong to the IMF. They contribute to its funds and have the right to its financial assistance. It is always a condition of this help, however, that the nation's government is prepared to accept the Fund's guidance on the economic and financial policies it considers necessary to improve the country's general economy and trade. In recent years this has usually meant cutting back on government spending and borrowing and restricting total demand within the country. For a certain period this usually makes conditions more difficult for most business firms and is not likely to be popular within the country concerned. Although the countries most likely to become subject to IMF supervision are the developing countries, advanced industrial nations may also have to seek the Fund's help. The United Kingdom was in this position in 1976 and the British Government was forced to modify its economic policies as a condition of assistance.

The European Community

The formation and growth of the European Community from the original six to twelve countries by 1986 is a political and social movement

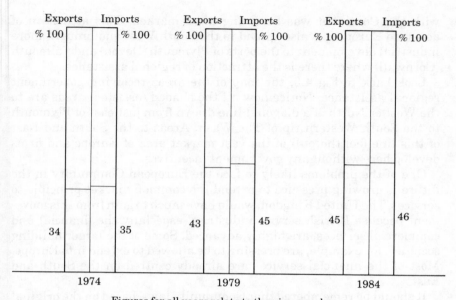

Figures for all years relate to the nine members

Fig 4.4   UK trade with the European Community. Source: United Kingdom
Balance of Payments HMSO 1985

as well as an economic trading bloc. The ultimate ideal is to provide
for the free movement of goods, people and money within all the
members but that ideal is a long way from being achieved.

Nevertheless there has been a substantial growth of trade between
the members of the Community. For industrial goods this has not been
accompanied by the barriers imposed against non-member trade that
has forced up food prices. This has important implications for the United
Kingdom. In 1984 around 45 per cent of British imports and exports
were traded with the European Community. As around a further 12
per cent of exports and 17 per cent of imports were with other Western
European countries this means that well over half of British trade
is now with Western Europe and Greece (an EC member). This affects
both the pattern and the location of production within the United
Kingdom. Britain is no longer an importer of food and basic materials
and an exporter of manufactured goods. Most of her trade is with other
developed, industrial nations and by 1984 Britain was paying more
for her imports of manufactured goods than she was earning from her
manufacturing exports.

At the same time trade with Europe had become so important that
the road and rail communication systems had to be adjusted to cope
with the traffic involved. Meanwhile the shift of firms towards the South
and East where they could have easy access to ports with close links

with the Continent was becoming more marked. This attraction of access to Europe has also spread to the South West and brought more industrial development to the ports of Plymouth (Devon) and Falmouth (Cornwall) where there is the attraction of regional assistance.

Look back to Fig 4.3, the map of the areas receiving government regional assistance. Notice how all the shaded (assisted) areas are to the West or North of a diagonal line drawn from just east of Plymouth to the South Western tip of The Wash. Areas to the South and East of this line feel the pull of the vast market area of Europe and firms develop here without any government incentives.

One of the problems likely to face the European Community in the future is growing pressure to extend the common market principle to services. The United Kingdom would have much to gain from this movement because British service industries, especially the financial and commercial services, are highly advanced. Some of the larger building societies, for example, are pressing to be allowed to extend into Europe. Most of the financial services are already centred on the South and East.

It should be remembered that Community laws, based on the original Treaty of Rome, forbid restrictions on trade between members but some exceptions have been made in recognition of the special problems of members. Hidden restrictions are more difficult to overcome.

Rapid review

1   What is meant by a balance of payments deficit?
2   What would be the effect on business if a government tried to reduce total demand to cure a balance of payments deficit?
3   If a government took no action to correct a persistent balance of payments deficit what would happen to the value of its currency in terms of other currencies?
4   Explain the difference between open and hidden restrictions on trade.
5   Describe three forms of open barriers to trade between countries.
6   What is the International Monetary Fund and how does it help countries?
7   How might Britain's membership of the European Community have influenced the location of British industry?

Social attitudes to business

The constraints on business behaviour

The public expects business organisations to pursue profits but to do this within certain codes of conduct. These codes are the reflection of the social attitudes of the day and are constantly being modified as society itself changes. The larger firms recognise this when they appoint public relations officers with the functions of showing the organisation and its members in a favourable light but also communicating to the organisation the expectations of the public. The owner-managers of small firms have always recognised that they have to operate within acceptable rules of conduct. They have to live within the communities they serve and indeed many self-employed business people seek positions of social status and influence within their communities, e.g. as magistrates, councillors, leaders of church, sporting or voluntary bodies. They cannot afford to undermine their private lives by their business conduct.

Interpretation of social attitudes is notoriously difficult. It is hard not to assume that one's own viewpoint is shared by everyone else. However, we may agree that modern business is expected to provide a good working environment for its workers, to maintain fair, ethical standards in its dealings with customers, to avoid destruction of and, if possible, to improve the physical environment within which it operates, and to avoid exploiting the weak either at home or in other countries.

Social attitudes and the law

To some extent the law clarifies and defines expectations of good business conduct. Sometimes it does not go as far as declaring certain actions illegal or making others compulsory, but in coming to legal decisions about the rights and wrongs of a particular dispute the courts may be required to examine whether the firm has observed certain codes of good business practice. This is one way in which the law has developed over relationships between firms and their customers and also between firms and their employees. Before deciding in favour of a firm which seeks to recover property from a debtor who has not paid the court will require evidence that the firm has made allowance for any special circumstances which caused the debtor to fail to pay as promised. Codes of conduct are also becoming increasingly relevant in labour relations, an area relatively new to the regulation of courts of law in the United Kingdom. There is a long history of law seeking to preserve reasonable standards of health and safety at work although this duty has been made much stricter since the early 1960s and has only applied generally throughout most private and public sector work since the mid-1970s.

In some cases the law still tends to support the firm's duty to make profits for its owners above other considerations. Before the provision of employee pensions became almost generally compulsory in Britain the law upheld shareholders' rights to profit above a company's moral duty to look after long-service workers in their retirement. More recently the law has supported the view that pension fund trustees should put the financial interests of the trust above purely moral or ethical considerations of how business profits might be earned.

Social attitudes and business management

Nevertheless most business managers are well aware that decisions must take into account society's view of what is and what is not accept-able behaviour. Few people wish to be exposed to public disfavour and when decisions have implications for workers, customers or the safety of the environment there is always the possibility of having to justify these in public through local or national press, radio or television dis-cussions.

Over some issues there are well-organised pressure groups. Anti-tobacco smoking groups have succeeded in banning smoking in the offices of many organisations. Other groups seek to publicise evidence of business exploitation of workers in some developing countries. Public sector management is just as likely, perhaps more likely, to find itself the target of criticism as their private sector counterparts. Pressure from the public has forced the nationalised gas and electricity boards to revise their procedure for cutting off power supplies in cases of non-payment of bills, particularly where customers are known to be elderly and infirm. Public action over the disposal of atomic waste is likely to change official policies on this difficult problem and has certainly led to increased managerial efficiency in maintaining safety standards.

We should, however, be very wary of assuming that public pressure always tends to improve standards of business conduct. Business is a reflection of the society within which it operates and changes in social attitudes are often subject more to fashions than to some mysterious law of moral progress. No doubt the nineteenth-century business owners who saw their firms as extensions of their families and who led their employees in morning prayers before embarking on the long and often brutally hard and unhealthy working day believed that they represented genuine social progress. We can now, perhaps, see their actions with greater clarity but before condemning them we must pause to wonder how our business (and private social) conduct will be viewed by future generations.

Rapid review

1   **How might social attitudes affect the objectives pursued by business organisations?**

2   Give two examples of changes in business practices resulting from the pressure of public opinion.

Exercises

1   'Business firms do not object to inflation because they can keep on increasing their prices.'
'Business firms fear inflation because they have to face constantly rising costs.'.
Which statement do you think is most likely to be correct? Give reasons for your answer.
2   'Changes in the country's exchange rate do not concern us as we are not involved in the export trade.' Explain why this statement from the owner of a small manufacturing company is likely to be wrong.
3   Apartheid and smoking are two issues over which social pressure groups seek to influence business decisions. You may think of some others. In what ways might business decisions be affected as a result of these and similar pressures?
4   Some large firms try to encourage their managers to take an active part in community life, as say, magistrates or school governors. Suggest reasons why the firms should take this attitude.
5   'We wish to reduce taxes in order to help business firms to produce more and to employ more workers.' How might a Government Minister justify this statement?
6   The chapter gives one example of a European Community decision (on reducing milk production) that affected farm businesses. Suggest other decisions that could be taken either by the Government or the European Community that would also have a major impact on particular industries.
7   What are the main business activities in your area? Suggest reasons why they are located in your area. List and discuss the locational advantages and disadvantages for (a) manufacturing and (b) financial services of your area.
8   To what extent has trade, the transport network, industry or agriculture been affected by Britain's membership of the European Community?
9   A Trade Union official is arguing that 'Britain must stop exporting jobs to foreign countries and impose strict controls over imported manufactured goods'. Prepare a letter in which you show the dangers that might follow from import controls.

Questions from examination papers

Short answer questions

1   Define invisible trade and give *two* examples of invisible exports which benefit the United Kingdom economy. AEB 0(A) 1983
2   Identify *three* differences between a public limited company and a workers' co-operative. AEB 0(A) 1983

3   Give *three* examples of how decisions taken by a local authority may affect firms already established in that area. AEB 0(A) 1983
4   Give *four* disadvantages of trading as a sole proprietor. AEB 0(A) 1985
5   Name *two* main documents which contain the regulations concerning a limited company and its members. AEB 0(A) 1985

Essay questions

1   *a*   Assess the advantages and disadvantages to the business sector of the United Kingdom of our membership of the European Economic Community.
b   How have these effects varied between different businesses and in different parts of the United Kingdom? AEB 0(A) 1982
2   *a*   Distinguish, with examples, between the public corporation and the public limited company as forms of business enterprise.
b   Discuss the disadvantages which may accrue to any business organisation as a result of increasing size. AEB 0(A) 1983
3   Casson Furniture Ltd is a company manufacturing office furniture.
a   Outline *four* ways in which this company will be affected by local government policies and decisions.
b   Examine *three* ways in which central government can influence the demand for the company's goods. AEB 0(A) 1985
4   A company's production processes are regarded by a pressure group as polluting the environment. Discuss how the company might be affected by the actions of the pressure group in this situation. AEB A Level 1984
5   Describe and discuss the problems experienced by a business trading both at home and abroad as the result of a depreciation in the external exchange rate. AEB A Level 1985

5 The production process

Even the simplest type of business involves the organisation of a number of different functions. Window cleaners, for example, do not just clean windows. They must build up a round of customers (sales and marketing) and collect and bank the money paid (finance). They must also work out an efficient way to do the round – which houses on which days. Above all they have to decide how much time to spend on each part of the business, how much time, for instance, to spend on cleaning windows and how much on looking for new customers. In effect they must manage themselves efficiently.

We saw in Chapter 1 that in most businesses there is likely to be some element of specialisation, that is, different people concentrating on doing different jobs. This will increase the problems of organising efficiently. In this chapter we will be looking at three related aspects of organising a business:

1   the major functions that may take place in the business;
2   the types of production system that we are likely to find in business;
3   the ways in which these functions and systems can be organised.

In a very large company managers can be served by a large number of specialists. Some of the specialist advisory and service departments within Unilever are illustrated in Fig 5.1.

Business functions

Students sometimes want to know, 'What is the most important function in a business? Is it production, marketing, finance or what?' It cannot be stressed enough that they all depend on one another and that a successful business ignores none of them. There is no point in making something no one will buy or in finding a market for something that cannot be produced.

Nevertheless, it is true that different functions may be more important in different businesses. This may be tied up with the type of product but it may also be different for firms in the same industry. For example, some car manufacturers are vertically integrated to a considerable

Specialist advisory and service departments

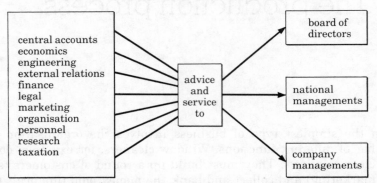

Fig 5.1   Specialist advisory and service departments. Source: 'Unilever's management and organisation'. Reproduced by courtesy of Unilever plc

extent. This is illustrated in Fig 5.2. In other words they produce many of the components they require themselves. The Ford Motor Corporation of America is a good example. Other motor manufacturers, including the largest of all, General Motors, 'buy in' many of their components. In this type of firm the purchasing function is likely to be more important than in the former.

With this in mind we can now examine the major business functions.

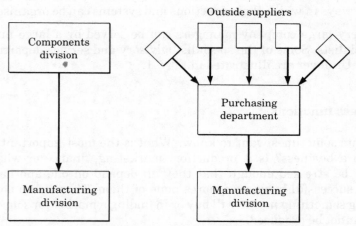

Fig 5.2   Sourcing from outside the firm increases the importance of purchasing

Purchasing

Most businesses need to acquire some goods such as raw materials or components and services such as insurance that will then be used in the firm's own production process. Skilful purchasing involves not only appraising the 'best buy' in terms of price, quantity, delivery time and so on, but also in ensuring that purchasing is interwoven with other important functions, such as manufacturing, which will be unable to proceed unless adequate supplies of materials are available.

On the other hand, it is the responsibility of the purchaser to ensure that too much is not bought. Quite apart from the financial implications of having large amounts of money tied up in idle stocks and earning nothing as a result of over-purchasing, the firm may not be able to handle too high a level of purchases. The firm might simply not have sufficient storage space. A purchaser needs to keep a very careful balance of stocks so that they are neither dangerously low nor expensively high.

Buying the key to selling

All the selling skill in the world will not help unless a firm is able to put the right goods literally 'in the shop window'.

The success of the big retail chains depends crucially not just on their skill in selling but in buying at keen prices and in buying the right goods at the right time. Some supermarkets aim to turn over their stocks twenty or more times a year. If they stock the wrong goods they clog up selling space. In order to get the right branded goods at the right price some of the large chains, such as Argos, employ buyers who operate throughout the world.

Production

In Chapter 1 we argued that anything could be regarded as productive as long as somebody was prepared to pay for it. This means that making goods and providing services are both 'production'. In business, however, the term 'production' is usually taken to mean making things: using equipment, people and raw materials to put together physical products as opposed to providing services.

Even this definition is still very broad and does not make it immediately clear what the work of the *production manager* typically involves.

Much will depend on the type of *production systems* and also on the formal organisation of the business. Both of these terms are examined later in this chapter.

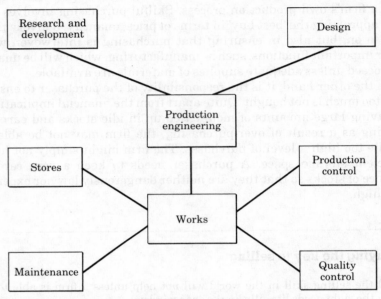

Fig 5.3   Some elements of production in manufacturing

Fig 5.3 shows a simple flow chart of some of the stages that are likely to be involved in the production process. Many or all of these activities are likely to be within the overall responsibility of the production manager.

Research and development

These are likely to be the responsibility of the technical department. Basic research on new materials, methods and products is then followed by a development phase in which new knowledge is developed to the point where it is commercially applicable. This is a crucial phase, as many new ideas turn out either to be too costly to carry out or not acceptable to the market on a scale large enough to make them commercially viable. More money is usually spent on development than on pure research. Some successful commercial development comes from spotting commercial possibilities in the research of others, sometimes in the published research of universities.

A further important phase is that of design. Detailed specifications of the new process or product are drawn up, along with plans, drawings, formulae and lists of materials. Design can be seen as the preparation of the blueprint for production.

How many ways can you lay bricks?

One of the earliest and most spectacular examples of the application of scientific work study and production design was carried out by Frank and Lilian Gilbreth in the building industry around the turn of the century. What could be more straightforward than laying bricks? Most people thought that after about 4000 years this task must surely have been perfected.

The Gilbreths reduced the number of movements in laying bricks from 18 to 5 by careful re-design of the whole bricklaying process. It might not be how you or I would build a garden barbecue but if you want to see the results of the Gilbreths' work simply visit any building site. The bricklayers there will be using at least some of their methods.

Production engineering

When the decision has been made what to produce the production engineer plans how it is to be produced. There may be several ways of doing a job. He or she decides which is the most appropriate and efficient. After this decision specifications and standards have to be laid down and tools selected or purpose designed and built.

The production engineer is also likely to be responsible for production planning which involves the rate and schedule of production, the ordering of materials and the utilisation of work force and machines. This obviously requires close co-operation with the people in the business who are responsible for selling the product.

Closely associated with production planning and often the responsibility of the same people, is production control. In brief, this ensures that the plans are being met, output maintained, schedules adhered to, quality maintained and so on. As we shall see a little later, although production and control go together their relative importance is likely to depend on the nature of the production process.

The works manager

Much important work has already been done before any goods are actually produced. The work of overseeing the actual process of manufacture is normally the responsibility of the works manager. As well as the various manufacturing activities the works manager's responsibilities include the stores department, work-in-progress and finished goods.

Inspection

We have already seen that it may be the responsibility of production control to check the quality of work completed. Another possibility is to have a separate inspection department. The object of inspection is to ensure that products that eventually go for sale are of a sufficiently high quality. The chief inspector's duties involve devising inspection techniques, determining the range within which slight departures from quality standards can be tolerated and communicating with the works departments about suggestions for improvements. For example, decisions have to be taken as to whether inspection should be centralised, i.e. all products inspected in a separate part of the factory, or decentralised, i.e. carried out as near as possible to the work place. The first method might simplify the actual process of inspection but the second would be likely to bring the results more quickly to the attention of the works manager who could then act to improve quality.

It must be stressed that a really effective inspection procedure is not one that results in the rejection of a lot of goods. This would be very costly for the business. The best procedure is the one that produces the smallest possible amount of waste material. The inspectors must be continually looking for ways to detect faults at an early stage and also should be able to suggest how they can be eliminated altogether.

Maintenance

In the same way the mark of good maintenance is not that plant and machinery are constantly being repaired, although repairs are part of the maintenance function. A schedule for the routine review of equipment should be followed so that breakdowns can be avoided. Maintenance might be organised as a separate department or, as with inspection, it might be part of another department such as works.

Marketing and sales

There now remains the crucial task of actually finding customers for the finished productions. Of course, as we have already seen, the production process could not have begun unless there had been some idea of what customers wanted and much production takes place in response to definite orders. In all events sales and marketing personnel are likely to work with other functions throughout the whole production process.

Why do people buy petrol?

Some years ago it was widely noticed that motorists tended to buy the same brand of petrol week in and week out. All sorts of sales campaigns were therefore designed to encourage and develop this 'brand loyalty'. Not many were very successful. Then it was realised that the reason why motorists bought the same brand was because they visited the same petrol stations – filling stations that they chose for convenience. Today oil companies put a lot less emphasis on supposed 'magic ingredients' in their petrol and a lot more on choosing good sites for their petrol filling stations, such as those near to housing estates, road junctions, after speed restriction signs and so on.

There is much more to marketing and sales than just putting a price on something and waiting for customers to turn up. As with production we can identify a number of different aspects. Marketing is examined in detail in Chapter 6 but at this stage we should recognise that it must involve:

   a   *market research* to discover customers' wants and to determine what sort of products and prices the firm can produce to meet them
   b   *advertising, sales promotion and public relations* all designed to foster favourable attitudes towards the firm and its products
   c   *sales activities* to make contact with the firm's customers and outside distributors in order to obtain actual orders for the firm's products
   d   *distribution* to get the goods to the customer and which involves
   e   *transport* and the making of decisions about the methods of distribution and transport to be employed, e.g. how far the firm will undertake these activities itself or leave them to other specialist organisations.

Any or all of these activities may be the responsibility of a separate department though as they clearly go together and depend on one another, there is likely to be a sales or marketing manager with overall control over these functions.

Many successful managers stress the importance of the firm's *market orientation*. In plain English this means deciding what business the firm is really in before committing the firm to specific decisions about product, sales technique and other marketing matters. This may seem fairly obvious but an example illustrates its importance. Is a successful brewery just in the business of making beer? We saw in Chapter 1 that Ruddles decided that the answer was 'yes' and therefore decided to specialise in this activity. Other successful breweries concluded that the answer was 'no' and that they were really in the business of providing a range of leisure and entertainment goods and services. Consequently they diversified into other activities such as travel and bingo halls.

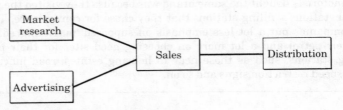

Fig 5.4   Some elements of marketing

Finance

Attention to the financial function is essential for the success of even the simplest business. The accounts books and financial records kept by a business are invaluable aids to control. For example, *budgets* may be drawn up to show how much it is planned to spend on each activity within the firm and *standard costs* will show how much it is estimated that each product will cost. By comparing the actual expenditure with the planned expenditure it becomes possible to spot where the firm is making and where it is losing money.

In a way this activity is rather like that of the inspection department which was concerned with the physical quality of the product. In the same way the mark of good financial control is that financial problems are identified at an early stage so that they can be put right. On the other hand the favourable trends need to be spotted sooner rather than later so that they can be fully exploited.

In many cases it is just as important to ensure that the business is profitable as it is to make sure that the *cash flow* is right. Look at this example.

The owner of a small business is persuaded that if he or she hires a machine for £500 per month, employs a worker at a cost of £500 per month to operate it and spends a further £500 per month on extra fuel and materials, he or she can produce goods each month that can be sold for £2000. On the face of it this appears a very profitable suggestion. By spending £1500 an income of £2000 will be received, to make a monthly profit of £500.

How to lose money

When Michael Edwardes took over as head of British Leyland one of the first things he did was to try and find out which of the company's products made money and which caused losses. The Mini, acclaimed as a world market leader in 1960 and year after year one of the company's top sellers, turned out to be losing £26 million a year. Other car firms had envied the market success of the Mini but had not introduced a competing car because they could not see how it could make money. They were evidently right!

But suppose that it is unrealistic to expect to sell any goods until at least the second month of operations and that trade customers, as is usual, will require time to pay. This may mean that income is not received until at least the fourth month. We can set this out in the form of a table (below).

Month	Outlay £	Cumulative outlay £	Receipts £	Cumulative receipts £	Cumulative deficit (−) or surplus (+) £
1	1500	1500	—	—	−1500
2	1500	3000	—	—	−3000
3	1500	4500	—	—	−4500
4	1500	6000	2000	2000	−4000
5	1500	7500	2000	4000	−3500
6	1500	9000	2000	6000	−3000
7	1500	10500	2000	8000	−2500
8	1500	12000	2000	10000	−2000
9	1500	13500	2000	12000	−1500
10	1500	15000	2000	14000	−1000
11	1500	16500	2000	16000	− 500
12	1500	18000	2000	18000	—
13	1500	19500	2000	20000	+ 500

This table shows that it takes a year before the business **breaks even**, i.e. before the earnings from the outlay just equal the total, cumulative cost. It is not until the second year of operation that there is a surplus.

This is a very important point. All the time the operation is, strictly speaking, 'profitable' because it is costing less to produce the goods than they will earn in sales. In cash terms, however, the firm is actually worse off throughout the first year of operation because of the pattern of cash flow. Before going ahead with this idea the owner of the business must ask questions such as : 'Can I afford to run these deficits for this long? Can I obtain credit from somewhere, such as a bank? If so, how much will this credit cost?'

In the recession of the early 1980s many firms failed not so much because they had been inefficient in the sense of being 'unprofitable' but because their cash flow was out of balance and they were unable to pay their bills.

The *financial manager* or *chief accountant*, if the firm has one, has other responsibilities, such as preparing accounts for people outside the firm, including the shareholders, tax authorities and the Registrar of Companies. He or she will also seek outside sources of finance for the business, an issue examined in more detail in Chapter 9.

Rapid review

1 Identify three ways in which the purchasing department contributes to the work of the firm.
2 How does the meaning of 'production' as a management function differ from 'production' in the economy as a whole?
3 What is the difference between 'research' and 'development'? Why are the two terms often used together?
4 What is meant by 'design'?
5 Explain the terms 'production planning' and 'production control'.
6 Name two possible systems of inspection.
7 State five elements of the marketing function.
8 What is meant by the term 'a market orientated firm'?
9 Briefly define the following terms: budget, standard cost, cash flow, break even.

Production systems

We have already seen that the relative importance of the different functions in a business and the way they are handled are likely to be affected by the nature of the product and by the production process. Consider the following examples.

Scale of operations

In a small business many of the functions are likely to be undertaken by the same person. Many of the *co-ordinating* activities of management are, therefore, likely to be less important than in a large company where the work of separate departments needs careful integration. For example, in a one-person firm the activities of production planning, control and inspection will be automatically, even unconsciously, undertaken by the one owner who is responsible for selling what he or she produces.

Service industries

So far we have been considering firms supplying goods rather than services. For the latter, however, the service often has to be adjusted to customers' special needs. Consequently the functions of marketing, design and production are closely linked. In general, the very nature of services ensures that the activities of sales and production go very closely together.

For instance, a customer needing his or her car serviced does not wait to be approached by a salesman from a garage. The motorist will probably make direct contact with the garage to obtain immediate information about when the work can be done and the likely price. In this kind of business there is, therefore, likely to be a *service manager* whose

Fig 5.5 The work of the service department is rarely routine

responsibilities will cover a mixture of sales, production planning and control, works management and so on. The service manager will co-ordinate the work of the service department in line with the wishes of customers. Schedules must be drawn up to ensure that work is carried out according to arrangements agreed with the customers.

Clearly this sort of activity is difficult to reduce to a simple routine and the co-ordination and supervisory roles of management are likely to be more demanding. For this reason service departments are often kept fairly small and indeed many of the most successful service businesses are small firms.

Different types of goods are likely to be produced in different ways.

Unit production

Whether one is making a bespoke overcoat or building an oil drilling rig the job is a 'one off' and tailored to the customer's special needs. Although certain parts of the process can be reduced to a routine, each job is essentially unique. Sales, design and production engineering must go closely together. Production planning is a fairly routine operation here, largely consisting of deciding whether the work is within the capabilities of the firm. Production control, however, is extremely important and demanding; indeed production co-ordination is likely to be the most significant managerial function in this type of production.

Mass production

Here we move to the other extreme with goods being produced in large numbers. At some stage there must have been co-ordination between marketing and production to ensure that there was a mass market for the goods to be produced. Thereafter, however, the link between the two functions can be fairly routine, simply a matter of agreeing schedules or the number of goods to be produced.

One of the major attractions of mass production is the possibility of reducing costs through *economies of scale*. Production planning, therefore, becomes extremely important. Careful attention at this stage can achieve cost savings which, applied to thousands of items, add up to an enormous total. Production planning here will extend to designing layouts, acquiring special equipment, to manpower planning, stores and so on. By contrast, production control becomes a routine activity. A well designed mass production system will virtually run itself and the work of supervision is much simpler than when dealing with unique unit production.

Batch production

The production of goods in batches falls between unit and mass production. Unit production, from the point of view of the production departments, is 'for customer' whereas mass production is 'for store', with goods being removed from store by the sales department. In batch production goods are produced neither entirely for store nor on receipt of customers' orders. Production levels, however, are continually adjusted according to the state of the market so that fairly close liaison is required between production and sales. Particularly important decisions concern the size of batches to be produced and the scheduling of which batches of which goods are to be produced at which time.

Continuous process production

This has much in common with mass production except that, instead of large quantities of individual items being made, the product is produced in bulk. Examples include oil refining, manufacture of plastic and the conversion of other raw materials. In many industries the automation of this process has gone further than in mass production so that, whereas a lot of mass production is carried out by relatively unskilled labour working on assembly lines, continuous process industries often employ fewer, but more highly skilled and qualified workers, largely for control and inspection purposes.

As we see later in this chapter, a change in the workforce may affect the nature of the organisation.

Production systems and specialisation

If you think carefully about the various systems of manufacturing production you will see that each is applying the principle of specialisation but adapting this to the scale of production best suited to the needs of the market. The common idea is that each worker is given a specific task and performs a small part of the total production process. When all the parts have been completed the process as a whole is complete.

If we look at this from the viewpoint of the worker we can see that it has the advantage that he or she becomes extremely skilled at one limited operation or set of operations but suffers from the monotony of endless repetition. This monotony is relieved to some extent by the smaller scale operations. In unit production, for example there are likely to be small differences with each separate item and these make

Potato crisps

A change in the production process made possible by changing technology can have a major impact on every aspect of a product's production, marketing and development. At one time potato crisps were manufactured in small plants scattered around the country using a process not far removed from that used at home for frying chips. A major company took over one small firm – Golden Wonder – and introduced a continuous, mass production method which enabled the product to be produced to a standard quality. A change in packing was also introduced to lengthen the shelf life of the packet and this moved the potato crisp out of the pub into the supermarket. More crisps were bought for children and different flavoured crisps were introduced. Further developments in technology enabled a much wider range of similar snacks to be produced and a large and highly competitive industry developed.

calls on the worker's skill and experience. Similar differences are also probable in batch production as products are modified to meet the needs of different customers.

It is continuous production that gives rise to the stories of people spending years doing exactly the same task with exactly the same set of tools. Sometimes the monotony is increased by the need to remain in roughly the same position for long periods of time and by constant noise which makes normal communication with other workers extremely difficult. Psychologists – and novelists – describe how people switch off from their surroundings and live in a dream world while they are working. Work then becomes solely a means to earn money in order to live during the hours spent not working.

When a particular job has been reduced to a purely mechanical operation it can probably be performed more efficiently by a machine which gets neither tired nor bored. Many mechanical jobs, especially those in continuous process production, have been taken over by automation. Robotics, the study and application of robots to industrial tasks, has become a major new service to manufacturing industry. The resulting fall in the number of unskilled or semi-skilled jobs on assembly lines has been one of the causes of increased unemployment in the 1980s.

When the scale of the production process does not justify the high starting costs of automation or of robots the mechanical tasks remain and the problem of monotony remains also. It then becomes a problem of management to resolve this by introducing variety, movement and opportunities for communication into work procedures. Some firms believe that the gain in worker morale from these changes more than outweighs any losses from reduced specialisation.

It is sometimes suggested that the specialised industrial worker is very vulnerable to changes in demand or production techniques that can destroy the demand for his or her special skill. There is some truth in this and the more limited the application of the skill the more vulnerable the worker. In a rapidly changing world there is a need for the worker to be adaptable; to be willing and able to learn new skills. In general the higher a person's level of general education the more adaptable that person is throughout life.

In a world which is having to adjust to high levels of unemployment this is a powerful argument for making the most of your opportunities at school and college!

Rapid review

1 Suggest one reason, relating to management, why many service
   organisations are small firms
2 Briefly define the following terms: unit production, mass production, batch
   production, continuous process production.
3 What benefits and what problems does specialisation bring to a production
   system?

Business organisations

There now remains the question of the best way to organise the functions of the business. Simply bringing together the best specialists will not necessarily make for a very effective business. You may have seen a football team, made up of 'star players' in almost every position, yet still struggling because co-ordination and organisation have been lacking.

Suppose we have a business with two departments, sales and production. How can their activities be co-ordinated and overall strategy for the firm be developed on such issues as developing new products or markets? We could do this in a number of ways, two of which are shown in Fig 5.6.

In the **line** structure the major strategic and co-ordinating decisions are taken by the managing director. The sales and production managers then plan their departments' activities in accordance with these decisions which are thus passed 'down' the line. In the **corporate management** structure the three work together as a team to make decisions

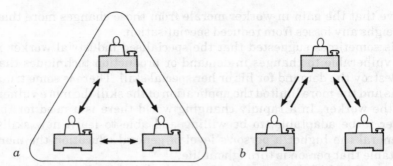

Fig 5.6*a*   Corporate management: problems tackled as a team effort. *b*   Line management: subordinates provide information and receive instructions relating to their own particular responsibilities

affecting the whole company. When making these decisions the departmental heads are, of course, expected to look at problems from the point of view of the firm as a whole rather than just their own departments.

Many years ago there were attempts to devise an ideal organisational structure that would suit all types of business. It is now generally accepted that there is no such ideal and that different types of structure suit different types of industry and business environment. However, it is very useful to look at some of the major aspects and determinants of organisational structure. We shall then be able to see how some of these are affected by the activities, size or environment of the firm.

Functional centralisation and decentralisation

So far in this chapter we have been considering firms where, typically, each department is organised along *functional* lines. That is to say that the departmental manager is responsible for a major business function such as production, finance or sales. This centralisation of functions into their own departments has a number of advantages. Notably it allows the maximum specialisation and exploitation of the cost benefits derived from economies of scale.

An alternative is to divisionalise the firm, for example by product or geography. This means that each senior manager is responsible for all the functions associated with a particular product or area. The advantage claimed for this is that, in contrast to the functionally organised firm, there is somebody responsible for ensuring that each product or market area is run in a profitable way. It is suited to large firms which produce a wide range of products. Many large manufacturers, those in the car industry, for example, adopt this type of organisation.

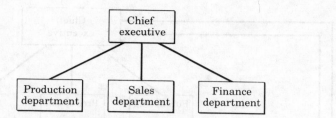

Fig 5.7   Example of functionally organised firm

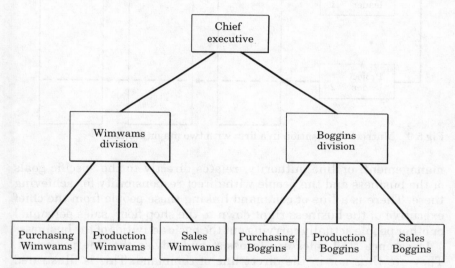

Fig 5.8   Example of divisionalised firm producing two products (wimwams and boggins)

Another kind of structure which attempts to gain the advantages of divisionalisation without complete functional decentralisation is the *matrix* organisation. Here, functional specialists are still concentrated into functional departments but personnel are then drawn from departments for particular projects, each project having its own co-ordinating manager (see Fig 5.9). This type of structure suits industries where individual projects have a limited life span. The aerospace industry is one where it has been used successfully.

Line, staff and functional organisation

A distinction is often drawn between line and staff management although the distinction may not always be clear in practice. Line

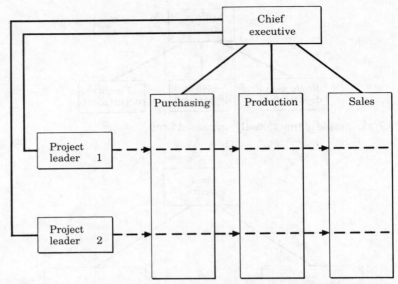

Fig 5.9   Matrix organisation in a firm with two major projects

management, or line authority, relates directly to the specific goals of the business and the people with direct responsibility for achieving these. There is a line of command linking these people from the chief executive of the business right down to the shop floor, sales personnel or other people actually carrying out the basic activities of the business.

In essence staff roles are to assist and advise the line personnel. They are thus not in the direct line of command. This is illustrated in the organisation chart of Fig 5.10. Staff are often experts or specialists in one field or another. Examples of roles often carried out on a staff basis include personnel assistants, research staff and finance officers.

Very often whole departments may have a staff relationship with the rest of the organisation, for example the department of the personnel manager or of the chief finance officer. Within these departments there is again a clear line of authority from the departmental heads to junior personnel but the whole department stands apart from the 'line' of the business as a whole.

The difference between staff and line activities is sometimes described as 'staff *say* what to do but it's up to the line *whether* to do it or when'. Clearly, in this sense staff are subordinate to line authority but, in practice, line managers will only reject the advice of specialist staff after very serious consideration.

One of the attractions of having a clearly defined line of command is that it makes for *unity of command* – that is to say each person

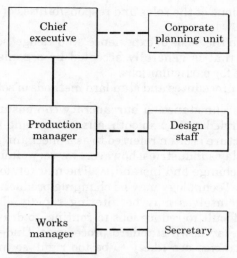

Fig 5.10   Line and staff relations. The solid lines show 'line' relations, the broken lines 'staff' relations

in the organisation has only one superior to whom to report and from whom instructions are taken. This prevents the kind of confusion that could arise if somebody were to receive contradictory instructions from two superiors.

However there may be circumstances in which it is felt that certain aspects of work should be authorised by someone other than the direct line superior. For example, expenditure over a certain amount might require the approval of the finance manager. In these cases we say that the specialist, here the finance manager, has *functional authority* for all major financial matters throughout the organisation in which-ever department they arise. The same sort of functional authority might be exercised by specialists such as purchasing, transport or public relations managers.

Bureaucracy and other types of organisation

When we hear the word 'bureaucracy' we often think of buck passing, rigidity, form filling and so on. Bureaucracy, however, in the context of organisation means a particular type of structure. Indeed, in the past, it has been the way that many of the largest and most effective firms have been organised. It has certain features:

1   A clear line of authority and command from the top to the bottom of the organisation.

2 Clear definitions of the roles and responsibilities of each individual and department.

3 Posts filled on the basis of experience, knowledge, seniority or some other attribute that is generally accepted by organisation members to qualify people for particular jobs.

4 Use of rules, procedures and standard methods of solving problems.

In the right circumstances a bureaucracy can ensure that business activities are carried on in a smooth, almost machine-like way; in fact this type of structure is often referred to as a 'mechanistic' one.

In many of today's industries, however, we very often encounter conditions of rapid change and instability. The market, for example, may be very volatile. Technology may be changing production methods and the products themselves may be altering rapidly. These conditions make it very difficult to reduce jobs to routine, to draw up precise job definitions or to lay down standard procedures. Under these circumstances bureaucracies are likely to be too rigid, so many firms have sought different structures. These are often based on groups or teams with the emphasis on participation and consultation. People are encouraged to consult with anyone in the organisation who can help solve their problems rather than go through 'approved channels'. They are expected to apply their own particular abilities to whatever problems come their way without being concerned by demarcation lines between their own and other people's spheres of responsibility.

Principles of management

The kind of changes we have just outlined obviously mean that there is no definite 'right' or 'wrong' sort of organisation suitable for all industries and markets, nor is there any definite 'right' or 'wrong' way to manage a business. Attempts to reduce the practice of management to a set of hard and fast rules are bound to be failures. It is impossible to lay down what should and should not done in all circumstances.

For instance, many years ago there were attempts to define an optimal **span of management** which would be appropriate in all circumstances. The span of management refers to the number of subordinates that are supervised by one superior. In Fig 5.11 we have shown two ways of structuring a firm where there are 16 people working at the lowest level. In diagram A the span of management is two. In diagram B it is four. Clearly, in an organisation of given size the wider the span of management the fewer layers of management there will be in the organisation.

We now know that there is no 'right' span of management which is associated with business success. Nevertheless, this does not mean

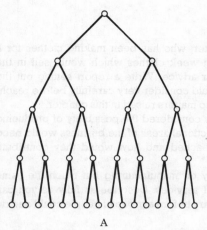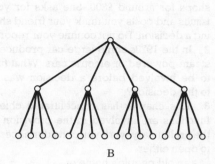

Fig 5.11   Tall versus flat hierarchies

that there is no point in studying and analysing the span of management. For example, a narrow span makes possible closer supervision and control but, because there are more layers in the management structure, senior managers are more likely to be 'cut off' from what is happening on the shop floor. On the other hand a wide span may improve communications but it makes the work of individual managers more difficult. A balance must be struck, appropriate for the individual firm.

The principles of management can be studied in the same way. While we cannot expect textbooks of management to turn anyone and everyone into first class managers, individual aspects of a manger's job will repay careful study. We cannot all be good sportsmen but even the best athlete benefits from coaching in the basics of his or her sport.

Rapid review

1   What is meant by 'corporate management'
2   What are the alternatives to a 'functional' system of organisation?
3   What is meant by 'matrix' organisation?
4   Explain the differences between 'line', 'staff' and 'functional' organisation.
5   List four features of bureaucracy.
6   Why can a bureaucratic structure cause problems in a period of rapid technological change?
7   What is meant by 'the span of management'?
8   What problems can arise if the span of management is kept narrow?

Exercises

1   A friend of yours, a skilled dressmaker, who has been making clothes for a hobby, believes that she can make each week clothes which would sell in the shops for around £300. She asks for your advice. Write a report setting out the issues and costs you think your friend should consider very carefully before reaching a decision. Do not confine your report to matters raised in this chapter.

2   In the 1970s some large car producers considered the possibility of producing steam-powered or electric cars. What functional areas of the business would need to be involved before a decision was reached and how would they contribute to that decision?

3   This chapter has concentrated chiefly on manufacturing but much the same functions are involved in the provision of services. Describe as fully as you can the preliminary work you consider necessary before a group of people could decide to open either

a an old people's home or

b a language school.

4   Classify the following activities according to whether you think they are likely to be service, unit, batch, mass production or continuous process:

food processing; printing; jobbing building; private practice accounting; electricity generation; electricity distribution; aircraft manufacture; industrial window cleaning; contract cleaning; computer hardware production; computer software production.

If you are not sure of the answer or if you think that an activity could be classified in more than one way, give your reasons.

5   Suppose your dressmaker friend became so successful that she obtained long-term contracts to supply a number of major stores. This would involve taking on help to share the workload. In what way would this be likely to change the nature of the production process and how might the change affect the relative importance of the various business functions?

6   Initially the dressmaking business was a one-person business. Then it grew (see question 5) so that a number of people were employed. Suppose it grew still larger to become a nationally important company and then larger again, to have production facilities in a number of different countries. Describe the sort of changes in organisational structure that you consider to be appropriate at each stage.

7   Look again at Fig 5.11. Describe the advantages and disadvantages that you feel apply to having either a 'tall' structure or a 'flat' one. Suggest two types of business that you would expect to be best fitted to each type of structure.

6 Marketing and distribution

In the previous chapter we have seen that marketing and distribution are vital activities in any firm, however large or small. It is not enough simply to produce some goods or services, put a price on them and wait for customers to appear. There are a number of important activities that any business has to undertake in order to ensure that it can sell what it produces. In this chapter we look at these activities in more detail.

Assessing the market

The importance of knowing the market

Fig 6.1 Know your market

When business people talk about the 'market' for their products they mean the actual and potential customers for the products. It is important to have some idea of the market before starting production and this is true even of the simplest and smallest business. Suppose, for example, you were thinking of setting up a window cleaning round. Will there be customers for your service?

If, for example, you live in a country area, there may be few customers and they may be a long way apart. On the other hand, if the potential customers include farmers and 'stockbroker belt' customers, they are likely to be able to afford a window cleaning service. In an inner-city area, there may be more houses closer together, but many people may be unable to pay for the service.

What, however, do we mean by customers being able to afford the service? Are they prepared to pay a price high enough to make it worth while providing the service? Remember, also, that the price people are willing to pay to have their windows cleaned will depend on the price being charged by other window cleaners.

To sum up, then, even for this simple service we have to recognise that the market will be influenced by:

a   The *number* of potential customers.
b   How much they *want* the service.
c   The *income* of potential customers.
d   The service being offered by *competitors*.

Furthermore, even people who buy the same product or service may do so for very different reasons and they can influence the way we try to serve the market.

It can be useful to identify the different types of customer. This is known as 'market segmentation' analysis. For instance, the people who are prepared to pay to have their windows cleaned are likely to do so for different reasons. There are those for whom it is simply convenient. There are some who cannot stand heights. There are people who employ a window cleaner once in a while, out of habit. Then there may be a number who want more frequent calls just to have somebody calling at the house!

If assessing the market is important for small firms, it is no less essential for large ones. Many of the goods that, as consumers, we take for granted today are only available at prices we can afford because they are mass produced, a process which tends to make the costs of producing each article much cheaper. Mass production methods are often very expensive to set up so that it becomes necessary, as we saw in Chapter 5, to ensure that there is a mass market for the product.

It is possible to think of more modern examples where the same problem that confronted Henry Ford has been faced, though not always as successfully. Today an enormous mass market has been discovered for home computers. There is also now a very large market for video tape recorders, though attempts to produce home video tape recorders 20 years ago came to very little. Attempts to mass produce and sell cigarettes with tobacco substitutes were another costly failure. In the mid-1980s Sir Clive Sinclair tried to launch an electric powered tricycle.

The Ford Story

What was the greatest contribution of Henry Ford to the motor vehicle industry? Most people would reply that it was the introduction of the assembly line and the mass production of vehicles. But there were hundreds of independent car producers at that time, most of them run by skilled engineers. It must have occurred to many of them that motor cars could be manufactured by mass production methods. It was Ford who saw that there would be a *market* for mass produced cars. Most producers felt that people would not be prepared to part with very large sums of money to buy a standardised product. After all, this is still the conventional wisdom in a number of industries. It is technologically quite possible to produce prefabricated houses in factories, and to mass produce grand pianos or boats by the hundreds of thousands.

Perhaps you can think of other examples where products have been launched either successfully or unsuccessfully.

Methods of market appraisal

There are a number of ways in which a firm can investigate the market either for a new or an existing product.

Using sales figures and reports

However well a product is selling, it is worthwhile keeping an eye on sales figures or reports from sales staff. First of all, sales personnel may report that customers are expressing a wish for something new. Secondly the trend of sales over a time can be illuminating.

Many successful people in marketing find the idea of a **product life cycle** useful. This is based on the experience that for many products sales over time do not remain constant, nor do they grow at a constant rate, but instead they fluctuate as shown in Fig 6.2.

Experience may suggest which stage a product has reached in its life cycle, whether future sales can be expected to expand or contract and at what rate. In addition it may be possible to anticipate when a new product will become necessary and, perhaps, what sort of product that should be.

For example, if it is predicted that sales will decline we might reasonably ask why. Is it because customers are becoming bored or the market saturated, or is some new product expected to become available?

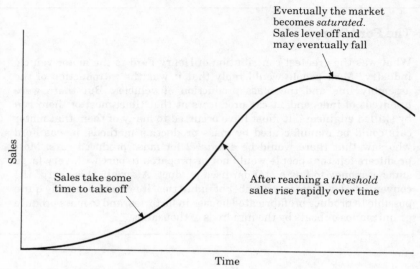

Fig 6.2   The product life cycle

Do we attempt to re-stimulate demand, find other uses for the product in order to attract new customers, or should we produce something different that customers can turn to?

It is not always a straightforward exercise to work out a trend even when there is reliable information. Some of the techniques used are described in the appendix at the end of this chapter.

Market testing

The most direct way that we could assess how well a new product would go would be to try actually selling it to people. This means carrying out an experiment in a particular town before trying to sell the product over a wider area. Cadbury's tried selling their new 'Wispa' chocolate bar in Scotland before launching it throughout the country. British Rail experimented with changes in its catering on a few services before extending them generally.

The advantage of this sort of experiment is that it is a direct test of whether people *really will* buy a product or pay a particular price rather than trying to work out what they *would* do. Its disadvantages include its cost, as the product has to be produced and marketed, if only on a limited scale. In addition we still cannot be sure that the results can be applied more widely. When any product is introduced there may be an impact effect, the product being bought initially for its novelty value which obviously wears off. Another problem is whether the area in which the tests are being carried out is really representative.

Will people throughout Britain have the same tastes in chocolate bars as those in Scotland? Will rail passengers in the North of England react in the same way as those on the South Coast?

Experiments under 'laboratory conditions'

A way of reducing costs and also making sure that the group of customers is truly representative, is to test out a product on a panel of selected customers who can be chosen as an average cross-section by age, income, occupation, sex and so on.

This may make the test cheaper and in some ways more reliable, but one major problem may be that people may try to be too helpful. In reality we may pay little attention, for example, to differences of a penny or two in product prices and choose an item for all kinds of 'irrational' reasons such as the packaging or because we like the brand name. If, however, we are closely examined about our choice we may start to stress things like its price or make great play of minor differences in such features as the texture or flavour of a soup.

That is not to say, for example, that the price, colour or flavour of soups are not important. Any one of these could be a major selling point. It is just that market researchers are aware of the tendency of panellists to make an exaggerated point of small differences. One subtle way round this may be to confront panellists with a number of varieties of tomato soup and ask them to choose which has the best texture when, in reality, all have the same texture but there are slight variations in colour. If customers express a significant preference for the 'texture' of one variety it is likely to be because subconsciously they have preferred its colour.

Questionnaires

Many of the same problems that beset panel tests are encountered in carrying out questionnaire surveys. However, with questionnaires we can get a picture of the tastes and preferences of a very large number of people chosen because they are believed to represent a true cross-section of the market.

On the other hand, whereas market tests and panel experiments deal with people's real reactions to real products, questionnaires tend to deal with hypothetical questions about what people would do, or would prefer or would buy. It is possible, by skilful questionnaire design to cross check on people's responses and to avoid asking leading questions which may prompt people to answer in a particular way. An example of such a question would be, 'Do you think you would probably buy more of this if it were a lot cheaper?' In order to avoid such pitfalls it is usually desirable to employ a specialist in survey techniques.

Another reason why specialist skills are necessary is the difficulty of making sure that the people answering the questionnaire are really representative of the market. Statisticians often talk about trying to obtain a truly **random sample** which will accurately reflect the market as a whole.

Getting a random sample might seem easy. Why not simply stop people in the street? But consider the way in which people may be *biased*. For example, if we conducted our survey on a Tuesday afternoon we would exclude anybody who was at work at that time. Our sample would include an undue proportion of housewives, mothers with young children, shift workers or unemployed.

Because of subtle problems like this, many firms that employ questionnaire surveys are happy to use outside experts. Specialist agencies like Gallup or National Opinion Polls often carry out work for business firms as well as their well publicised political surveys.

Using published data

Rather than carry out or commission their own market research, many firms prefer to study published data and then to draw their own conclusions or to learn from the published analysis of experts.

The British Government publishes a large amount of useful information. For example, *Social Trends* contains a wealth of information on topics as diverse as size of families, ownership of cars and how people spend their leisure time. All of these topics convey important information to business firms. The *Business Monitor* contains detailed analyses of individual trades and industries. There are, in fact, so many official sources of information that it is difficult to know where to start looking. The government's own *List of Government Publications* is usually a good starting point.

Many trade associations conduct surveys and publish information useful to their members. In addition the specialised trade press is a valuable source of information and analysis. More general publications such as the *Economist* and *Financial Times* often publish material useful for particular trades.

Rapid review

1 List four influences on the size of a market for a product.
2 What is meant by 'market segmentation'?
3 State one necessary condition for mass production to be successful.
4 What is meant by a product's 'life cycle'?
5 How is it possible to 'test a market'?
6 Why may information from market research enquiries be unreliable?

7 **What is meant by the term 'random sample'?**
8 **Name two British Government publications that contain information useful to marketing managers.**
9 **Name two other publications which are also useful to marketing managers.**

Promoting sales

The sort of information that can be obtained from the methods we have just outlined can be used to show not only what customers do want but also what they might want. It is a feature of modern business that producers do not simply trail behind consumers, providing something for which a demand has been built up. Many modern industries have developed on the back of inventions for which it was not immediately obvious that there was a powerful consumer demand.

Electric lighting had to be introduced against an unpromising background in which the market was already very well served by gas lighting. Telephones were introduced to an accompaniment of rather derogatory press comments that they were hardly necessary in a market already well served by telegraph services and five postal deliveries a day. You might also consider the difficulties of getting anyone to pay to have a telephone when hardly anyone else has one!

Advertising and other techniques of sales promotion must, therefore, be seen not just as devices for informing customers about a product but also as ways to create or develop demand.

Advertising

Advertising fulfils a number of useful functions.

a It passes on useful information to customers and can present this information in the most favourable and persuasive way. For example, not only can a price be given but it can be stressed how cheap this is in relation to the price previously charged or to the prices of competitors.

b The image of the product can be favourably enhanced. For example Macdonalds have skilfully adapted their television advertising to particular markets. In early evening the emphasis is on fun and games to appeal to children. Later in the evening the advertisements change to emphasise service and pleasant surroundings to attract adults.

c Advertising, and other forms of sales promotions, are useful methods of combating competition. The most obvious way of competing with business rivals may appear to be to cut prices. The problem, however, with price cuts is that it is very easy for competitors to retaliate by cutting their prices. The result may simply be that profits all round are reduced and no firm is better off. It is much more difficult for competitors to respond to advertising campaigns. One firm's slogans and campaigns may be very successful. Another firm may spend the same amount of money on its campaign and it is much less successful.

d Advertising may be aimed not so much at existing rivals as at competitors who may appear in the future. Any firm wanting to launch its new product into a market already well served by others will find that it has to overcome the images which have been built up by years of advertising and marketing effort.

It is not surprising that advertising may achieve a number of different ends. Business managers are not always clear why exactly they are advertising. Advertising budgets are often set as a fraction of forecast sales. This implies that higher sales may cause more advertising rather than the reverse!

Nevertheless, such rule-of-thumb approaches are not entirely to be ridiculed. Businessmen may be correct in assuming that advertising is important, even if they are not sure exactly why.

Advertising media

Advertising can take a number of forms of which the following are examples:

national or regional television; national or local newspapers and magazines; commercial radio; cinema; billboards; circulars; point of sale displays. The choice of medium for advertising will be influenced by a number of factors:

a *Cost* This includes the cost of both designing and developing the advertisement and of the medium. For example, the cost of television advertising includes that of making the commercial and that of the television time.

b *Size and nature of the target audience* The potential customers may be spread throughout the country, making national advertising sensible. On the other hand they may be concentrated in one area so that local or regional advertising would be more effective. Moreover, customers for some kinds of products may require different types of advertising. Advertising of financial services often requires considerable detail and this makes press advertising more suitable than, say, commercial television. Other potential customers may best be reached through specialist magazines or through circulars. Building services, for example, can be advertised in detail directly to selected households. Changes in technology can alter the pattern of advertising. If cable television becomes widespread this is likely to open new and potentially valuable avenues for selective forms of advertising.

The cost of advertising and the nature of the target audience go hand in hand. Commercial television advertising may appear very expensive, £26 000 per minute, for example, on national TV at peak time in the early 1980s, but in terms of potential customers reached it may be very cheap. The 'exposure cost', i.e. the cost per potential customer likely to see the advertisement, may amount to just a fraction of a penny.

Other forms of sales promotion

There are many other ways of promoting a product.

Participation in major exhibitions or trade fairs

This may be particularly appropriate if the potential customers are commercial buyers who attend such shows and look upon them as an important way to make contact with suppliers and find out about new products.

Sponsorship

Sponsorship of the arts, public works or sporting activities can be very effective in putting a product or company name before the public. Sports sponsorship has been a useful way of getting product names mentioned on the BBC, which does not carry formal advertising. Cornhill Insurance are believed to have benefited substantially from the sponsorship of Test cricket matches.

Packaging and display

Attractive packaging of a product, advertising in shops (point of sale), special displays in shops and other aspects of **merchandising** such as special offers and free samples, can not only maintain existing sales but are also useful devices for encouraging first-time buyers. The hope is that the costs, especially of special offers and promotions, will be recouped through repeat sales.

Public relations (PR)

Skilful 'PR' can obtain media coverage which may, in some ways, be even more successful than conventional advertising. After all, customers can recognise advertising for what it is, but may be influenced to a greater extent by favourable mention of a product in the editorial or news content of TV, radio or the press. Many companies, therefore, cultivate careful contacts with specialist journalists and issue press releases which, they hope, will be reported in the media. Record companies send free copies of records to disc jockeys and authors appear on TV chat shows when they have a new book released.

Analysing the market

If you propose to carry out some market research or to try to market a product it is essential to analyse the market and to be sure about who it is you are trying to reach. For example you will have to ask yourself questions like:

Are we trying to sell directly to the public or to trade customers?
Is our product for general sale or is it aimed at a special group such as firms in a particular trade or hobby enthusiasts?
Is there a substantial export market?
Is our business such that we want to sell a few products to many customers or sell in large quantities to a few customers? Should we change this balance in the future?

Our market research may suggest that a market that we have previously ignored could provide us with plenty of sales in the future. Careful market analysis can assist in making sales promotion much more effective and also help us to choose appropriate forms of distribution, an aspect that is examined in the next section.

Rapid review

1 **List four functions of advertising.**
2 **List the main advertising media.**
3 **What are the main influences on the choice of advertising medium by business firms?**
4 **What is meant by 'advertising by sponsorship'?**
5 **What is the role of public relations in the business organisation?**
6 **What questions is market analysis seeking to answer?**

Distribution

Efficient production methods, coupled with skilful marketing, may have ensured that we can produce goods or services cheaply and that there is a market for them. There remains the vitally important question of how we actually get our goods and services to the customer.

Channels of distribution

Direct sales to customers

This, of course, is the oldest form of distribution and in many trades it remains the most important. However, it can be a very awkward one in some businesses such as manufacturing. Customers, especially private buyers, are unlikely to go to a factory to buy what they want, and manufacturing firms, at least in the past, have not wanted to spread their energies into retailing by opening their own stores. Manufacturers, therefore, have tended to use a number of intermediaries to get their products to the customer.

Manufacturers in some sectors have run their own retail outlets. The major oil companies, for example, have extended beyond oil refining into controlling their own retail distribution systems. This has not always been successful and there were reports of at least one company seeking to sell its chains of petrol filling stations in the mid 1980s.

There are other trades where producers sell directly to customers. In some cases this is because producers find it advantageous to control the final retail stage and be in a position to offer a complete service, including after-sales service, to the customer.

In other industries producers may sell directly to consumers through factory shops, farm shops, 'pick-your-own' arrangements at farms, by mail order or any other scheme that business ingenuity may devise.

In the main, however, it still suits the majority of producers to specialise in what they know best, the physical production of the product, and to leave its distribution to other specialists.

Organised markets

After direct selling, markets represent the oldest form of trade from producer to consumer. Here we have in mind not the retail markets found in many towns on 'market days' but the markets where producers and traders, especially the traders in **commodities** make their deals. These markets, located in many of the world's major trading centres, including London where most of the main British commodity exchanges

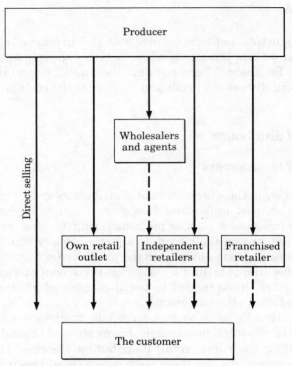

Fig 6.3   Channels of distribution

are found, bring together producers and traders who wish to buy in bulk for onward distribution to the final customer.

By commodities we mean goods such as tin, copper, zinc and other metals or bulk foodstuffs like tea, coffee, wheat and cocoa. What distinguishes commodities is that they tend to be sold on the basis of objective descriptions, such as 'Brazilian coffee' or 'Sri Lankan tea', rather than according to some brand name, though, of course, the experienced buyer will be able to distinguish high and low quality goods according to their source.

However, at the end of the day one tonne of tin is much like another tonne of tin and one individual seller will not be able to get a much higher price than the going market price, nor will an individual buyer be able to obtain a substantially lower price.

One interesting feature of many organised markets is the facility for dealing *forward* or in *futures*. This very specialised activity is described in Chapter 8.

Organised markets also exist for fresh foods, such as fish or vegetables. Speed is essential in getting these goods to market and these wholesale food markets provide convenient facilities for the producer or importer to sell his output in bulk either to a retailer or to a wholesaler.

Wholesaling

The markets we have just outlined are wholesale markets. Wholesaling involves purchasing goods in large quantities from the producer or importer and selling in smaller quantities to the retailer, or sometimes, to another wholesaler or dealer. A service is provided as the producer prefers to deal with large orders and the retailer in smaller purchases. There are, however, other services provided by wholesaling besides this 'breaking bulk'.

a *Warehousing*   Demand for goods may be seasonal but production may take place all the year round. Toys, for which there is peak demand before Christmas, are an example. Wholesalers can absorb supplies throughout the year. Optimum use of storage space can be made by stocking several types of goods whose demand shows different seasonal patterns. Sports goods, for instance, have peak demands in the summer months and could be stored alongside toys.

b *Transport*   A manufacturer may have sales throughout the country, though not at a sufficient level to warrant shipments to different areas and the maintenance of small depots in these localities. Wholesalers, able to break bulk for a number of manufacturers, can find it worthwhile to distribute goods around the country and maintain depots of efficient sizes in the various areas.

c *Marketing*   The wholesaler may be a key figure in weighing up the market and influencing the patterns of production. This is true, for example, in the clothing fashion trades where small manufacturers often produce in response to requests from the larger wholesale houses.

d *Finance*   By taking stocks from manufacturers in advance of demand and allowing credit to retailers while stocks are being sold the wholesaler is, in effect, helping to finance production. Without this service manufacturers and retailers would have to employ more money.

e *Other services*   The position of wholesalers, enables them to provide other services to both manufacturers and retailers. Both can be provided with information about market trends; retailers can be made aware of new products. Some goods may be packaged by wholesalers. The Co-operative Wholesale Society, though this may be thought to be a special case as technically it is owned by its own retail customers, provides a wide range of retail services, from expert advice to advertising. The wholesale members of the 'symbol' chains such as VG and Spar, who also have close relationship with the retail members, offer similar services.

Conventional wholesaling has declined in importance in recent decades. The *functions* of wholesaling still have to be undertaken but are now often less important than in the past and where they remain essential are often carried out by manufacturers, or, more noticeably, by retailers. The growth of large chains in retailing has often been made possible by the incorporation of wholesaling and retailing within the one organisation.

Developments in production methods, in transport and communications have all contributed to this process. When flour was sold by millers in large sacks, breaking bulk was a necessary service for small shops selling to ordinary households. Modern machines have no difficulty in packing flour in paper bags at the end of the production line. Motorway transport, the telephone and telex have brought retailer and manufacturer closer together and the wholesaler's warehousing is not always essential to bridge the gap between them. Computer-assisted stock control helps manufacturers to plan their production more efficiently without having to keep large stocks in reserve.

The financial system has now become very efficient and well able to meet the needs of firms which have to carry stocks or which must buy stocks before money is received from sales. Large manufacturers and retailers are highly skilled in obtaining finance and do not need this aspect of wholesaling.

However, some independent, smaller wholesalers have survived by concentrating on specialised services to producers or retailers. For example, a wholesaler may provide extensive refrigerated storage for local retailers. 'Cash and carry wholesalers' have been vital for the survival of small retail shops.

Agents

Agents may offer an alternative to wholesalers. An agent acts on behalf of another, the principal. The role of the agent in distribution is to take over the work of distribution from the manufacturer. In some ways agents may act much like a wholesaler; in other ways they may act like a retailer and sell to the final customer. Agents can be particularly important in servicing foreign markets where they have special local knowledge.

Franchising

This is a growing form of distribution. A franchise gives the sole right to serve a locality with a particular good or service. Agents often hold sole franchises.

The modern trend in franchising is for producers carefully to develop and market the product, including the organisation of advertising, and then to leave the retail stage to a franchised independent firm. The franchise holder normally has to pay for the franchise. In return they receive a wide range of services from the producer. The shop will be laid out according to a distinctive pattern. Special equipment will be provided, training given and exclusive supplies of materials provided.

Franchising has been particularly important in some service trades such as fast foods. Its supporters claim that it combines the individual 'entrepreneurship' of the independent franchise holder with the economies of large scale production, advertising and so on. It also provides a role for small firms and personal initiative in an economy which often seems to be dominated by large organisations. The system's critics claim that large producers favour it as it gives them retail outlets and retail management at very low cost. It can also lead to frustrated expectations among the franchise holders who will never truly be 'their own bosses'.

The marketing mix

As with all business decisions, there is no one right form of distribution and no one right approach to marketing a firm's products. Indeed a single firm may choose different ways of marketing different products. Marketing and distribution managers must choose a combination of different strategies in response to an environment in which a number of forces, many of them beyond their control, are at work. The chosen **marketing mix** (or market mix) of price, distribution channel, advertising and product promotion must be the result of careful analysis of the environment, the available strategies and the nature of the firm's product.

Rapid review

1 List the main channels for the distribution of manufactured products.
2 List some of the goods traded in organised commodity markets.
3 List the main functions of wholesaling.
4 What is the difference between an agent and a wholesaler?
5 What is meant by the following terms: franchising, marketing mix?

Exporting

British firms as a whole export a higher proportion of the goods and services they produce than in any comparably sized country. The proportion is around 30 per cent.

Fig 6.4   The marketing mix

Exporting is a very powerful source of extra business. However depressed or static the home market may be, there are always opportunities in foreign markets. For many firms, however, the extra problems involved in exporting appear daunting and the British Government has made considerable efforts to encourage more firms to export.

Problems in exporting

Exporting confronts firms with the same problems as serving a domestic market but there are additional difficulties. These include:

a   Assessing the needs and tastes of customers in a different country, with different cultural, political and religious backgrounds
b   Transport and distribution over longer distances and under a range of different conditions.
c   Pricing and receiving payment in foreign currency.
d   Different legal systems and procedures for settling disputes.

Serving foreign markets

Some larger firms serve foreign markets in the same way as the domestic market by setting up overseas branches. Problems such as market research, advertising and distribution can then be handled in the same way as the home market.

This approach is not open to most firms. The following are some of the possible alternatives.

Export associations

A group of firms may collaborate in the costs of operating an overseas branch.

Export agents

A manufacturer may use a firm based in the export market as an agent to organise distribution. In this arrangement the ability of the agent to feed back information about the foreign market to the principal is of great importance. The exporter, however, is very much in the hands of the agent and very great care has to be taken in the choice.

Export merchants

These specialise in coping with the problems of exporting. For a producer that deals only with export merchants, business is much the same as dealing with a domestic wholesaler, except that it may be found necessary to carry out further, overseas market research.

Import houses

An import house in the foreign market may serve much the same function from the producer's point of view as the export merchant except that the producer must actually arrange transport to the foreign country.

Buying agents

These may operate in the UK on behalf of foreign companies. Once again, from the producer's point of view, the transaction is much the same as dealing with a domestic buyer.

Government assistance for exporters

Part of the functions of the Department of Trade is to help develop British exports and to help individual exporters to overcome particular difficulties. Much of this work is carried out through the agency of the British Overseas Trade Board (BOTB).

The Board is run by a group representing business, financial and trade union interests as well as those of government and it is responsible for co-ordinating a range of export promotion services. Operating with the help of sixteen area advisory groups it provides advice and assistance for solving many of the problems of exporting identified earlier in this chapter. It arranges trade fairs and special British promotions in many parts of the world and publishes booklets which provide both general and specialised information essential for exporters. It also operates an export marketing research scheme that offers useful help to smaller firms wishing to enter export markets, and further assistance may also be available under its market entry guarantee scheme.

The BOTB provides information about special problems in particular areas, e.g. with import licences and restrictions, and is also a channel through which exporters can communicate their problems to government and seek the government's aid in easing barriers in overseas markets.

One particular worry for exporters who trade directly with foreign markets, in preference to relying on export merchants, is the uncertainty that attaches to payment. Is the foreign buyer reliable? Is the market stable? Will currency fluctuations threaten payment? Some of these risks can be insured through a government agency, the Export Credits Guarantee Department whose work is examined more fully in Chapter 9, and many currency exchange risks can be reduced by dealing in currency markets in ways which are outlined in Chapter 8.

Rapid review

1 List the main problems of export selling.
2 What is the difference between an export merchant and an export agent?
3 List three services provided for exporters by the British Overseas Trade Board.

Exercises

1 Magazines sometimes publish questionnaires on matters of interest to their readers and invite readers to complete these and send them in. The results are then published as representative of readers' views. How representative are these results likely to be?
2 Suggest ways in which you could obtain useful information about patterns of expenditure of members of your class, for example, on clothes or entertainment?

3   Using *Social Trends* (available in most public reference libraries) as your main source of information, write reports on one of the following:

  a   changes in drinking habits in the past five years

  b   regional differences in income in the United Kingdom

  c   ownership of household durables such as washing machines, fridges, freezers in the United Kingdom

4   Make a collection of press advertisements, or a log of television commercials. Use these to discuss the particular objectives of the advertisements.

5   In Chapter 5 we traced the development of a dressmaking firm from a one-person business to a major concern. Suggest appropriate forms of advertising and sales promotion for different stages of the firm's growth.

6   How might the methods of distribution of the dressmaking firm we analysed earlier change as the firm grows through time?

7   A major fast-food chain has developed in the USA by franchising outlets whereas in the UK its first hundred or so stores were fully integrated within the firm and were run by managers. Later it started to open franchised stores in the UK. Explain, analyse and discuss this strategy.

8   Discuss the opportunities and problems that might be presented for our dress-making venture if it contemplated entering the export market.

9   Choose one of the following and with the help of any booklets you can obtain describe and comment on the services they provide for exporters, paying particular attention to the requirements of small firms with little experience of the export trade.

  a   A High Street clearing bank.

  b   The British Overseas Trade Board.

  c   The area Chambers of Commerce.

  d   The Export Credits Guarantee Department.

  e   A freight forwarder.

7 The firm and the customer

This chapter is closely concerned with matters of the law and with legal machinery. While it will concentrate as much as possible on issues of broad principle and general trends it has had to describe the law and legal system as it exists in England and Wales, and for the most part in Scotland. Other countries have different laws and systems of consumer protection. Readers in other countries, therefore, should note for themselves differences between their own and the British systems outlined in this chapter.

The need for consumer protection

Any trading transaction involves an agreement between two people or groups of people whereby one side agrees to deliver goods or perform a service and the other agrees to make a payment. An agreement enforceable at law is a contract and most trade transactions, therefore, are subject to what is known as the law of contract. In its basic principles the law is concerned to ensure that people should do what they have agreed to do, i.e. to uphold contracts freely entered into. For this principle to operate fairly certain important conditions are necessary. These include the following:

a The agreements are legal and the people making the agreements are capable of entering into legal contracts;
b Each side is equal in strength and each side enters into the agreement freely and is aware of what is involved.

Given these assumptions which apply to all contracts, agreements between traders and individual private consumers are based on the further principle that the buyer should be on guard against the possibility that the seller is hoping to get the best of any agreement. This is expressed in the well-known phrase of 'let the buyer beware'. This is often interpreted to mean that the buyer should check that the goods bought are in order and do not contain faults that should have been discovered on normal inspection. On the face of things, therefore, the position of the ordinary buying consumer is legally rather weak. On the other hand there is a very long history of attempts by governments and legal systems to modify this basic position in favour of ordinary consumers.

If they did not have any special protection consumers today would be very much weaker than most of the traders with whom they deal. Many of the goods bought are made in such a way that it is impossible to find faults without putting them to normal use. The only way to find out if a holiday brochure accurately describes a package holiday is actually to go on the holiday! An assumption of equality hardly describes the relative strength of the average individual householder and a giant multinational company with its legal staff and the finance to fight cases through the full machinery of the law courts. The large supplier always has much more at stake than the single buyer. A supplier, faced with a claim for £100, knows that if they accept responsibility for one case they are likely to be faced with similar claims from hundreds more people and a final loss of many thousands of pounds, so that it is worthwhile risking heavy legal costs in defending their position. The buyer, acting alone, is unlikely to risk turning a loss of £100 into a much greater one. Where substantial purchases are involved buyers are rarely experts because they buy only occasionally, but the supplier is constantly involved in similar transactions. If the supplier does not develop special knowledge and skills it is often worth employing specialist advisers.

From time to time, therefore, Parliament has sought to redress the balance of equality by changing the legal relationship between trader and the individual customer. It has done so in a number of important ways.

Rapid review

1 What assumptions are made when people make legal contracts?
2 State three reasons why consumer protection law is necessary.

Consumer protection laws

Laws and contract conditions

As modern consumer society has developed the law has adapted to changed conditions. It is still based on the law of contract and indeed there are very few modifications when buyers and sellers are both private individuals or both regular traders. However, when the individual buyer is dealing with a trader in the normal course of business, certain special conditions are assumed to be contained in the trading agreement and these provide him or her with special protection.

Much of the law relating to the conditions of trading contracts is contained in the Sale of Goods Act 1979. This Act did not itself create any new law but it brought together the provisions of a number of statutes including the famous Sale of Goods Act 1893 and the Unfair Contract Terms Act of 1977. The Act applies to goods bought by individual buyers from traders whose normal business it is to sell goods of that type. It is implied that such goods:

a *are of merchantable quality* – a difficult phrase that has not yet been defined to the full satisfaction of everyone concerned with consumer law, but which means roughly that the goods should be in good working order at the time of sale, taking into account the price paid, the nature of the goods and the way in which they were described. There is, however, some uncertainty over goods that develop faults after a period of use.

b *are fit for a particular purpose* made known to the trader. If, for example, a buyer asks for an article capable of performing a particular task and the trader states that it will, then it must do so for there to be a valid contract.

c *correspond to their description,* which in these days of prepackaging is a matter of some importance because machine or human errors can easily lead to misdescriptions of size, type or quality of goods.

Failure to meet these requirements may entitle the buyer to a refund of money or compensation, including compensation for damage caused by faulty goods, e.g. a faulty washing machine.

These rights may be lost if the buyer:

1 Examined the goods and failed to notice an obvious fault.
2 Was told about the fault before buying, ignored the seller's advice or his/her admission of inability to give advice.
3 Was given the article as a present (the actual buyer being the one who has the rights).

Traders, of course, have a right to refuse a refund to buyers who simply change their minds about buying when there is nothing wrong with the goods.

It is no longer possible for traders to evade the obligations imposed by laws such as the Sale of Goods Act by persuading customers to sign guarantee forms that take away buyers' legal rights. Completion of a guarantee card cannot reduce the extent of protection afforded by the law but it can strengthen it by providing evidence of purchase and may give entitlement to any additional promises made by manufacturer or trader. It may also, of course, ensure that the buyer is placed

Fig 7.1   Manufacturers' warranties cannot remove the customer's legal rights

on a computer marketing list and ensure receipt of sales literature for a number of years.

In 1982 the Supply of Goods and Services Act extended protection to agreements for the sale of services, thus recognising the growing importance of services, such as package holidays, in modern life. The Act also gave the same degree of protection as that afforded to other shoppers to those who hired articles, bought them in part exchange, had them supplied along with services or bought them with sales promotion coupons.

Fig 7.2   Services such as holidays are now covered by consumer protection legislation

Quality and safety

It is generally recognised that quality is a very difficult area for legislation. No trader can be expected to sell a Rolls Royce for the price of a Mini and quality is a legitimate subject for competition. On the other hand it is also recognised that for many modern goods and services quality cannot be identified by simple examination and will only become apparent as the product is actually used or the service enjoyed.

Efforts have, therefore, concentrated on persuading manufacturers and traders to establish acceptable quality and grading standards and to find ways of signifying these on the product or as part of a sales description. Many devices have now become familiar and widely accepted. Most motorists recognise the difference between two and four star petrol although few may be aware of the precise technical distinction. Most tourists are also familiar with the star system of grading hotels.

Any quality grading system requires a method of determining and describing quality which is consistent, capable of precise definition, comprehensible to buyers and seen as practicable and fair by sellers. It also needs a body with powers to police the system and to deal with complaints and award penalties in cases where the system can be shown to have been abused. In many cases traders' own associations operate the necessary machinery and while this may be rather less satisfactory than a genuinely independent body it must be remembered that reputable and honest traders have a strong interest in preserving the reputation of their trade because they also suffer from the activities of rogues and from the public hostility that they arouse.

There is an independent body whose work in establishing minimum quality and safety standards for a wide range of products is widely respected and whose standards are adopted by many traders. This is the British Standards Institution whose 'kitemark' (shown below) is a well-known symbol. Its appearance on an article indicates that the product conforms to a standard established and tested by the Institution.

BS 857

Some goods are potentially so dangerous or they may have caused such problems in the past that Parliament has given a Government

Minister powers to establish legally enforceable safety standards. Such powers were granted under the Consumer Protection Act of 1961 but were later strengthened by the Consumer Safety Act 1978. This legislation tends to be concerned with such issues as the protection of children against fire risks, the sale and use of faulty heaters, unguarded fires and inflammable clothing.

Food and drugs

There is a long history of laws designed to protect people against dangerous and unhealthy food, drugs and food preparation. Unfortunately the law constantly seems to lag behind changes in business practice and food technology. Threats to health no longer arise chiefly from local attempts at fraud. We can buy our flour secure in the belief that it has not been adulterated with powdered cement or arsenic. On the other hand we cannot be sure that the frozen chicken bought in the local supermarket has not, at some stage in its journey from the factory farm, been allowed to thaw out and then been re-frozen to become a highly dangerous article. Nor can we be sure that during its brief life the chicken has not been injected with drugs that are then passed into the bodies of those who eat it, sometimes with unpleasant consequences. Efforts to reform the law so that it is better able to protect consumers from the misuse of modern food technology are not assisted by the tendency of governments to use spurious 'safety' regulations to protect their own producers against more efficient foreign competition, or the attempts sometimes made by food producers to ridicule European Community proposals (themselves not always well directed) aimed at securing Community conformity to general safety standards.

Weights and measures

This is another area with obvious opportunities for fraud where the law has long been active. The major British statute is the Weights and Measures Act 1963 but this has been modified a number of times to bring the law up-to-date with modern methods of packaging and distribution. The Weights and Measures Act of 1979, for example, strengthened the law on pre-packed goods. Efforts are made to ensure that goods are sold in standard sizes so that fair price comparisons can be made and prepacked goods must be marked with their weight or measure. Selling short weight or measure is a very old criminal offence and offenders in some societies have often received rather harsh treatment.

Advertising and describing

There is no general law on advertising and some degree of exaggeration, sometimes known as advertising 'puff' has always been tolerated and expected. After all, consumer advertising can be seen as entertainment – the participants are often familiar as film or TV actors. It could be claimed that a society which learns to live with, and treat with scepticism, the wiles of the advertiser is less likely to fall under the spell of political advertising, the propaganda of the totalitarian state. There is no mass consumer advertising in any totalitarian regime whether of the extreme left or the extreme right.

Nevertheless certain aspects of advertising and the description of goods and services are subject to legislation. Some are subject to regulation by special bodies and all have to take account of the law as it has been shaped by some important Court decisions.

The nearest British statute to a general advertising law is the Trade Descriptions Act 1968. Trade descriptions legislation is also interesting in that it crosses the normally strict division between criminal law which deals with offences against the community as a whole and prescribes punishments for those guilty of criminal offences, and civil law which seeks to protect and define the rights and obligations of individuals and creates the means whereby a wronged individual is able to seek redress and compensation from those causing the injury. Thus, for example, a trading standards officer may have the power to take action against a motor trader who sold a vehicle with a false mileage on its indicator and assist a purchaser who had bought the vehicle on the basis of the falsely declared mileage to gain redress.

In general the Trade Descriptions Act makes it a criminal offence fraudulently or carelessly to give a false description, written or verbal, of goods or services in the course of sale. Fairly specific rules apply to descriptions of prices, especially when it is claimed that they are 'reduced' or 'sale' prices. It is difficult, however, for any law to overcome the ingenuity of traders who wish to give customers the impression that the price asked is more favourable to them than it really is. Price displays are also subject to the provision of the Prices Act 1974 and the Consumer Credit Act. Price display legislation usually seeks to ensure that:

   a   Any price quoted is the price buyers pay and that there are no hidden costs.

   b   Buyers know exactly what they are getting for a quoted price and are then able to compare prices on a like-for-like basis.

   c   Buyers are not misled into believing falsely that they are getting the benefit of special reductions or discounts.

Another act with important implications for advertising and sales promotion is the Misrepresentation Act 1967. This does not create any new criminal offence but it does strengthen the legal rights of buyers of goods or services who have suffered loss as a result of a false or inaccurate description which was a basis on which a purchase was made.

The courts and consumer protection

Consumer protection is one branch of the law where much is owed to the decisions of judges in the courts, that is to what is known as the Common Law, perhaps because judges are also buyers of goods and services. The famous Sale of Goods Act of 1893 was itself largely a codification and clarification of the law as it then stood after years of judicial decisions on buyer–seller disputes.

Probably the best known of all legal cases affecting consumers is that of *Donoghue v Stevenson, 1932* – the snail in the ginger beer bottle case. Mrs Donoghue visited a cafe with a friend who bought for her a bottle of ginger beer in the traditional dark and opaque bottle so that the contents could not be seen. After consuming some of the ginger beer Mrs Donoghue poured the rest into a glass and out came the decomposed remains of a snail. Not surprisingly Mrs Donoghue felt ill and later became sick and subsequently claimed damages which she was eventually awarded. This was a significant decision because:

1 Mrs Donoghue had not herself bought the drink and so she had no contract with the cafe owner nor with the manufacturer. The Sale of Goods Act did not, therefore, apply. The decision did not depend on the law of contract but was far wider and affected anyone injured by a product.
2 Mrs Donoghue had no way of knowing that the product was defective other than by consuming or using it. The defect was latent (hidden) and the retailer could not know of its existence. In such circumstances the manufacturer has a duty to take reasonable care to ensure that the ultimate consumer is free from any defect likely to cause injury. Later cases have extended the duty to anyone suffering injury whether or not he or she was actually using the article.

Another famous and interesting case directly concerns advertising. This is *Carlill v Carbolic Smoke Ball Co, 1893*. The company issued an advertisement in which it promised to pay £100 to anyone who used the smoke ball for a specified period and who caught influenza. With amazing persistence and some considerable discomfort a Mrs Carlill did use the smoke ball for the required time and she did contract influenza. She sought the £100. This she eventually obtained after going to the Court of Appeal and the case has remained as a stern warning to advertisers that specific claims must be upheld. Thus a claim that, after eating a certain food, 'your cat will live longer' is too vague to give rise to any legal action on the part of cat or owner. After the Carlill case no advertiser would be foolish enough to claim that a cat fed on the food for a specified period would live for any stated time thereafter!

Small claims and the County Court

Business firms now have to recognise that some encouragement has been given to customers to pursue claims by the institution of a special small claims procedure. This can apply to claims that do not exceed £500.

The procedure uses the most common civil court, the County Court, and allows people to bring their own cases without having to employ a solicitor. Cases are settled by **arbitration**, a less formal and imposing procedure than the normal court hearing.

Solicitors can be employed but the court will not allow costs for claims under £500. Claims between £500 and £5000 are heard by the County Court in the normal way. Larger claims have to go to a higher court.

Booklets explaining the small claims procedure can be obtained from most consumer advisory bodies.

Rapid review

1 State three implied conditions of most normal retail contracts which are subject to the Sale of Goods Act 1979.
2 What rights has the buyer if any of these conditions are not met?
3 How might the buyer lose these rights?
4 State one important change in consumer law resulting from the Supply of Goods and Services Act, 1982.
5 Draw the 'kitemark' of the British Standards Institution and state what it indicates.
6 Why is it still necessary to have weights and measures laws?
7 Why is *Donoghue v Stevenson, 1932* an important case in the history of consumer law?
8 What important point of law was established by the case of *Carlill v Carbolic Smoke Ball Co, 1893*?
9 What are the usual aims of price display legislation?
10 What is the advantage of the small claims procedure in the County Court and when can it be used?

Consumer credit

Principles of consumer credit law

Laws to protect people making use of hire purchase to acquire goods date, in Britain, from 1938 but present law rests chiefly on a major statute, the Consumer Credit Act 1974. This extended the law as it had developed for hire purchase and credit sales to almost all forms of instalment credit. An agreement which falls within the scope of the Act is known as a *regulated agreement* and, in 1986, this meant any agreement under which credit of not more than £15 000 was provided to an individual (including a sole trader and partnership but not a company) other than exempt agreements which are mostly non-commercial agreements, bank overdrafts and those where the amount of credit is not more than £50. Cash loans where the customer is free to spend the money as desired are not exempt even if below £50. House mortgages were originally exempt from the legislation but in 1984 they became subject to the provisions relating to advertising the cost of credit.

The Act is based on a number of fairly clear principles including:

a The licensing of dealers in credit, with the licensing power granted to the Director General of Fair Trading who thus gains a measure of control over the conduct of those engaged in the consumer credit industry.

b Control over the terms and conditions of instalment credit agreements so that the Court has powers to set aside unreasonable provisions and creditors have to apply to the Court before they can recover goods under certain circumstances, notably after a third of the total purchase price has been paid. There is also some protection against high-pressure selling in that some forms of canvassing for credit are forbidden and in other cases the debtor is given a short period during which the agreement can be cancelled as outlined in the section relating to cancellable agreements.

c Suppliers of credit such as finance houses have to accept liability for faulty goods where transactions fall between stated limits.

d Supplying to debtors full and accurate information including a copy of the agreement within a stated period, full details of cash and credit price and details of the true cost of credit, based on the annual percentage rate (APR), calculated according to a formula and tables issued by the Office of Fair Trading. This allows borrowers to identify and compare interest rates in spite of differences in the frequency of interest payments or charges and the repayment during the loan term of the sum borrowed.

It's only £25 down and 24 easy monthly payments of ....

Fig 7.3   You are entitled to know the true cost of credit

Consumer credit law imposes certain obligations on the part of debtors who, for example, should not sell goods without the approval of the creditor and who should notify changes of address or location of goods, but the main intention of the 1974 Act was to provide the conditions under which a responsible and competitive consumer credit industry could develop and play its part in extending the widespread ownership of property. It was also hoped that extending a fairly liberal law to the whole industry rather than to limited parts would check the earlier spread of consumer credit schemes and agencies and bring it more firmly under the control of the main banks and the more responsible financial institutions. This hope has, in the main, been realised.

Cancellable credit agreements

A cancellable credit agreement is one which can be cancelled at the request of the borrower. It is one that has been discussed by the trader and customer and which is signed by the customer off trade premises. The trader can be the supplier of either the goods or the credit or an agent of either.

For it to be enforceable without a court order such an agreement must be in writing and must contain certain stipulated information set out in a specific form. Among other matters the agreement must contain:

a A heading stating that the agreement is one regulated by the Consumer Credit Act 1974.

b The name and postal address of both trader and customer.

c Details of any charges which the customer has to pay if he/she breaks the agreement.

d Financial particulars such as the cash price of goods, any advance payment, the amount of credit to be provided, the total charge for credit, the timing and amount of repayments and the annual percentage rate (APR) which was explained earlier in this chapter.

e A statement of the customer's protection and remedies. This must be shown as a whole with the financial details and they must not be printed in such a way that they are overshadowed by other information.

f Signatures of customer and trader and date of signing. The customer's signature must be in a box set out in a form established by the Office of Fair Trading.

The Consumer Credit Act requires that all terms must be readily legible. The agreement, for example, must not be fastened in such a way that the terms are difficult to read.

An important provision is that there is a **cooling-off period** which is 14 days where goods are bought from a mail order catalogue but in other cases five days from the day the customer receives either a second copy of the agreement or separate notice of cancellation rights.

If the customer decides to cancel, a written notice to this effect must be sent or taken to the trader within the cooling-off period and both trader and customer should then try to restore the position between them as nearly as possible to what it was before the agreement was signed. Detailed rules have been set out concerning obligations relating to goods, including perishable goods, but in general the customer should either return goods or keep them safe and unused until collected and repay any money loaned under the agreement. Goods may be retained until any money repayable by the trader has been returned. The trader must return any money paid as deposit or first payment, etc., and any goods taken in part exchange.

Rapid review

1 State four principles established by the Consumer Credit Act of 1974
2 What is a cancellable credit agreement?
3 List six matters that must be contained in a cancellable credit agreement.
4 What is a 'cooling-off period' in relation to consumer credit?

The institutions of consumer protection

For some years the British Government has recognised a degree of responsibility for consumer affairs and there is normally a minister concerned with this field within the Department of Trade or of Trade and Industry. (These two departments seem to marry and divorce from time to time.) In the belief that one of the best forms of protection for the consumer is the ability to choose between genuinely competing suppliers the Government in the early 1980s has placed less stress on legal intervention in the market but has sought to encourage business competition, e.g. through the Competition Act 1980 which widened the grounds on which reports could be called for on 'uncompetitive practices'.

The Office of Fair Trading

The Government's main agency for the implementation of its consumer policies is the Office of Fair Trading which was set up by the Fair Trading Act, 1973. The OFT has a number of functions including:

a keeping a general watch on commercial practices as they affect consumer interests;

b collecting evidence and making recommendations to the minister if new laws or powers appear to be needed to check practices that are against the consumer interest;

c keeping a general watch on the development of monopolies or uncompetitive practices;

d observing developments in consumer affairs and law in other countries, including the European Community and advising the government on their implications for Britain and recommending action to the Government;

e encouraging improved consumer education and awareness of consumer rights and responsibilities;

f special licensing functions, mentioned earlier in this chapter, under the Consumer Credit Act 1974.

Monopolies and Mergers Commission

Working closely with the OFT, the Monopolies and Mergers Commission is the official body for the investigation of monopolies, proposed mergers and uncompetitive practices as defined in the various relevant statutes. The most important of these are the Fair Trading Act of 1973 and Competition Act of 1980. Investigations are carried out on the instructions of the Secretary of State for Trade, or by the Director General of the OFT. In practice only a very small proportion of industries, firms, mergers and business practices which could be made the subject of reports under these laws are ever, in fact, investigated. Even fewer become subject to government action following the report although there may be a great deal of private negotiation to change practices of which the Government disapproves.

Other bodies concerned with standards and practices

The work of the British Standards Institution has already been mentioned. Apart from the OFT there are very few official bodies with general responsibilities for regulating business practices.

The Advertising Standards Authority

This is one body with authority in a difficult area of business practice. The Authority seeks to enforce a British Code of Advertising Practice and a Code of Sales Promotion Practice. It receives and investigates complaints from the public and negotiates with individual firms to stop bad and illegal practices.

Trade bodies

In Britain there is a strong emphasis on self-regulation through bodies representing particular industries and trades. Codes of practice are often negotiated with the OFT and procedures established for dealing with complaints against firms. Some of the best known of these bodies are: the Independent Broadcasting Authority which oversees television and radio advertising, the Retail Trading Standards Association with responsibilities in retail advertising and sales practice, the Mail Order Traders' Association of Great Britain, the Law Society which, however, is perhaps better known for its defence of lawyer interests, and many others in a wide range of different product areas.

The Consumers Association

This is itself a commercial body selling its services in defence of consumers. The Association is well known for its publication *Which?* and its investigations in product and service standards. It is a general champion of consumer interests and publisher of information useful to consumers and taxpayers.

Press, television and radio

Apart from competition, publicity and the exposure of damaging practices are among the strongest weapons of consumer interest. These modern equivalents of the pillory and the stocks can, of course, be abused but, for the most part, 'investigative journalism' regulated by a strict law of libel and responsible editorial management, can and does play an essential and healthy part in improving business standards and exposing rogues who prey on over trustful (but sometimes over greedy) consumers.

Rapid review

1 List five functions of the Office of Fair Trading.
2 What is the main function of the Monopolies and Mergers Commission?
3 List four organisations concerned with consumer protection other than the OFT and M&MC.

The business firm and the consumer

The obligations of the customer

The success of all businesses, other than those seeking a 'quick buck' and a quicker flight to South America, depends ultimately on the goodwill of the consumer. Most reputable firms work hard at promoting good customer relations and, if anything, err on the side of giving customers more than their strict legal rights. Most shopkeepers can quote examples of goods returned allegedly imperfect but fairly certainly misused. Stores with a policy of accepting returned goods know that they have to allow for some abuse of this policy.

It is, perhaps, too often overlooked that buyers, as well as sellers, have obligations. All contracts are based on good faith by *all* parties to the agreement. This means that buyers should give correct information, especially where credit is involved, should take reasonable care of the product if they wish to rely on the implied conditions of merchantable quality and fitness for purposes and make payments as agreed with the seller.

In practice traders cannot assume that the buyer's duty of good faith will always be maintained. In one form of agreement, that for insurance services, the seller (the insurance office) is legally able to rely on a stronger duty, that of the *utmost good faith* which imposes a duty on the person requesting insurance not only to tell the truth but also to disclose without necessarily being asked, any information that could be considered material to the nature or degree of the risk to be insured, i.e. if a house proposed for fire insurance has a thatched roof or a motor car proposed for insurance has been modified to give increased power or performance. Failure to reveal such material information could enable the insurance office to repudiate an insurance agreement and avoid meeting a claim.

In other cases traders investigate the truth of buyers' statements. Insurance companies, for example, often survey property to be insured. Where any form of credit is to be given the seller will normally check the 'credit worthiness' of the buyer or hirer. This they can do by obtaining bank references or by checking through specialist credit reference agencies which keep records of people with a history of non-payment of debts. Traders who accept payment by credit card will telephone the card company before concluding sales where the amount of credit exceeds a set limit. Failure to do so would usually mean that the trader would have to suffer any loss through failure to pay or other reason such as the use of a stolen card. The growth of large-scale retailing has forced firms to develop specialised systems to replace the local knowledge of the small shopkeeper.

Implications for employees

The existence of consumer law and the need to balance what is legally correct with what is practicable in daily business life places some burdens on employees, who must also balance their feelings of obligation to customers with loyalties to the employer. After all, the continuation of their own jobs depends on pleasing the customer and also on ensuring that the business operates at a profit. On the other hand the removal of this apparent conflict is no guarantee that standards of customer service improve as the experience of some nationalised industry services suggest. Nevertheless there is clearly a need for employers to ensure that their employees are trained to cope with the problems. All employees engaged in selling should receive training in the following main areas.

An adequate knowledge of their particular trade

If customers can legally rely on a seller's skill and judgement the seller must be assumed to possess this. A trader cannot escape from liability on the grounds of a sales assistant's inexperience but is fully responsible for the actions and statements of every employee working on his or her behalf.

A working knowledge of consumer law

This does not mean that every shop assistant should have a law degree but it does mean that the assistant should be aware of the general nature of the trader's responsibilities and the buyer's rights and responsibilities. The amount of knowledge expected depends on the extent of the employee's own responsibilities. A manager would be expected to be better trained in this area than an assistant.

Human relationships

This is a difficult area to define but most employers know the kind of employee they can trust to have direct contact with the public and those who, however skilled, they need to keep away from customers. Nevertheless this is an important aspect. When a customer starts to take formal action to exercise his or her legal rights under consumer law then there is likely to have been a failure in human relationships as both traders and buyers normally prefer to avoid the costs of legal action. There will certainly have been a breakdown in customer relationships. No person is likely to continue to trade with a firm that it has had to take to Court. Consumer law, like most other forms of law, is at its most successful when it is least in evidence.

Rapid review

1   **Name one type of agreement that is subject to the principle of 'the utmost good faith'.**

Exercises

1   It is often stated that consumer protection is as much in the interests of reputable business firms as it is to the benefit of consumers. How would you argue that this statement is correct?
2   Assume that you are the manager of a shop and that a customer who has just bought an electrical appliance has said to you that he cannot understand why manufacturers still asked people to fill in and return guarantee cards because they did not affect a buyer's legal rights. What arguments could you use to persuade the customer that it might be in his interests to complete the card?
3   Use the Office of Fair Trading's publication *Fair Deal* to answer the following questions:
   a   Can a trader refuse to refund money for returned goods?
   b   Must you accept a credit note if this is offered when you have returned faulty goods?

c   Does the Sale of Goods Act apply to goods sold privately?

d   Must goods be marked with the correct price?

e   What is the difference between an 'estimate' and a 'quotation'?

4   What are a trader's obligations in respect of weights and measures? Who is responsible for ensuring that traders meet these obligations?

5   What is meant by APR in connection with instalment credit trading? What are a trader's obligations concerning APR and how can a trader calculate it?

6   Why are *Donoghue v Stevenson, 1932* and *Carlill v Carbolic Smoke Ball Co, 1893* two of the most important legal cases in the history of advertising and consumer law?

7   Choose one of the organisations listed below and obtain leaflets describing their activities. With the help of these leaflets write a comprehensive account of your chosen organisation's contribution to consumer protection.

The British Standards Institution

The Consumers Association

8   Choose one television or radio programme which you consider assists consumer protection and describe the part it plays.

9   Assume you are the manager of a shop selling a range of household goods. Prepare a set of simple guidelines suitable for giving to a new sales assistant to help the assistant in dealing with complaints from customers about goods which they claim are faulty.

8 The firm and its suppliers

The purchasing function

Purchasing, in business, is concerned with the legal acquisition of the equipment, materials, supplies and services required by a private or public sector organisation for the fulfilment of its production or public service activities. It is concerned with more than just buying and includes any other method, such as hiring, that enables the organisation to gain the use of the goods and services it needs.

Whereas purchasing is one of the managerial functions which, in small firms, owners or their principal managers have to undertake as part of their duties, it has become a specialised division of management in larger organisations. Some writers distinguish different classes of purchasers. These include:

a *Industrial purchasers* who operate in private sector or State-owned organisations which have commercial, profit-seeking objectives.

b *Institutional purchasers* who are mostly in the public sector and who operate in organisations such as local authorities, government departments, the health and education services and the armed forces, which have statutory functions to perform and which are not required to earn profits or achieve purely commercial objectives.

c *Intermediate purchasers* who operate in organisations such as those in the distributive trades whose chief function is to buy for re-sale.

Because the purchasing department is required to contribute towards the overall objectives of the main organisation, purchasing officers in each of these three sectors of activity are likely to approach their tasks in rather different ways. Purchasing equipment for the Royal Navy, for example, is likely to pose different problems from those faced by purchasers employed by a shipping company operating cruise liners. Nevertheless, the fundamental objectives of purchasing remain the same. These may be loosely outlined as:

'To obtain goods and services of the right quality in the right quantity from the right source and to ensure that they are available for use at the right place at the right time for the right cost.'

What the word 'right' implies in each case, however, and which of the various 'rights' take priority over the others in cases where they cannot all be satisfied at the same time must depend to a very high degree on the objectives and priorities of the main organisation. This chapter is chiefly concerned with industrial purchasing and the contribution made by the purchasing function to the profitability of the business enterprise. While cost must always be an important consideration it may well take second place to other issues in many public sector institutions.

The importance of purchasing

In many small firms purchasing is a relatively neglected aspect of management. The pressures of ensuring survival are often so great in the early years of a firm's life that the greatest emphasis is placed on marketing and producing the product. If the firm does survive and prosper these remain the dominating activities because they give rise to the most urgent problems. Senior managers have to give their attention to selling and production because the penalties for failure in these are only too evident. Consequently busy managers frequently tend to reduce purchasing to a matter of routine. Having found suppliers who can be relied on to supply the required materials on conditions that appear satisfactory the actual work of ordering and re-ordering is frequently left to junior office staff or undertaken by managers at times when other matters are less pressing.

If the firm continues to grow the consequences of this neglect can become increasingly serious. The firm may be operating with equipment that is less efficient than that used by competitors. It may not be aware that materials in regular use can be obtained at lower cost. Suppliers may not be aware of the importance of some delivery times so that costly delays occur in production. Those ordering materials may not fully understand the quality requirements of the production department so that materials of the wrong quality are purchased leading to further problems and sometimes to heavy losses or claims for compensation from customers.

It is the function of the specialised purchasing manager to eliminate these and other avoidable costs which can arise out of inefficient purchasing.

The objectives of purchasing

The specialist must ensure that the needs of the departments using materials and services are clearly understood and appropriate goods and services supplied. In addition he or she contributes specialised knowledge and skill in the following areas.

The right level of supply

Purchasing officers are expected to make sure that production and the satisfaction of customer requirements are not held up by lack of necessary materials or services. At the same time it is necessary to avoid the financial costs of having an unnecessary quantity of materials standing idle for too long within the organisation. These two requirements are, to some extent, in conflict. On the one hand there must be sufficient stocks of materials to keep production going and to cope with unexpected increases in the flow of production and to guard against unexpected interruptions in supply caused by accidents or other events outside the control of the firm and supplier. On the other hand materials in stock represent 'idle money' in that money used for their purchase could have been used for other purposes and may have been borrowed at a high price in interest charges. Stocks also use up space which could be used for other purposes and have to be guarded against theft at further expense. The costs of keeping stocks may also have to be compared with savings that can be achieved by buying goods in bulk. These conflicting pressures somehow have to be reconciled.

They are more likely to be successfully balanced if supplies are obtained from reliable sources. The possible consequences of failures in quality and supply have already been made clear. Choice of supplier is often an important responsibility of the purchasing manager.

Cost control

Taking into account all the above considerations, purchasers must ensure that materials and services are obtained for the lowest possible cost. This not only involves bargaining with suppliers, seeking less costly sources of supply and the general use of whatever buying power the firm has but also in making use of other methods of acquiring goods if these offer lower total costs than outright purchase. This can be especially important in obtaining machinery and equipment. In some cases it may be less costly to hire or lease equipment than to buy it. Under a leasing agreement the equipment is technically purchased by the leasing company and then leased to the user for an agreed period after which ownership generally passes to the user. Among the advantages of leasing as opposed to buying are:

a Capital does not have to be borrowed or it may be used for other productive purposes.
b It may be easier and less expensive to keep equipment up-to-date.

c   The equipment will be contributing to the earnings of the firm and so helping to 'pay for itself'.

Hiring direct from a supplier, leasing or buying under a hire purchase agreement are all different ways in which a firm can have the use of goods while paying at intervals during the period of use. They are ways of avoiding having to pay the full purchase price in a single lump sum before the equipment has started to increase the earnings of the firm. These different methods of acquiring goods may seem very similar but, in practice, different taxation rules or different rates of interest or other features can make one method less expensive than the others. The purchasing specialist is expected to know what is best for the firm.

Purchasing and uncertainty

Business management has been described as the process of making decisions under conditions of uncertainty. The purchasing function is no exception to this general problem. One natural reaction of the manager is to try and reduce the degree of uncertainty and the purchasing specialist can seek to achieve this in a number of ways.

Fixed price agreements

In return for an agreement to buy an agreed quantity of materials over an agreed period of time it is sometimes possible to negotiate with suppliers a fixed price. This has advantages for both seller and buyer and can reduce the total costs of trading so that both sides can obtain some benefit from the cost saving. The seller gains the benefit of definite sales over a future period so that marketing and advertising costs can be reduced or switched to new markets and transport and warehousing can be carefully planned ahead. The buyer gains a definite price which will hold good over the period however market prices move and whatever happens to inflation. In periods of very great uncertainty the seller may insist on keeping a right to change the price under certain agreed eventualities such as wages rising over an agreed amount or, in the case of goods imported from other countries, a very large movement in the rate at which the home currency can be exchanged for foreign currencies.

Tenders

If the purchasing firm is large and an important customer in the market it may be able to stipulate the precise quantities and quality of the goods it wishes to buy and to invite offers or tenders from possible sellers. It can then choose the most favourable offers it receives, bearing in mind the reputation of the supplier over matters of keeping to agree-ments as well as the price. In some cases the buying firm may even be able to state the price it is prepared to pay and ask for proposals from suppliers wishing to supply on the terms stated.

Where the buying firm is much larger and more powerful than the supplier it will wish to have some guarantee that quality standards will be maintained and goods supplied as agreed. It may arrange for its own quality inspectors to visit the supplier's factory and inspect the production process from time to time.

Dealing in futures

Uncertainties are increased when the firm is buying basic or raw mater-ials from other countries. World market prices for the basic metals such as tin, copper and zinc and commodities such as rubber and cocoa can fluctuate greatly. There can be a large change between the time when production is planned and actually started. Firms can arrange long-term contracts or buy 'forward', i.e. in advance of production needs, but long-term contracts can put the firm at a disadvantage against competitors if prices fall, and buying stocks in advance and keeping them until wanted is expensive.

A possible solution is to deal in futures. For example, a firm which knows that it will be wanting copper in, say, three months' time can delay purchasing the copper and paying for it until it is needed, or it could arrange a 'futures' contract to purchase a similar amount of copper at an agreed date in the future. When the time arrives to buy the precise quantity and grade of copper needed the futures contract is reversed – the firm sells the fictional futures copper it had earlier agreed to buy. If during this period the copper price has risen then the futures copper will be sold back at a profit and this profit will be set against the additional cost of the actual metal bought. If the price falls the futures deal will show a loss but the copper will be bought at a price lower than that allowed for in the production plan.

This may seem a very complicated way to remove the risk of price movement – a process known as **hedging**, but in reality it is flexible and suits the needs of many firms.

Financial uncertainties

Another source of uncertainty when buying goods from other countries is the exchange value of the home currency. Much international trade takes place using the United States dollar as the means of valuation and payment. If the exchange value of the British pound falls so that

£1, say, can be exchanged for only $1 instead of an early exchange value of $1.30 then a British importer is going to have to spend more of his own pounds to obtain the dollars needed to pay for any given quantity of goods. For example a trader in January agrees to buy goods priced at $10 000 and with £1 = $1.30 he works out the cost at about £7692. However, in April when the goods arrive and payment is due the pound has fallen so that £1 = $1. The trader now has to pay £10 000.

There are several possible ways to overcome this difficulty. An international trader or multinational company can keep bank accounts in foreign currencies, though few companies like to keep large sums of money in bank accounts when they can earn more by employing it in production. The firm can arrange to buy currency 'forward', i.e. for delivery at an agreed future date at an agreed forward price or it can buy financial futures in the London International Financial Futures Exchange (LIFFE). Dollars and some other leading world currencies can be traded on futures terms in much the same way as described for copper in the older metals and commodities futures markets. Dealing in financial futures can be more flexible and less expensive than the other ways of reducing the risks of exchange rate movements.

Rapid review

1   What is the function of purchasing in a business organisation?
2   What are the objectives of purchasing?
3   How can the purchasing manager try to reduce the element of uncertainty in buying?
4   What is a tender?
5   What is meant by 'hedging' and how can dealing in 'futures' help a purchasing manager to hedge against the risk of a price rise?
6   In which British market is it possible to deal in financial futures?

Purchasing organisation and procedures

Purchasing organisation

The importance given to specialised purchasing in an organisation depends on the type of industry in which the firm operates and the risks and uncertainties associated with purchasing. As noted earlier, it also depends on the size of the organisation and the amount of materials and services acquisition that is required.

The more important buying is to the activities of the firm, the greater its possible contribution to profit or loss; the greater the degree of risk and uncertainty, the more likely is the purchasing function to be given a high place in the management structure. An example where purchasing is likely to be high in the level of management might be a large retail stores group selling a wide range of goods which can be bought from home or foreign producers. The more skilful the purchasing the more attractive will be the stores to customers and the greater the freedom of store managers to offer attractive and competitive prices.

At the other extreme might be the case of a highly specialised manufacturer of advanced electronic equipment where raw materials form only a very small proportion of the total value of the final product and where the main purchases are electronic components made only by a few suppliers in the world. The success of this firm depends on its employment of highly skilled people rather than on its purchase of materials or services from other firms. When it has to acquire very expensive and specialised equipment this is likely to be attended to by the most senior managers who will be advised by the accounts managers. There is little scope here for the normal purchasing specialist and the purchasing function is likely to be seen as a routine task of no great importance to the profitability of the organisation.

Where purchasing exists as a recognised specialist activity then it is a *staff* function of management as explained in Chapter 5. The extent of the purchasing manager's authority will depend on his or her place in the structure of management.

Centralisation and decentralisation

Both centralised and decentralised organisation are found in relation to purchasing and the terms are used both in relation to departments at the same location and to firms which operate from a number of different locations. Practices differ even between organisations in the same sector of activity so that opinions clearly differ on the relative advantages and disadvantages of the two types of organisation.

In favour of *centralised purchasing* it is claimed that it is easier to gain cost economies of large-scale buying and the use of the firm's market power as a large customer. Buying policies and activities can be better co-ordinated to achieve common quality standards and prices throughout the organisation and the physical distribution, transport and warehousing of stocks can be better planned. Purchasing officers may be given a better training and helped to understand the organisation's activities as a whole. It is also argued that the performance and costs of the purchasing department can be better monitored and controlled when centrally organised.

On the other hand *decentralised purchasing* can reduce the cost and quantity of administration and keep the purchasing officers more closely in touch with the needs of people in the production departments.

In practice there is often a mixture of centralised and decentralised buying. For example a hypermarket group may centralise the buying of groceries where customer demand is fairly constant throughout the country and where profit margins are so small that all possible economies of scale have to be exploited. In contrast the same group may allow its wines and spirits managers to buy their own stock in line with the special features of their own local areas and where there is more scope for individual buyers to show their initiative without risking large losses.

Materials management

This is the term used to define the total work involved in bringing external goods and services into the organisation and in administering their storage and movement within it until they are used in the process of production, the activity of the organisation or until their sale. It is often considered to be part of the purchasing function. Clearly it covers a very wide range of possible work including planning the whole process and preparing suitable procedures for buying, stock control and internal movement, obtaining the required goods and services including negotiating conditions of purchase and ensuring that they are met, storage and internal distribution to the point of use and checking that the goods and services are as required by the eventual user.

Rapid review

1   **Is purchasing part of line or staff management?**
2   **State one advantage and one disadvantage of decentralised purchasing.**
3   **What is meant by 'materials management'?**

Stock control

Stock control is an essential element in general purchasing policy. Its purpose is to achieve the best possible level of stock within the organisation taking into account conflicting needs – to guard against production delays due to stock shortages, and to avoid unnecessary expense of stock holding. At the same time the firm will wish to plan its purchases so that the payments it has to make to suppliers become due at times when there is revenue available to meet them. Careful planning can often reduce the borrowing requirements of the firm. This is part of what is often called planning the **cash flow** of the firm and this is where there has to be close co-operation between the purchasing specialists and the finance officers.

Security is another important aspect of stock control. The greater the quantity of stock held the more difficult and expensive security becomes. It is important that authorised people should be able to obtain stock quickly but if withdrawals from store are too simple then stocks tend to 'shrink' and pilfering becomes widespread. To prevent this stock records must be an accurate reflection of what is physically in stock and must, therefore, be kept up-to-date. At the same time care must be taken to ensure that the records are not falsified to cover up disappearances. One of the problems with computerised systems is that although records can be kept up-to-date much more easily they can also be manipulated by those who understand the system in ways that are difficult to spot by those less familiar with it.

It is not the intention in this chapter to consider stock control procedures in any detail but a broad outline of some of the best-known methods is helpful in gaining an understanding of what is involved.

Methods of control

Most stock control methods rely on some system whereby stock levels are kept between a maximum and a minimum level. These levels are worked out on the basis of the amounts needed to maintain production for stated periods. For example the maximum level might be based on the supplies needed to maintain operations for four months and the minimum on the level needed for two months. The skill of the purchasing officer then lies in planning orders so that these are placed as stocks approach the minimum and bring them up close to the maximum while at the same time taking advantage of discounts that can be obtained from suppliers for bulk orders and keeping the firm's own administrative costs as low as possible. It must be remembered that placing orders involves costs in communication, preparing invoices, making records and making payments. There is always a danger with max–min methods that purchasers try to keep stocks constantly around the maximum level with constant small 'topping up' orders with all the additional administrative expenses this involves for both buyer and supplier who is then less likely to allow the most favourable prices and discounts. Figure 8.1 illustrates a typical max–min control system.

If max–min methods are not employed then some other regular purchasing system is necessary because it is too dangerous to leave orders until requests are received from production or other departments. Often

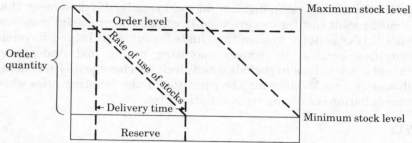

Fig 8.1   A possible system of stock purchase

there is a regular periodic system when departments are asked to put in requests at, say, three-monthly intervals.

Where stock is held centrally there are sometimes procedures for periodic physical inspection of stocks so that orders can be placed to bring them up to the required levels. Even where procedures for ordering are not based on physical inspection this is still necessary at regular intervals to ensure that actual stocks are what the firm's records say they are. It is only by physically checking stocks that it is possible to discover if discrepancies are due to thieving, or dishonest purchasing practices or just simple errors in recording.

Valuation of stocks

It is the responsibility of the purchasing department to ensure that the finance officers are supplied with accurate and realistic valuations of stock held although this responsibility has to be exercised within the principles established by the firm's senior management. It has to be remembered that there have been very many cases of sudden collapse of apparently successful firms where investigation has revealed that the accounts showed unrealistic valuations for worthless stocks. At the same time undervaluing stocks can provide managers with hidden reserves of profit which effectively deprive shareholders of dividends or allow them to claim success at times when the firm is really trading rather badly. There is a legal requirement that business accounts should show a 'true and fair view' of the financial condition of the enterprise. This requirement cannot be met if the stocks held by the firm are not correctly and fairly valued. Three common approaches to stock valuation are known as LIFO, FIFO and AVCO.

LIFO

This stands for 'last in first out' but, in valuation terms, does not mean that the most recently bought stocks should always be used first –

a policy that would mean disaster for most retailers! It does mean that the most recent cost figures are used in calculating material costs and profits. LIFO is not a system that finds favour with Inland Revenue authorities because it reduces operating profits and understates retained stock values in periods when stock purchase prices are rising, although some allowance may be permitted under taxation rules when severe inflation is causing constant price rises.

FIFO

This represents 'first in first out' and means that the earliest stock figures are used to calculate material costs so that operating profits are reduced at times when material prices are rising but are increased if prices are falling.

AVCO

This relates to an average costs basis for calculating material costs in periods when they are changing.

Consequences for profits

The effect of the three methods is illustrated by the following example.

Valuation of material costs

	Tonnes purchased	Price per tonne (£)	Cost (£)
January	10	40	400 FIFO
March	10	42	420 (820)
June	10	46	460 LIFO
December	10	50	500 (960)
		Average	Total
Total	40	44.50	1780

Suppose that by the end of December 20 tonnes have been sold producing a sales revenue of £920.

If materials costs are based on LIFO they are shown as £960 and there is a loss of £40, ignoring all other costs, and remaining stocks are valued at £820, well below the current replacement value.

If material costs are based on FIFO they are shown as £820 to produce a profit of £100.

If AVCO methods are used there is an average cost of £44.50 and a total cost for the 20 tonnes sold of £890 to show a profit of £30.

This simple example helps to show how different accountants are able to show different profit figures for the same firm. Firms may use whatever methods are believed to give the fairest picture of their true financial position but they are not allowed to keep changing valuation methods in order to reduce their liability to pay taxes or to give a distorted picture to their shareholders.

Rapid review

1 **What is the purpose of stock control?**
2 **What is meant by 'max–min' in relation to stock control?**
3 **State the differences between LIFO, FIFO and AVCO as methods of valuing stock.**

Modern technology and purchasing

Stocks held by firms are constantly changing, as are their prices and replacement costs. Records, therefore, have to be constantly revised and checked. At the same time accurate records of purchases and payment liabilities have to be kept to ensure that payments are made correctly for goods and services received and found to be satisfactory. A system based on manual methods is time consuming, 'labour intensive' (uses a large amount of labour) and liable to error. The manual work involved in keeping records up to date is very repetitive and monotonous. It is often carried out by junior staff who do not realise the consequences of errors. Consequently checking and inspection procedures have to be introduced and these increase costs further.

Purchasing and stock control, therefore, are activities which lend themselves to the application of modern technology based on the microchip, including computers and other electronic equipment.

Computer systems

Purchasing and stock control systems have been developed for mainframe, mini- and microcomputers and for integrated systems using any combination of these. Systems can be individually designed for the needs of the firm but generally it is possible to modify standard systems to meet the individual needs of particular organisations. The advantage of the microcomputer is that it brings the computer into closer contact with the storeman and purchasing officer. It loses its mystery. Programmers can learn more easily the full needs of people in the departments and programs are easier to adapt and modify as needs change. Most systems are likely to have the following features:

a Programs which actually operate the system and which produce, maintain and update records and instructions in accordance with the information supplied to it.
b VDU display units which enable operators to read information contained in the computer's memory in response to commands given to it through a keyboard which is usually very similar to the ordinary typewriter keyboard. The operator can quickly and easily obtain such information as details of items in stock, where located in stores, prices, VAT rates and so on.
c Procedures for inputting information on such matters as the sale of items or their use in production, i.e. the information needed to keep records up to date and for ensuring that payments and fresh purchases are made. Most systems still rely on information being entered via a keyboard and this often remains a time-consuming process during which errors are likely to occur. Laser scanning of specially prepared labels and marks reduce both time and errors, and further developments are likely to improve methods of inputting information directly by typed matter or by the human voice.
d Records kept usually on magnetic tape or discs. These, of course, have to be kept in an ordered manner so that the correct computer files and programs are available as required.

Computer systems offer many benefits to the purchasing function. They vastly reduce the amount of manual manipulation and alteration and the quantity of physical records kept. They update material speedily and accurately – if supplied with accurate information. Calculations carried out by tested programs do not have to be checked. Computers do not forget, nor do they get bored or misinterpret instructions. Reminder systems can be used to remind purchasing officers when to re-order or check stocks or to bring to their attention stocks falling to minimum levels. Some of the services offered by a computerised system are shown in Fig 8.2

On the other hand computer systems are only as good as the programs prepared for them and the information fed to them. People often seem to credit them with powers and intelligence which they do not possess. It is still essential to have regular physical checks of stocks to ensure that errors are not occurring and multiplying. Systems are also open to abuse. The criminally minded can deliberately feed in false information in order to steal stock or money. It is desirable to have random checks and to change procedures and programs from time to time.

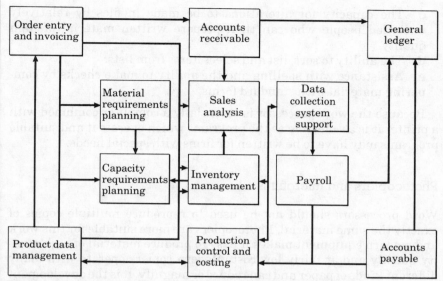

Fig 8.2   Information flow among program packages. Source: The
Manufacturing Accounting and Production Information Control System.
Reproduced by courtesy of IBM Corporation

However, a good computer system should free managers and senior
staff from purely routine work so that they can concentrate on those
aspects of their work that only they can carry out effectively, e.g. negotiating with suppliers, researching sources of supply and checking that
they are meeting the needs of production departments as effectively
as possible. Computers do not replace human managers. Properly
employed they make them more efficient.

Word processors

Much of the information processed by computers still has to be produced
and used in written form. The word processor enables this to be done
extremely quickly and accurately. A word processor is basically a pre-
programmed computer linked to one or more printers for the purpose
of producing material in paper form. It has many advantages including:

a   The capacity to store and reproduce accurately standard forms
and letters.
b   The ability to incorporate individual details and variations in
otherwise standard forms and letters so that a large number of paper
communications can be produced which nevertheless have the
appearance of being individually prepared.

c The capacity for alterations to be made in files by relatively unskilled people who can then prepare written material of high quality.
d The ability to sort, list and select items from lists.
e Assistance with spelling and the ability to make checks by comparing material with standard forms.

Because the word processor is essentially a computer combined with a printer it is as effective as the programs which operate it and suitable programs may have to be written for firms with special needs.

Photocopiers and microfilms

Word processors should not be used to reproduce multiple copies of exactly the same material. Photocopiers are more suitable for this work and modern equipment makes it easy to produce material of high quality quickly and at fairly low cost. Modern copiers operate with many different kinds of paper and can reduce or magnify. It is the development of microphotography, however, that is of particular benefit to purchasing and stock control departments. As an alternative to or to supplement computers the microfilm technique provides readily accessible records which can easily be read on screens. You are probably familiar with this type of material because many libraries now keep and maintain their records of books on microfiches which are available in place of the old card indexes which had to be maintained and sorted by hand.

Rapid review

1 Why are purchasing and stock control very well suited to the use of computerised methods?
2 What features are usually found in computer systems of stock control and purchasing?
3 List five advantages of a word processor.
4 What is a microfiche and why is it often preferred to a card index system of record keeping?

Exercises

1 Why is purchasing an important activity for a business organisation?
2 'The cheapest supplier is sometimes the most expensive.' How might this be?
3 By referring to journals such as the *Financial Times* list six commodities that are traded on 'futures' markets. Choose one of these and check its price once

a week over a period of at least six weeks. Discuss your findings and explain how trading in futures can help a manufacturer or importer to avoid losses through price changes.

4 Explain what is meant by stock control. How can computers make the process of stock control more efficient?

5 Explain how it is possible for a firm's stock to be to be valued in different ways. How might these differences affect the profits of the firm?

Questions from examination papers

Short answer questions

1 Mention *four* tasks that a marketing department in a large company is likely to undertake. AEB 0(A) 1982

2 Give *three* major considerations which should be taken into account when a firm makes purchasing decisions. AEB 0(A) 1982

3 From the viewpoint of an employee, list *two* advantages and *two* disadvantages of being employed as part of a mass production process.

4 State *three* features of the protection offered to consumers by the Sale of Goods Acts. AEB 0(A) 1984

5 Describe briefly *three* ways in which a wholesaler may help a small retailer. AEB 0(A) 1984

Essay questions

1 *a* From the manufacturer's point of view, what are the advantages of distributing his products through a wholesaler?

  b In view of these advantages, why have general wholesalers become relatively less important in the distribution of goods? AEB 0(A) 1982

2 'The work of the marketing department of a manufacturing firm begins after a new product has been produced and is concerned mainly with advertising it.'

  a Analyse this statement carefully, making clear the extent to which you agree or disagree with it.

  b In what ways would you expect the marketing department of such a firm to work closely with other departments of the firm? Refer to *three* other departments in your answer. AEB 0(A) 1983

3 'In recent years many companies have accepted the need to exhibit greater social responsibility.'

Discuss this statement and in your answer make reference to a company's responsibility towards its customers and its own employees. AEB 0(A) 1985

4 Discuss the factors a manufacturing organisation would consider before deciding to change its location. AEB A Level 1984

5 Outline the main aspects of consumer protection provided by the law and discuss the consequences of such protection for the consumer. AEB A Level 1985

9 Finance and the firm

The need for and sources of short-term finance

The need for funds

In Chapter 8 we saw how the firm has to keep and control stocks and to plan the flow of materials to be used in production. People have to be employed to do all this work and they have to be paid. We can see that the firm has a great deal of expense just in producing its goods and before it even has the opportunity to sell them and earn money to meet its expenses. Employers cannot say to their workers, 'You help me make goods and I will pay you when they have been sold.' Workers also have their own expenses to pay and they need their wages to be paid regularly.

Of course, once a firm has been in business some time there is a regular flow of cash coming in from sales of goods produced in previous periods to pay for present production costs. If it were to cease production the revenues would continue to come in after many of the costs had stopped. However, firms do not want to stop producing and as long as they stay in business they are always having to suffer from the time lag between meeting costs and receiving revenue from sales. If, as most firms wish, they increase production levels then the amount of outstanding costs is likely to increase.

To cover this gap many firms borrow money and as long as the profits earned as a result of this borrowing are greater than its cost then, clearly, it pays them to do so. Normally it is safe for firms to borrow on a 'short-term' basis to meet operating expenses and to maintain stocks. This means that they may be called upon to repay money so borrowed within a short period of time, say within a year, or on receiving short notice, say a month, that the lender wants the money repaid. If it has to repay to one lender a successful and profitable firm is usually able to borrow from another or to delay some of its purchases or other spending in order to find the necessary money.

Firms may also wish to borrow money on a short-term basis in order to acquire certain types of equipment or vehicles or to provide finance during the period when they are arranging to obtain long-term funds. These rather different cases are examined later in this chapter.

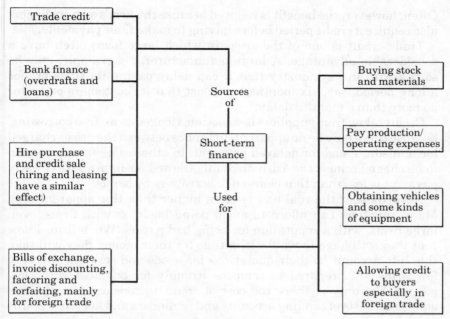

Fig 9.1   The finance of production and trade

Sources of short-term finance

The efficient firm will seek to arrange its flow of cash so that it does not have to borrow any more money than is necessary and so that it retains the confidence and support of its financial advisers. A careful study of the times when money is received and when it has to be paid may reveal ways in which changes could reduce borrowing costs. If there are some months when cash accumulates in bank accounts and others when it has to be borrowed then, because banks always charge more to borrowers than they pay to lenders, the firm will cut costs by re-arranging payment dates to produce a smoother flow of money through the business.

Trade credit

However skilfully it manages its cash flow, the firm is still likely to find it necessary or profitable to obtain money from outside sources. A practice adopted by almost all business organisations is to trade on other firms' money by taking trade credit. It is common practice in business to require payment at the end of a stated period after delivery of the goods or after the date the order is received. This helps to share the burden of financing production over all the firms involved.

Often, however, the benefit is reduced because the firm's own customers also require a credit period before having to make their payments.

Trade credit is one of the areas in which large firms often have a considerable advantage. A large manufacturer, for example, may be so powerful in its industry that it can delay paying its suppliers for a long period, say, six months but insist that its customers pay after no more than a month's delay.

Credit taken from suppliers is sometimes looked on as 'free borrowing' because there may be no apparent difference between the prices charged for immediate and for delayed payment. In other cases it may be seen to be cheap because the 'cash discount' allowed for immediate or early payment is less than that charged to borrowers by banks.

Nevertheless, the real cost is often higher than this apparent cost. Many suppliers can afford to avoid doing business with firms, even large firms, with a reputation for being bad payers. When firms know that they will have to wait a long time for their money they will take this into account in their quotations for goods and services and very few firms are prepared to compete strongly for business with slow payers. Not only is there the cost of credit to consider but also the additional costs of sending accounts and reminders and keeping records open. Suppliers are much more anxious to compete and offer keen prices for good and reliable payers. Consequently the true cost of excessive trade credit is often much higher than some company accountants realise.

Bank finance

The most common source of short-term finance is the clearing bank, now often known as the High Street bank, e.g. Barclays, National Westminster, Lloyds and Midland. Firms, both small and large, are likely to turn first to one of these banks when they want to borrow money. Where possible the banks prefer to lend money for definite terms at rates of interest agreed for the whole term or at the bank's base rate plus an agreed percentage. Most business firms, however, prefer to negotiate the more flexible overdraft whereby an account holder is allowed to make payments up to an agreed limit above the balance of the account. Interest at the bank's current rates is charged on a daily basis on the actual amount overdrawn. Again, however, the true cost of an overdraft can be higher than the interest charged because banks tend to increase service or account handling charges where overdrafts are in force and, of course, the customer with a large and persistent overdraft is in a relatively weak position to bargain over bank charges. Banks, however, make most of their profits from lending money and are always anxious to lend to successful, profitable and efficient business organisations. They do compete for good business customers so that bank finance is usually the most flexible and least costly way to raise short-term finance.

Finance to obtain equipment

Firms often seek to finance their acquisitions of office and other types of equipment and vehicles out of their normal revenue. They can do this if they can spread the cost over periods from one to around four years. Finance for these purposes may be provided by the suppliers themselves, or, more usually by specialised finance institutions. Many of these are themselves owned or closely associated with one of the large banks. The precise way in which the financial arrangement is made often depends on the needs of the individual firm and on the current taxation laws. Because of the peculiarity of taxation and the allowances that can be set against taxation, some methods can sometimes cost less than others even though interest charges are the same.

The main ways of financing equipment acquisitions are:

a Hire purchase whereby, legally, the firm hires the equipment or vehicle for an agreed term but has an option to purchase it and usually does so when the final payment of an agreed number of instalments is made.

b Credit sale, which is similar, in practice, to hire purchase, but the firm buys and gains legal ownership of the equipment on signing the agreement and making the first payment.

c Leasing, which is another very similar method but here the leasing company buys the equipment and leases it to the firm for an agreed term and agreed number of payments. Ownership normally passes to the firm with the final payment.

d Hiring, where there is often no firm agreement that the firm will ever acquire legal ownership of the equipment but will simply acquire its use in return for an agreed, regular hire charge. Indeed the firm may prefer not to buy it but replace it from time to time and renegotiate the agreement. If purchase is desired this can usually be arranged by negotiation.

Some advantages of leasing and hiring were identified in Chapter 8 and the scale it can sometimes reach is illustrated in Fig 9.2.

It may seem strange that there should be so many different ways of achieving the same object which is essentially to pay for equipment out of the revenue that the equipment itself will help to earn. This diversity is partly the result of a complex taxation system but is also evidence of the ingenuity of a modern financial system in devising ways to provide business firms with money in forms that meet a great range of different needs and circumstances.

> Forward Trust Group
> is pleased to announce
> that it has arranged a
> leasing facility of £50,000,000
> on behalf of Nissan Motor
> Manufacturing (UK) Limited,
> to finance the development
> of a new automotive factory in
> Washington, Tyne and Wear.
>
> This concludes the first
> phase of the financing
> of manufacturing plant.
>
> November 1984
>
>  **FORWARD TRUST GROUP**
> A member of Midland Bank Group

Fig 9.2   Leasing can be on a vast scale. Source: Advertisement in *The Sunday Times* Business News, 2 December 1984

Firms will thus often be presented with a choice of different ways to finance an intended acquisition. In making that choice they are likely to be guided by considerations of cost and flexibility.

The net costs of a particular form of finance will depend chiefly on interest rates and taxation.

Interest is the charge made for having the use of someone else's money. When comparing interest rate costs firms should compare the true rates, now known as the **annual percentage rates**. The APR is the equivalent annual rate if interest is paid once a year on the actual amount of money owing during the year. It takes into account repayments of the original amount borrowed and payments of interest made more frequently than once a year.

Taxation is often fairly complex and liable to change, especially if the Government considers that it is losing too much tax revenue because of the use of particular devices. For some years leasing was popular because the leasing companies were able to claim very substantial allowances to set off against tax when they legally bought the goods that they leased to users. The companies were then able to pass on some of their savings through reduced interest charges. When the tax rules were changed there ceased to be any cost advantages compared with hire purchase or the use of a bank overdraft.

Flexibility is often considered to be important, especially when equipment is constantly being modernised. A firm may prefer to hire rather than buy something such as a copying machine or a word processor if it thinks that better versions will be available in a year's time. On the other hand the hiring company will have to take into account that, if this does happen, it may have on its hands large quantities of nearly new equipment that no one will wish to hire or will only hire at very low rates. This possibility will be reflected in the hire charges that it makes on new equipment.

The choice of credit is a business decision and like any other it usually has to be taken under conditions of some uncertainty.

Rapid review

1 For what purposes might a firm wish to borrow money on a short-term basis?
2 Why might a profitable firm need short-term loans?
3 List the main sources of short-term business finance.
4 List four ways to finance the acquisition of business equipment.
5 State two matters likely to influence the choice of method to finance the acquisition of equipment.

The need for and sources of long-term and permanent capital

The need for capital

It is a basic principle of business finance that short-term borrowing should not be used for purposes that make it impossible to recover the money if the owner wishes to exercise his or her rights to regain it. Many perfectly profitable firms have failed because they could not provide cash when it became due without harming the activities of the business. If a business owner borrows money for a year and uses this to set up specialised buildings and equipment that they hope will provide sufficient revenue to repay the loan at the end of the year, they are in very great trouble if production and sales are delayed and they fail to achieve the revenue within the time expected. If they sell the equipment they lose their chance to produce anything and are likely to lose heavily because the market value of the equipment has probably fallen. Any firm which needs to rely on substantial physical assets such as buildings and large amounts of machinery or which needs to spend a long period engaging in research before goods or services can be produced needs to have the use of finance on a long-term basis and preferably needs to have some finance that it need not repay at all as long as the business is operating effectively.

The investment decision

Before making a decision whether to acquire or use capital resources for new development the firm must have some means of working out whether this is likely to be worthwhile. It must be able to calculate the cost, the probable increase in net revenue that it will bring and be able to compare these in a realistic way. Modern firms have available a number of techniques of investment appraisal that can help them to reach the decisions.

One very simple method is to calculate the cost of a proposed project, make the best estimate possible of the additional revenues it is likely to produce and then calculate the length of time before the expected revenues just equal the cost. This time is known as the 'payback period'. Firms may decide that they will only consider projects with payback periods of less than a stated length, say four years, or they will show preference for those with the smallest periods.

For example, suppose a project, costing an initial amount of £100 000, is expected to produce additional revenues of £1000 at the end of year 1, £15 000 at the end of year 2, £84 000 at the end of year 3 and £70 000 at the end of year 4. Then the initial cost of £100 000 is paid back by the end of year 3, so 3 years is the payback period. One problem of using this method is that many projects are ignored because they might take a long time to reach their payback period but they could be extremely profitable in subsequent years.

More scientific techniques use what are known as **discounted cash flow** methods. These involve calculating the present value of future flows of revenue and comparing this with the cost.

For example, if we assume that £100 invested for a year would earn interest of 10 per cent, then the present value of £110 payable in a year's time is now £100. The present value of future revenues can be calculated with the help of discount tables or computer programs.

One difficult decision that the firm has to make is to choose the interest or discount rate. The higher the rate chosen, the lower the present value. The present value of £110 payable at the end of a year and discounted at a rate of 20 per cent rather than the earlier 10 per cent is £91.67. Because firms will have to choose rates which are related to the earning power of money, any general rise in interest rates used by the banks and other financial institutions will tend to reduce the number of investment projects that business firms find acceptable.

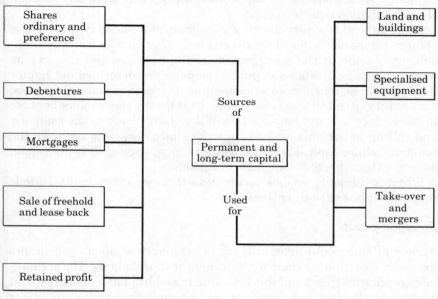

Fig 9.3   Business capital

Forms of capital

Very small firms have to rely on the capital that their owners can introduce from their own savings or can borrow from relatives, friends or banks. Partnerships may require a new partner to contribute a certain sum of capital as a condition of joining the firm. Small family companies will bring in capital in the form of shares. If, say, two people, Bill and Anne, decided to form a small private company to produce computer software and each contributed £500, they would start with total capital of £1000. This they might decide to divide into 1000 shares, each of £1, and they would each hold 500 of the shares. Suppose that after a few years success had brought them accumulated unspent profits of £2000 and they had also bought equipment valued at £3000. Their business would now hold assets (cash and equipment) with a total value of £5000 so that the value of each share could now be said to be equal to £5. If they decided to stop trading, sell the equipment and pay out the capital, each could receive £2500.

Suppose Anne wanted to leave the business but Bill decided to carry on. One way to do this could be for Anne to sell her shares to Bill or to someone else entirely. Alternatively, the shares could be left unsold and Anne could remain a shareholder but cease to work in the company. As a shareholder she would still be entitled to any division of profit (dividend) decided upon.

Share capital is a very useful way to finance a company. In the case of large companies sales of shares can be taking place constantly without any change in the management of the business and the way its work is carried on. Shares in public companies as described in Chapter 2 are, of course, much more saleable than shares in private companies. This ability to sell shares is very important for the shareholder because in most cases it is not possible to sell the shares back to the company and selling is the only way to turn the share back into cash. To the company, share capital is normally permanent capital. It is not repaid as long as the company continues in existence.

When a company wishes to increase the amount of capital funds it can use it has various options.

Retained profit

Almost all successful firms will try to keep back some of their profits instead of distributing them to the owners or shareholders. The accumulated profits are then available for acquiring additional assets to expand production. It must not, however, be imagined that these profits are necessarily cheaper than money borrowed from outside the firm. The funds could have been invested elsewhere to earn interest and this sacrifice of interest must be taken into account in any appraisal of a possible investment project.

Additional shares

As long as the firm is successful and is able to increase its profits its shares will increase in value. This is likely to attract investors who want to buy a stake in that increase in wealth. The firm, therefore, may be able to sell more shares and increase its total share capital. If it does so, however, it is 'diluting' the value of the existing shares because the shareholders will have a small proportion of total shareholder votes and there is the risk that dividends per share will have to be reduced if profits do not rise in proportion to the number of new shares.

To overcome this problem it is normal to offer any new shares first to the existing shareholders at a price that is below the market price at the time of issue. Existing shareholders are given the 'right' to buy the new shares in a stated proportion to the shares already held. For example rights based on two new for every five existing shares held would give the holder of 500 shares the right to buy 200 new ones. Shareholders not wanting any more shares could sell their 'rights' to anyone else who wanted to buy them at whatever price obtainable.

Borrowed funds

It is not always possible to issue additional shares. Many people prefer to receive a definite rate of interest on their investments rather than dividends which can fall as well as rise. Companies can issue loan stock which can be divided into units and sold in very much the same way as shares. Loans are stated to be repaid at a definite future date or within stated dates but the ability to sell is still important for investors who need to recover their money before the repayment date.

The term **debenture** is a general one used to refer to **company loans** and the two terms can be regarded as interchangeable. More important are the rights of the loan stock or debenture holders should the company be unable to pay the interest it has contracted to pay or even should the company fail completely. If the loan is 'secured' by rights to specific assets such as a particular factory building then the stockholders are entitled to the proceeds from the sale of this building. If the loan is 'unsecured' then the stockholders have no special rights beyond those of other creditors.

Holders of debentures may contribute to the success of the company by the money they provide, but not share in that success other than through the fixed rate of interest they receive. To make loans more attractive companies sometimes issue **convertible loans**. These operate as normal loans for a stated period after which the holders have the right to change the loan for an agreed number of shares.

Mortgages

If a business organisation owns land or property it may, like the private householder, borrow on the security of the property by means of a **mortgage**. The mortgage transfers some of the legal rights of ownership to the lender during the period of the loan but the practical rights of occupation and use of the property remain with the borrower.

Sale and leaseback

A more extreme way to raise money through land or property is actually to sell it and lease it back again. This is more attractive from the

	£ million		
	Combined		Unilever Group
	1983	1984	
			Borrowings
	577	830	Debenture and similar loans
	498	1 001	Bank loans and overdrafts
	1 075	1 831	
			The repayments fall due as follows:
			Within 1 year
	71	118	After 1 year but within 2 years
	285	357	After 2 years but within 5 years
	186	187	After 5 years but within 10 years
	16	56	After 10 years but within 20 years
	59	75	After 20 years
			Amounts repayable after 5 years
			Repayable by instalments:
	167	133	Debenture and similar loans
	29	23	Bank loans and overdrafts
	196	156	
			Not repayable by instalments:
	64	142	Debenture and similar loans
	1	20	Bank loans and overdrafts
	65	162	
	261	318	
			Total amount due on borrowings repayable by instalments:
	290	259	Debenture and similar loans
	68	71	Bank loans and overdrafts
	358	330	
			Secured amounts are:
	22	43	Debenture and similar loans
	68	128	Bank loans and overdrafts
	90	171	
			of which:
	38	104	Secured against tangible assets
	52	67	Secured against other assets
	90	171	

Fig 9.4   The finance borrowed by a large multinational organisation. Source: Unilever Report and Accounts for 1984

	£ million	
Combined		
1983	1984	**Unilever Group**

1983	1984	Unilever Group
		Borrowings (continued)
		Debenture and similar loans
		Unilever N.V.
27	26	6% Bonds 1972/91
11	6	$8\frac{3}{4}$% Bonds 1981/85
69	86	$9\frac{1}{4}$% Bonds 1987 (United States $100.0)
69	86	$9\frac{3}{4}$% Bonds 1986/90 (United States $100.0)
32	31	$4\frac{1}{2}$% Bonds 1984/91 (Swiss Frs. 100.0)
32	33	$6\frac{3}{4}$% Bonds 1991 (Swiss Frs. 100.0)
32	33	$7\frac{1}{2}$% Bonds 1993 (Swiss Frs. 100.0)
272	301	Total Unilever N.V.*
		Group companies:
		Netherlands
3	2	$4\frac{1}{2}$% Loans 1968/87
4	4	$9\frac{3}{4}$% Loans 1980/89
5	4	$9\frac{3}{4}$% Loan 1989
		U.S.A.
14	15	$9\frac{1}{8}$% Notes 1982/91
19	–	$7\frac{9}{20}$% Notes 1982/97
10	11	$8\frac{2}{5}$–$9\frac{7}{8}$% Loans 1982/93
93	257	A series of other loans at variable interest rates
420	594	
		*Guilder equivalent in millions (see page 36) (1983–1 205).
		Unilever PLC
10	10	$6\frac{3}{4}$% Debenture stock 1985/88
2	2	$5\frac{1}{2}$% Unsecured loan stock 1991/2006 ⎱ Rank
55	55	$7\frac{3}{4}$% Unsecured loan stock 1991/2006 ⎰ parity
–	36	8% Unsecured loan notes 1992
67	103	Total Unilever PLC (see page 38)
		Group companies:
1	1	Canada: $6\frac{1}{2}$% Debenture Series A 1985
9	10	$8\frac{5}{8}$% Debenture Series B 1993
3	3	Australia: $7\frac{3}{4}$% Debentures 1982/87
6	7	$10\frac{1}{2}$% Debentures 1985/89
71	112	A series of other loans at variable interest rates
157	236	
577	830	
128	288	of which repayable within one year:
		Bank loans and overdrafts
311	776	Loans
187	225	Overdrafts
498	1 001	
330	750	of which repayable within one year:

financiers' point of view because they gain actual ownership and the right to increase the amount of rent payable at agreed intervals. Insurance offices have been important providers of finance by these means.

Rapid review

1 **Why should short-term borrowing not be used to finance the purchase of a specialised business building?**
2 **What is the payback period of a proposed investment project?**
3 **What is meant by 'discounted cash flow'?**
4 **List the main ways in which a business firm may raise permanent and long-term finance.**

The capital market

The market in permanent and long-term finance is usually called the **capital market**. In fact there are several different markets though they are closely connected. The capital markets are also linked quite closely to the short-term financial markets through institutions such as merchant banks and the clearing or High Street banks which have important functions to perform in whatever way money is raised.

Banks and specialist organisations

When the small organisation needs money it often has little idea what form of money it requires and it is likely to go first to its High Street bank. The bank can often supply the finance itself in the form most appropriate for the organisation. The banks are more ready today to provide start-up and venture capital for small firms offering specialist advice as well as finance. Some banks co-operate with a government loan guarantee scheme under which, in return for a charge made by an addition to the loan interest the Government undertakes to repay the bank loan if the borrower fails.

In some cases, the bank may introduce the firm to a specialist corporation or the firm may itself approach the corporation. One of the best known of these is Investors in Industry PLC, commonly known as 3i, the descendant of the former Finance Corporation for Industry. Investors in Industry has a number of specialised divisions including ICFC (Industrial and Commercial Finance Corporation) which exists to assist small- and medium-sized firms in industry and the services and claims to be the world's largest source of private venture capital (capital risked in new business venture). ICFC will make loans or take ordinary shares in companies it decides are worth supporting at any point in their development. It can provide long- or short-term finance and help to open up export markets. It also has access to European Community sources. In addition to finance it can provide skilled financial and managerial assistance.

Merchant banks, some of which are owned by the large High Street banks but which also include some very large independent institutions, can cover a wide range of activities including advising business firms and helping them to obtain the finance they need. They operate in both short- and long-term finance markets and are the main channels whereby firms enter the various capital markets. They usually operate as issuing houses and accepting houses as described later in this chapter.

The new issue market

This is concerned with the provision of new or additional shares or loan stocks to companies. Much of its work involves the conversion of private to public companies. Such conversion usually helps a company to raise more finance and it makes its shares and debentures more readily saleable so that money can be raised from a much wider public.

A new issue (issue of new shares or debentures for the first time) involves the sale of shares (which, for simplicity in this section we shall assume includes loans) by the company to members of the public. The money raised goes to the company and increases its capital. This is highly specialised work and the company is normally advised by an **issuing house** or the issue department of a large merchant or clearing bank. The issuing house assumes responsibility for the issue, the terms of the sale and its timing and all the steps necessary before the new shares become saleable or marketable in whichever section of the capital market has been selected. The relationship between company and issuing house is an important one because the professionals in the markets will judge the issue on the reputation of the house – which, in most cases is part of or very closely linked to one of the main merchant banks.

The Unlisted Securities Market

Most new public companies in Britain today are likely to have their shares traded in the Unlisted Securities Market (USM) which is an offshoot of the main Stock Exchange. The issue is likely to be less costly than for the full Stock Exchange although the cost has risen

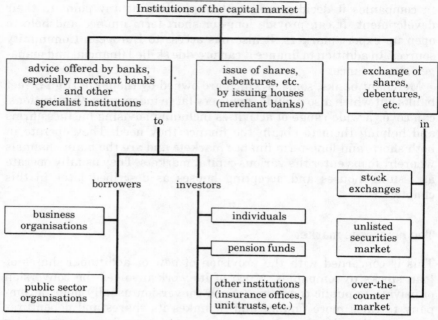

Fig 9.5   The capital market

considerably since the market has grown. The rules of the market are a little less stringent than for the main Stock Exchange and it is generally recognised that investment through the market will be in the shares of smaller and riskier companies. Investors willing to take the greater risks gain the chance to buy shares in new and growing companies. Potential profits can be much greater.

The function of the USM is to give smaller companies the chance to raise capital and have their shares traded at a much earlier stage than would be possible if they had to wait for entry to the full Exchange. It operates as a market to bring investors to new and growing enterprise in a way that is essential for the efficient operation of a market economy.

The market opened in 1980 and it has proved to be very successful. Its share prices are now regularly featured in the main financial journals.

The Stock Exchange

The London Exchange is closely linked to the provincial exchanges in cities such as Birmingham, Glasgow and Manchester, but it is London which dominates the British financial scene and which provides the main market for buying and selling shares in the larger, well-established public companies.

London, however, can no longer assume that it can remain the centre of the financial and commercial world. It is facing increasing competition from markets in the USA, Europe and the Far East. Shares in the largest multinational companies are traded in all the main world exchanges and some of the larger firms of stockbrokers are also represented in all the main markets. Investors and companies now have more choice and there are more people competing for the business of the really large-scale dealers.

To meet this competition the London Stock Exchange is having to become more flexible and to raise the level of efficiency of its administration. Traditional practices can no longer be retained out of respect for tradition alone. The catalyst for change was the Office of Fair Trading which accused the London market of restrictive practices and started an action in the Restrictive Practices Court. The action was eventually dropped after intervention by the Government and after the Council of the Exchange undertook to commence reforms in its practices. In early 1985 discussions took place as to what changes were to be made. The outcome was that the strict division that existed between the roles of the jobber and the broker disappeared and firms are now able to undertake both functions – as they have done in all other exchanges for many years. Thus firms can represent clients as brokers and buy and sell shares on their own account as 'market makers'.

Fixed scales of commission have also been abolished. Only a few broking firms will now be able to secure the business of the large investors such as the insurance offices and pension funds. Some of the others are likely to develop specialised services for small individual investors simply in order to survive. Members of the Exchange can also be owned by approved British or foreign banks and financial institutions. This revolutionary 'Big Bang' took place in October 1986.

Over-the-counter markets

These are developments on the American pattern and they exist as markets for a small number of company shares outside either of the main divisions of the Stock Exchange. They operate as private markets run by individual firms which specialise in the shares of a small group of companies. The best markets observe a common code of practice but over-the-counter trading is very risky although the Stock Exchange may take over much of this trading in its own 'Third Market'.

Speculation

All stock markets are speculative. People buy shares in the hope of profit. The true speculators are those who seek short-term profit and who are prepared to buy and sell with that objective in mind. They are not really making their money available for investment in business enterprise. Nevertheless it can be argued that speculation has a function in capital markets. It ensures that there are always people prepared to deal so that those who wish to convert their shares to cash can do so quickly and conveniently without affecting the finances of the company. Shares become an almost liquid asset to the investor while remaining fixed capital for the company.

Speculation also arouses interest and improves communications. We know a great deal more about the use and misuse of business capital than we do about investment in the public sector!

It also leads to the development of active and disciplined markets in which individuals are protected by precise laws and codes of professional conduct.

It can only be justified as long as it does fulfil such functions. If capital markets become dominated by a relatively few large public companies and financial institutions such as the large banks, insurance offices and pension funds then the benefits of a competitive market give way to the restrictions of monopoly. This is why new developments such as the USM and over-the-counter markets are important. They are helping to keep the financial markets alive and active in the service of business enterprise.

Rapid review

1 What is the main function of the Industrial and Commercial Finance Corporation?
2 What is an 'issuing house'?
3 What are: (a) the Unlisted Securities Market? (b) Over-the-counter markets?
4 What functions can be claimed for speculation in stock exchanges?

The finance of overseas trade

This is a highly specialised but most important part of the financial system. It also represents an important area of co-operation between the commercial banks and the Government through the agency of the Export Credits Guarantee Department.

Exporters face the problem that they sell in highly competitive world markets where prices are keen and it is often necessary to give generous credit terms but the risks are high and the profits often slim. The exporter needs to obtain his money as quickly as possible after goods

have been dispatched though few importers are willing to pay until
the goods are received. It is the banking system that helps to meet
both needs. The banks have developed payment systems that look complicated but, in fact, operate, for the most part, very smoothly and
effectively.

Commercial bills and documentary credits

The commercial bill of exchange is still an important means of payment
in foreign trade. An exporter may agree that payment can be in the
form of, say, a 90-day bill. The exporter (or the bank acting for them)
drafts the bill stipulating how, where, when and in what currency payment is to be made. The draft is then sent to the importer who arranges
that the undertaking to pay as stipulated by their bill draft is *accepted*
by an approved bank or accepting house on their behalf. The accepted
(signed) bill is then returned to the exporter's bank which, by arrangement with the exporter, usually discounts it, i.e. credits the exporter's
account with the face value of the bill less a discount. The bank can
hold the discounted bill or re-discount it with a discount house. Whoever
holds the bill when payment is due collects the full amount.

The banking system thus:

a Administers the transaction.
b Accepts the bill on behalf of the payer and in doing so guarantees
that payment will be made. A bill accepted by a recognised bank
is much more valuable than one without this guarantee.
c Arranges discounting which, in effect, is a loan to the payee on
the security of the accepted bill.

In this way the exporter gains speedy payment. The importer gets time
to pay and the banks gain profitable business.

When firms are trading regularly with each other it is common to
arrange a system of payment by documentary credits. A bank in the
exporter's country holds an accepted bill on behalf of the importer with
authority to release it on receipt of satisfactory shipping documents
showing that the goods have been safely dispatched to the importer.
The bank checks the documents and if they are in order releases the
accepted bill to the exporter who lodges it with his own bank for discounting as already explained.

Factoring, invoice discounting and forfaiting

A simpler, though often more expensive method of financing exports
can be for a specialist financial institution to take over responsibility

for collection of a trade debt as a factor. The factor, usually a subsidiary company of a commercial bank, effectively buys the debt and assumes the risk of non-payment. This service enables the exporter to receive speedy payment – at a cost.

Invoice discounting is very similar but the risk of non-payment remains with the trader. This service is usually a little less costly. Both services are only available for approved trade debts usually with well-known international companies.

Banks will often allow overdrafts to exporters to cover the period between manufacture and payment. The banks, therefore, offer a range of services to suit all kinds of trading firms.

Forfaiting is a bank service available to suppliers of capital goods (equipment, etc.). The bank buys bills of exchange or promissory notes signed by an approved importer. The bank will prefer the bills or notes to have been guaranteed by an internationally reputable bank.

The Export Credits Guarantee Department

Providing credit for exporting is doubly hazardous. There is the normal risk of the failure of the bank customer who may not be trading wisely or efficiently and to this is added the risk that he or she will not be paid for reasons outside his or her control. The overseas buyer might fail or payment might be blocked by government action in either country – or even in some third country.

To protect their customers' money the banks would normally have to charge very high interest rates on any loans made to exporters. Exporting, however, is considered to be in the national interest and governments are prepared to help. The ECGD is an important agency for such help. It provides insurance for exporters and guarantees to banks making loans to exporters and so reduces the risks run by banks and enables them to keep their interest charges competitive.

Although a department of government, with losses made good by the taxpayer, the ECGD has the duty to try and operate on a commercial basis with costs met by charges to customers. In the world depression of the early 1980s it suffered some very heavy losses and it may be forced to cancel some of its schemes and reduce the amount of protection it is able to offer.

All trading countries have agencies similar to the ECGD and there are international agreements designed to discourage governments from using such departments to provide concealed subsidies to their exporters.

Rapid review

1 **What is a commercial bill of exchange?**
2 **State three ways in which the banking system assists in operating payment systems that depend on bills of exchange.**
3 **State the differences between: factoring, invoice discounting and forfaiting.**
4 **List two ways in which the Export Credits Guarantee Department assists exporters.**

Exercises

1 Explain why even the most profitable of business firms is likely to want to borrow money.
2 Suppose the dressmaking firm mentioned in earlier chapters decided to acquire more equipment. Describe the various ways in which it could finance the acquisition of the equipment. Choose one of these ways and explain its advantages and possible disadvantages for the firm.
3 Suppose the dressmaking firm was offered a new factory with more space which would enable it to increase its production by 50 per cent. Describe how the firm would set about reaching a decision whether or not to buy the factory. What considerations would influence that decision?
4 If the firm did decide to buy the factory how might it raise the necessary finance? Why are the methods of financing a factory purchase likely to be different from those used to acquire equipment?
5 Find an 'offer for sale' of company shares in one of the financial journals. Study it closely and answer the following questions:
   a Why are the shares being issued?
   b What inducements are being offered to possible buyers of the shares?
   c What is the business of the company and what has been its trading record over the previous five years?
6 Obtain a booklet describing the work and services of the ECGD and describe the cover granted by the Department's normal comprehensive policies. (The ECGD itself publishes a suitable booklet.)
7 Describe as fully as possible the services offered to business firms by either
   a a merchant bank or
   b the ICFC.
8 Describe and discuss the part played in the British capital market by the Unlisted Securities Market.
9 Should gambling in company shares be made illegal? Justify your answer.
10 With the help of a suitable booklet obtained from one of the large banks, describe the system of documentary credit payments as used in foreign trade.
11 Describe as fully as you can the work of the Export Credits Guarantee Department.

10 The costs of production

An important element in business survival and success is an under-standing of your real costs of production. Unless you know how much something is costing to produce it is difficult to know how to price it or whether to accept an order at the price offered. For example, in earlier chapters we used the example of a small but growing dress-making business. Suppose this business receives an enquiry from a customer for a 'rush order' which would involve having to pay workers overtime rates. What sort of price would have to be charged to make it worthwhile taking the order? To work this out we must analyse costs.

Types of cost

Even a small business incurs a wide range of costs. There will be rent, rates, heating and lighting for the premises; costs of materials; buying and maintaining equipment; wages and National Insurance charges; transport, postage, telephones, insurance premiums and so on. One of the first requirements for the small business owner has to be to make sure that all costs are known. Profits can melt away when unex-pected bills arrive. The prudent business owner always plans carefully to ensure that the business can meet its bills.

It is often useful to distinguish different types of cost, such as fixed and variable, overhead and direct, or average and marginal. Of course, at the end of the day the business will only be successful if it can pay *all* its costs. It also has to be recognised that the practical division of costs into different types can sometimes be rather forced and artifi-cial. However, the real value of making these distinctions is that they help in making business decisions.

Fixed and variable costs

To set up in even a small-scale tailoring or dressmaking business will involve costs such as buying a sewing machine. This cost is incurred however many or few clothes are made. Because the cost does not change whenever the production or output level changes it is termed a **fixed cost** of production.

In contrast, the amount of material used to make the clothes will vary according to how many garments are made. This, therefore, is a **variable cost**.

The distinction between fixed and variable cost is not always clear cut. For example, the cost of labour is often treated as a variable cost but, in practice, most labour costs are fixed unless workers are being paid piece or overtime rates. The depreciation (fall in value over time of machines, equipment, etc.) of capital equipment is often treated as a fixed cost. Some depreciation occurs solely because of the passage of time (most cars, for instance, are worth less as soon as they are driven away from the showroom by the buyer) but some is related to the extent of use (a one-year-old car with 20 000 miles 'on the clock', other things being equal, has a lower value than one known to have been driven only 4000 miles). In effect, then, depreciation is really a mixture of fixed and variable cost.

Furthermore, whether a cost is fixed or variable depends on the time period we are looking at. Given a sufficiently long period *all costs are variable*. Our clothing company would have to purchase more machines if its sales continued to increase. If the number of machines it could keep fully employed required more space then, another building would have to be hired or built. The amount of capital used by the firm is dependent on the scale of its production output.

If you have studied any economics you will recognise here that we are describing what economists call the **long run** which they define as that period during which the quantity employed of *all* factors of production can be changed. The **short run** is defined as that period during which at least one production factor is held constant, the others being variable. The actual length of time involved depends on the production process. The long run for a window cleaner is somewhat shorter than for an oil company!

There is believed to be a limit to the extent to which variable factors can be added to fixed factors without a serious loss of efficiency. Machines can operate effectively within certain levels of output. Attempts to exceed these by more and more intensive use will result in **diminishing returns** as breakdowns increase or the standard of output becomes unreliable. Similarly a piece of land can be worked more intensively but eventually the variable costs of obtaining additional output from that one piece must start to rise.

One useful way we can use our classification of fixed and variable costs is in **breakeven analysis**.

Suppose that the product 'boggins' can be sold for £1 each. The fixed costs of production are £2000, however many or few boggins are produced. The variable costs are 50p for each boggin. We can show this information diagrammatically as in Fig 10.1. We can then read off the profit or loss that will be made at different levels of output. The point at which the combined fixed and variable costs (total costs) are just equal to total sales revenue, so that there is neither profit nor loss, is called the **breakeven point**.

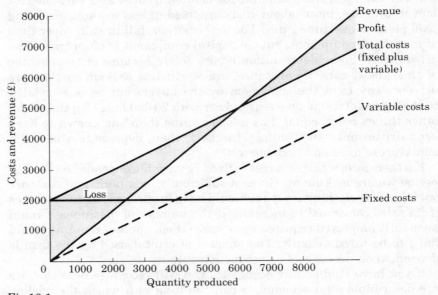

Fig 10.1

One attraction of this sort of analysis is that we can see how sensitive the results are to change in costs or revenues. We can redraw the diagram and recalculate the breakeven point. Work out for yourself the new breakeven point for boggins if, for example:

a   The price of boggins rose to £1.30.
b   The fixed costs of production rose to £3000.
c   The variable costs of production rose to 60p.

You can see that an analysis of fixed and variable costs can be a useful aid to deciding what and whether to produce and in what quantities.

Overhead and direct costs

Direct costs are those that are directly attributable to the production of particular goods and services. For example, the purchase of a 'boggin-making machine' is a fixed cost but it is also directly related to the production of boggins. On the other hand, heating the factory which is likely to be a variable cost – the more hours per week the factory stays open the higher the heating bill – will be difficult to attribute to any one product if several are being produced in the same factory. Such a cost is, therefore, known as an **overhead** cost.

It is clearly important to cover (be able to pay from revenue) all overhead costs. One way that cost accountants try to ensure that all costs, including overheads, are covered, is to calculate a contribution that all production should make towards paying the overhead costs. For example, if we produce £1000 worth of product A and £2000 worth of product B, one accounting convention (customary practice) would be to attribute twice as much of the overheads to product B as to product A. The object would be to ensure that if we achieve our planned levels of output and sales then all the overhead costs can be met from the revenue earned.

This is sound practice in keeping account and financial records. We want to be able to show all the costs incurred in earning revenue and we do not want to discover that we have incurred costs without any idea what these costs were for.

Nevertheless, we should be careful not to use this kind of analysis in the wrong way. It can be misleading if rather arbitrary ways of allocating past charges are used for deciding what to do in the future. For example, suppose a farmer is considering whether to open a farm shop. The correct way to work out the financial implications of this would be to calculate the fixed and variable costs which directly result from the decision – converting a shed, hiring labour, the cost of heating and lighting the shop and so on – and then relate these to the likely income from the venture to see if a profit can be made. The decision should not depend on whether or not the shop can make a 'fair' contribution to the general farm overheads which have to be met whether or not the shop is opened.

The point is that keeping accurate records and making sound decisions are both essential business activities. However, the way we record and analyse information, such as the details of costs, may have to be different for different purposes.

Standard costs

In a similar way it can be useful to work out the *standard costs* of producing each unit of production. The standard cost is the amount, calculated in advance, that it should cost to produce something if we are operating efficiently. It can be subdivided to show, for example, the *standard labour cost* or the *standard material cost* of production. This is useful for several reasons:

a   To calculate standard cost we must have some idea how costs are likely to behave for different levels of output and therefore we must undertake some research and clear thinking about the production process.

b   The calculation of standard costs enables us to compare these with actual costs and so identify the sources and causes of discrepancies and inefficiencies in the use, say, of labour or materials which may have been less productive than we had expected.

Average and marginal costs

Have another look at Fig 10.1. Total costs are made up of fixed costs and variable costs. We can work out the **average costs** of production at each level of output by dividing the total costs at that level by the quantity produced. Try working these out for yourself at different numbers of boggins before reading any further. For example,

1000 boggins cost £2500, so the average cost per boggin = £2.50
2000 boggins cost £3000, so the average cost per boggin = £1.50
4000 boggins cost £4000, so the average cost per boggin = £1.00

The variable cost per boggin is constant so why is the average costs coming down as output rises? The answer is that the fixed cost is being spread over more and more boggins so that the average fixed cost is being reduced each time output is increased. This fall in average cost can be shown in a diagram such as that of Fig 10.2.

Another way of looking at this is to ask, 'How much does it cost us to produce more boggins?' The answer cannot be the average cost of production because this includes the fixed cost which, by definition – being fixed – does not change whether we produce more or less. The cost of producing one extra unit (or the reduction in cost resulting from the production of one less unit) and which results only from changes in those costs that do vary with the amount produced, is the **marginal cost**. The marginal cost is shown as a broken line in Fig 10.2.

We can look on the marginal cost as being the difference between the total cost of producing, say, 1000 boggins and the total cost of producing 1001. In this case it is equal to the variable cost attributable to one unit, which here we said was 50p per unit. Because, in this example, the variable cost per unit stayed the same for all levels of output the marginal cost is equal to the unit or average variable cost but this will not always be the case.

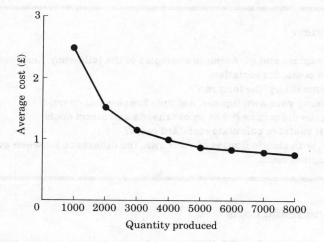

Fig 10.2

The great merit of knowing the marginal cost of production is that, once again, it can help us to make correct decisions. Suppose we were already making and selling 8000 boggins and received an inquiry for an additional bulk order for which the potential customer was prepared to pay 70p per boggin instead of the usual price of 75p. Would it be worthwhile accepting this order?

If we look at our breakeven chart we might say 'No'. The average cost of producing 8000 boggins is 75p (£6000 divided by 8000) which is more than the price offered. We might think that meeting the order would produce a loss.

However, if we look at the marginal cost of producing the extra 1000 boggins from an output level of 8000 we find that the increase in total costs is only £500 (1000 multiplied by 50p). Since the additional revenue gained from the order is £700 (1000 multiplied by 70p) to take the order would increase our profits by £200 and we should accept it.

This decision assumes, of course, that we can produce the additional 1000 boggins without our having to purchase any additional machines or hire more workers, i.e. that the fixed costs remain fixed throughout the increased level of output. This reminds us of the difference between short and long run noted earlier and you can now begin to see that certain output changes may be critical. At these levels we have to decide whether to acquire additional fixed production factors and so move into a higher level of fixed costs. Everything depends on whether or not we can maintain sales at the higher production level and so achieve a sales revenue that will cover the increased total costs. A wrong decision can destroy a business so we can see how important it is to analyse costs accurately.

Rapid review

1 Briefly explain and give simple examples of the following: fixed costs, variable costs, depreciation.
2 What is meant by 'the long run'?
3 Draw, using your own figures, a simple break-even chart.
4 Explain the difference between overheads and direct costs.
5 Why is it useful to calculate standard costs?
6 Explain, with simple figures of your own, the difference between average and marginal costs.

Falling and rising costs

We have seen one reason why costs might fall as output rises – the spreading of fixed costs over larger and larger quantities of output. There are many other reasons why average costs might fall in this way. Some of these are due to the average fixed cost being reduced and some due to reductions in average variable costs. The reasons average costs might fall include:

a *The use of larger capacity equipment* Sometimes bigger or more advanced pieces of equipment are more efficient than smaller ones. They may use less energy, fuel, materials or labour for each unit of output. This means that, although the fixed cost is higher, the variable cost tends to fall as output increases. The effect is noticeable with large-scale plant and equipment such as blast furnaces, earth diggers, oil tankers or double-decker buses. The latter can carry twice as many passengers as single-decker buses but do not use twice the fuel and they still have only one driver!

b *Producing over longer time periods* If the same production process continues over an extended time workers become highly skilled and all the 'bugs' can be 'ironed out' of the system. This will tend to make for smoother operations and reduce variable costs. This kind of effect is so well established in the aircraft manufacturing industry that engineers talk of an '80 per cent rule'. Each successive batch of aircraft costs approximately four-fifths of the previous batch.

c *Production concentrated in larger firms* In many activities large organisations have numerous cost advantages over small ones. They can practise the division of labour more fully, using specialists more extensively. They can make more efficient use of their stores and maintenance teams as the requirements and demands on these become more predictable with the increasing scale of production. Large firms can also make use of their market power as important customers obtaining favourable discounts from suppliers and gaining access to sources of finance not open to small organisations.

All the above effects are sometimes referred to as **economies of scale** which, in general, mean a tendency for average costs to be reduced as production is increased. Sometimes people classify different kinds of economies of scale. Cost savings of the kind described under **a** and **b** are often called *production* or *technical economies* whereas those described in **c** would be *administrative* and *financial* and perhaps *managerial*. All would be termed **internal economies** because they arise from conditions within the firm itself.

If there are internal economies there must also be **external economies** and these arise out of the specialised services which develop to serve all firms within an industry or within a particular industrial area. Such services might include firms specialising in repairs to certain types of equipment or special design or marketing services. External economies assist all firms, large and small, within the industry or area.

There is also the opposite effect, a tendency for average costs to rise, which is termed **diseconomies of scale**. These usually result from organisational problems arising from the growth of the firm. Lines of communication in the organisation become longer, management can be overstretched and the workforce may become demoralised, feeling like 'small cogs in a big wheel'. These are often called **managerial diseconomies**. (At this point you might like to refer to the discussion on organisational structure in Chapter 5 and especially the diagrams on p. 93.)

In practice there are always going to be some elements both of economies and diseconomies of scale in production. Increased output, for example, is always going to spread fixed costs over a greater quantity, but a larger number of workers will increase problems of co-ordination. Whether or not the net effect is going to be to make average costs fall or rise, or whether economies and diseconomies will cancel each other out is likely to depend on the industry and the level of production under consideration. There is reason to believe that the overall effect is the one illustrated in Fig 10.3.

More about marginal cost

If variable costs are themselves not constant the marginal cost of production is not going to be equal to the variable cost. Suppose that the average variable costs of producing wimwams were to fall as output rose from very low levels, then to stay constant and eventually to rise, we then might have the position as shown in the following table which, for simplicity assumes that there are no fixed costs.

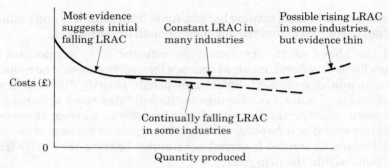

Fig 10.3   Long-run average cost (LRAC) in reality

A	B	B/A
Number of wimwams	Total variable costs (£)	Average variable costs (£)
1	10	10
2	16	8
3	21	7
4	24	6
5	30	6
6	36	6
7	42	6
8	50	6.25
9	63	7
10	85	8.50

The marginal cost is the difference in cost, for example, between producing four wimwams and three wimwams, or between eight and seven. Thus the marginal cost of the fourth is £3 and of the eighth it is £8. We can show the difference between average and marginal costs and their relationship to each other diagrammatically as in Fig 10.4. A number of points are worth noting. If average costs are falling then marginal cost is less than average cost. If average costs are rising then marginal cost is greater than average cost. These can be important points to remember, especially if we are making decisions about output levels or, as earlier, about accepting additional orders under conditions when economies or diseconomies of scale are causing average costs to rise or fall. However, if average variable costs are constant then marginal costs are equal to average variable costs. If average fixed costs at these output levels are very small then marginal costs can be said to be approximately equal to average total costs. Because firms are very often producing at output ranges where these conditions are

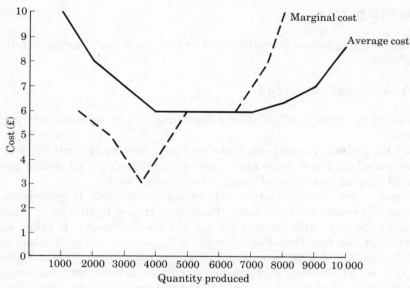

Fig 10.4

found it often does not matter in practice whether decisions are based on average or on marginal cost.

Rapid review

1 List three reasons why average costs might fall as output rises.
2 Distinguish between internal and external economies of scale.
3 Explain, with simple examples, the terms 'production', 'administrative' and 'managerial' economies of scale.
4 If average costs are rising which of the following statements is true? 'Average cost is greater than marginal cost.' 'Average cost is less than marginal cost'.

Cost and price

In everyday life we often use the words cost and price interchangeably. When making business decisions, however, we need to draw a clear distinction between them. **Cost** is the amount paid out on components, materials, labour, fuel, machines and other expenses incurred in production. **Price** is the monetary amount for which the product is sold.

Cost-plus pricing

Sometimes firms use a formula which links price to cost. Such a formula might be:

Price = direct cost × 130%

where 30 per cent is allowed as a contribution to overhead costs and profits.

We have already seen some of the problems involved in making decisions based on direct costs and a desire to ensure that all production should make a proportional contribution to overheads.

There is another drawback to this kind of approach. It ignores the customer's reaction to the price the firm is trying to charge in order to meet its costs and achieve its desired level of profit. It takes no account of the fact that *higher levels of output are not only likely to affect costs through economies and diseconomies of scale, they are also likely to affect the price it is possible to charge.* If we want to increase the amount we can sell in a given market then we are very likely to have to reduce the price in order to attract more customers.

A more satisfactory approach may be one which has been termed *incremental pricing.* This involves using the sort of techniques we looked at in Chapter 6 to estimate the state of the market and how much customers are prepared to pay. We can then compare the revenue we can hope to earn with the costs of production and decide the most profitable level of output. In effect this is very much what we were doing in the breakeven analysis outlined earlier in this chapter.

It has to be said, however, that one merit of the cost-plus approach is that it reminds us that, in the long run, the firm must be able to meet all its costs in order to be able to survive. In the short run we might cut prices as long as we are covering marginal costs but in the long run we must make sure that revenue is sufficient to cover *all* costs. This may make us cautious about the price we charge today in case it makes it more difficult in the long run to charge a price that will enable us to pay all our costs.

Rapid review

1 In relation to business production distinguish between cost and price.
2 What is meant by cost-plus pricing?
3 What is meant by incremental pricing?
4 State one merit of cost-plus pricing.

Further aspects of costs

Estimating costs

By now it is clear that it is essential to be able to make an accurate estimate and forecast of costs for such important business purposes as pricing, fixing standard costs or for accurate cost accounting. Cost estimates can be made in a number of different ways each being appropriate for a particular purpose.

For the purposes of record keeping we need to record costs that have actually been incurred. This involves reference to stock inventories, to purchases, wage and fuel costs, estimates of equipment depreciation and so on.

For pricing purposes or for fixing standard costs we have to try and estimate what future costs will be. We can do this by referring to estimates prepared by production engineers and designers and costing these. One problem with this type of appraisal is that it often tends to be over-optimistic. Engineers are usually more ready to recognise potential economies of scale than the organisational diseconomies which managers are either reluctant to admit exist or believe that they can overcome.

Another approach to forecasting costs may be to calculate trends from past information or to look at costs that are being incurred in other plants or firms. Both these have their hazards. Calculating statistical trends is a sophisticated process involving technical problems beyond the scope of this book. If we look at the costs of other plants or firms we need to be sure that we are comparing like with like. For example, a firm wanting to set up a factory to produce electric cars on a small scale should be very wary of making too much use of cost estimates based on the experience of the giant motor vehicle producers.

Opportunity costs

Before making any decisions involving costs we need to be sure that we have taken account of all costs. One cost to be aware of is the **opportunity cost** of doing something. This is the cost of whatever of value has had to be given up to make it possible. A factory used exclusively to make motor cars cannot also be used to make motor cycles. A field growing wheat cannot, at the same time, be used for growing barley. A worker or manager cannot be in two places at once!

Thinking along these lines can alert us to various costs that we might otherwise overlook. For example, a small business owner should not assume that finance drawn from personal savings rather than borrowed from a bank is 'free'. Although no interest is being paid for the use of the savings the owner is being deprived of the interest that would have been earned had the savings been deposited outside the business, with a bank, say, or building society.

The cost of credit

In similar vein all businesses should realise the cost of credit extended to customers and recognise the value of credit received. If we are supplied with goods on the basis of '60 days to pay' at a price which is the same whether we pay now or in 60 days' time, then this is the equivalent of being given an interest-free loan for 60 days.

If, therefore, we give credit terms to a customer at the price we would charge for immediate cash payment, we are effectively giving them an interest-free loan. If, to allow this credit, we ourselves have to borrow or have an overdraft from a bank, then the free credit represents a very real cost to ourselves. Accordingly there are a number of options we might wish to consider:

a *Whether to offer a cash discount* Once we have an idea of the real cost of credit we can work out how much discount it is worth our while to offer to induce the customer to forego credit terms. The more cash payments we receive the lower the amount we need to borrow and the less our own interest payments.

b *Instituting a system of credit control* We want to be aware of how much credit we are giving and for how long a period. There are various ways of running a credit control system; one is illustrated at the end of chapter exercises.

This is a system suitable for a firm with repeat business with a fairly limited number of customers. The business invoices to each customer can be shown under the month in which a statement is sent. As payment is received, the amounts can be adjusted. The system can be used to show:

- the amount of credit outstanding to each customer
- the pattern of likely repayments in the next few months
- the total amount of credit outstanding
- which customers are particularly quick or slow payers
- long-standing debts which may need special attention

Costs, budgets and planning

Throughout this chapter we have stressed the importance of analysing costs for the purpose of sound decision making and planning. Costs must be carefully estimated and forecast and then related to revenue to see whether certain courses of action should be pursued.

One way of checking the likely outcome of plans is to work out sets of accounts for time periods in the future *as if* plans had been fulfilled. In other words at the start of, say, 1988 we could draw up trading and profit and loss accounts, balance sheets, appropriation and any other accounts we feel are relevant to 1 January 1989 on the assumption that our plans and forecasts are met. These are known as **budgeted accounts**.

From these accounts we can also work out the various costs of our proposed programmes, for example material, labour, office overhead and fuel costs. These can then be expressed as *budgets* for the various managers, showing target expenditure.

Care has to be exercised in drawing up and using budgets. Clearly some costs are estimated on the basis of a given forecast level of output. If this turns out higher or lower, costs may be different. Just as it is useful to estimate a standard cost, it may also be useful to give managers a standard quantity figure with the understanding that the budget is estimated on this figure.

There is a danger that budgets may be used as a 'stick to beat people with'. In other words, managers may be disciplined for failure to stay within a budget. This can lead to undesirable consequences. For instance, managers may regard staying within budgets as their prime objective above all else, even where this gives rise to inefficiency or wasted opportunities. It is more desirable that a 'budget overshoot' should be examined in a spirit of co-operation to try and identify its causes and to see if it can be justified.

Another undesirable type of behaviour can be managers attempting to see that their budgets are all spent inside the budget period. This can arise if senior management reacts to an underspend one year by cutting the budget for the next. This leads managers to feel they are penalised instead of rewarded for reducing costs.

Budgets can be further criticised on the grounds that they give managers an indication of the minimum level of achievement which will be satisfactory and thus encourages them to aim only for satisfactory rather than stimulating the best possible performance. This can also occur if senior management concentrates only on punishing budget overshoots rather than rewarding undershoots.

Notwithstanding these objections, however, budgets, carefully used can be invaluable. Managers and departments are often cut off from the overall decision making of the firm. For example, it may not be clear to the transport manager what sort of expenditure and activity on the part of his or her department is likely to assist the profit making of the whole business. Giving the manager a budget provides the department with a useful focus for its objectives.

Budgets can also be used as a way of providing senior management with early warnings of likely cost increases or potential savings. As long as subordinates have confidence that under or over-spends on budgets are not going to be penalised in the ways described earlier, they will be in the best position to point out where budgeted costs are unrealistic and should be adjusted. This improves the flow of information and makes for better decision making.

The term budget is also used in business in a slightly different sense of an allocation of funds for a specific purpose. Even here, however, there is the same idea that the budget is prepared in consultation between the user of the fund and the supplier of the finance and the user has to account for the way the fund is actually used in relation to the proposed use.

A marketing manager may be allowed an advertising budget to cover all proposed advertising during the year or, perhaps, a promotional budget for the purpose of launching a new product. Other managers will have budgets for such purposes as investment, for training and re-training or for technical research. The idea behind any budget is that proposed expenditure is carefully planned with specific objectives in mind so that eventual actual spending and its results can be compared with these proposals.

Rapid review

1 What is meant by a statistical trend? Why might such a trend be misleading as a basis for estimating future costs?
2 What is meant by credit control?
3 List two advantages and two dangers of using budgets as a method of business planning.
4 What is the fundamental purpose of any budget?

Exercises

1 Chris runs a hairdressing salon. Rent and rates are £80 per week. Two assistants are employed at a cost of £70 per week, including employer's National Insurance, for a 40-hour week. Overtime at £2.00 per hour is payable. The salon is open six days per week, eight hours a day, except where demand makes it worthwhile staying open. This usually means two hours extra for two nights each week. The assistants have one day off mid-week.

Gas and electricity work out at £1.00 per hour while the salon is open. Chris spends about £400 per year in repairs, decorations and so on. Shampoo, conditioner and other materials cost about 5p per customer and customers are also provided with free coffee.

It takes about 20 minutes for a straightforward hairdo; up to about 45 minutes for more elaborate work.

Identify the items of fixed cost, variable cost, direct cost and overhead. Can you suggest guidelines for pricing? What would be the weekly number of customers for Chris to break even?

2   What sort of economies of scale would you associate with the following: a supermarket chain; a steel blast furnace; a jumbo jet; the amalgamation of separate car companies into British Leyland, operating on different sites; the amalgamation of three colleges into a Polytechnic; assembly line manufacturing; the advertising of Kellogg's Corn Flakes?

3   Examine the table. Advise the directors of the Woggleworth Widget Co as to what action, if any, they should take in respect of credit outstanding. Bear in mind that different action might be appropriate for different customers.

WOGGLEWORTH WIDGET CO – CREDIT CONTROL, OCTOBER 19—									
	Sept.	Aug.	July	June	May	April	March …	Oct (last year)	Total
ABC Retailers	1200	1200							2400
Federated Boggins	750						100		850
Kwikbuck Sales	900	1000							1900
Mammoth Racket Co	2000	1200	2500						5700
Southern Widgets	400								400
Tardy & Co	750	300	660	400	500				2610
Useless Enterprises								300	300
Total	6000	3700	3160	400	500		100	300	14160

4   Chris's business having been a success, a decision is made to expand it. Chris will run a new city centre salon and the existing salon will be run by a manager. Outline some of the problems involved in costing for the new expanded business. Should the manager be given a budget and if so, what?

5   The Forward Enterprise Company Limited is preparing to launch a new consumer product manufactured in its own factories. The Company's Management Accountant is instructed to prepare a budget for this venture.

   a   What is the purpose of the budget?
   b   What information will the accountant need?
   c   Show how a breakeven chart could be produced and discuss the usefulness of such a chart.

11 People at work I

The employment contract

The basic relationship

When one person works for another the law assumes that they have
entered into a legally binding agreement. Such agreements are often
termed contracts and employment law is a very specialised part of
the general law of contract. Since the early 1960s there has been a
general trend towards clarifying the nature of the employment contract
so that employers and workers can have a clearer understanding of
their rights and responsibilities.

The whole subject can be a little difficult to comprehend unless we
also understand something about the law in general and how it operates. In the first place it is desirable to recognise the difference between
criminal and civil law. Criminal law is concerned with people's relationships with the State, representing society in general. The State can
decide that we should do certain things, such as buy a licence for a
TV set or insure certain risks, or that we should not do certain things,
such as commit murder or sell dangerous heating appliances. Failure
to obey the rules established by the State is likely to result in a breach
of criminal law, i.e. in committing a crime, and exposes a person to
whatever punishment has been established by Parliament.

Civil law, however, is concerned with people's relationships with one
another, such as actions causing injury to other people or failure to
keep to agreements. A great deal of British civil law has developed
in two ways. In one way it has been formed as a result of judgments
made in the courts when these have had to settle actual cases involving
disputes between people. This is often called the common law of the
country. In addition the law has resulted from Statutes, the Acts of
Parliament. These two sources of law do, of course, operate together
because many statutes also have to be interpreted by the Courts when
disputes have arisen because of differing views as to what an Act of
Parliament actually meant or how it applied to a particular situation.

Before 1960 there were very few statutes that had any direct bearing
on the employment contract and most employment law was based on
common law, in fact on decisions made by judges who, it was often

felt, tended to see the world more through the eyes of employers than of employed workers. Consequently the employers' responsibilities to their workers were not very clear nor did they seem to be very extensive. They had a general duty to pay wages as money rather than 'in kind' (as goods and services) and to provide reasonably safe working conditions and adequate supervision. Statutes established specific duties in some cases, such as when potentially dangerous machinery was used, and indirectly set minimum wages in a few trades where Wages Councils operated, but on the whole any individual worker was likely to have a difficult and expensive time trying to prove that employers were not meeting their legal responsibilities.

The workers' obligations were about equally as vague. Their duty was to carry out the instructions of the employer and to show the degree of skill expected by workers with their particular training and qualifications. Failure to do so justified dismissal in most cases. In practice, as shown in Chapter 12, the relationship was likely to be modified by trade unions but individual workers had very few rights beyond the right to the agreed money wage and to any special conditions they were able to negotiate with the employer.

The modern relationship

This situation began to change from 1963 when the Contracts of Employment Act obliged employers to draw up a written contract and to ensure that all workers received either a copy or opportunities to inspect it. A whole series of later statutes have sought to clarify the nature of the employment contract and to establish definite terms and conditions so that both workers and employers now have more precise rights and responsibilities. Legislation has also tried to set up suitable machinery for the settlement of disputes.

The employer's legal duty to communicate terms of the employment contract to employees is outlined in Chapter 13.

It is not necessary to have a detailed knowledge of the law as it has become established since 1963 but it is essential to be aware of the main aspects which are subject to the law, to know the general legal position and know where to look for further details.

Recruitment and opportunities at work

The law does not go as far as ensuring that everyone has a fair and equal chance to obtain any job for which he or she is qualified. It is concerned with two forms only of possible discrimination. These relate to race and sex. With very few exceptions, advertisements for jobs should not contain any discriminating element in relation to these.

Advertisements may, however, discriminate over age – setting a minimum or a maximum age – a position that many regard as unjust. If a person feels that failure to secure a job, or to secure promotion at work was caused solely by race, that person may complain and seek redress through an industrial tribunal but should first obtain advice from the Commission for Racial Equality which might be able to provide legal and other help. People who consider that they have been discriminated against solely because of their sex should seek advice from the Equal Opportunities Commission and, if there is evidence of such discrimination, also go to an Industrial Tribunal. Employers should be aware that, under the Sex Discrimination Act 1975 it is unlawful to discriminate because of a person's sex in the areas of employment, education, consumer services (including housing) and in advertising.

It can be very difficult to prove that there has been discrimination. Employers and managers can even be genuinely unaware that racial or sex prejudice has influenced their judgement. If there is clear evidence relations are likely to be sufficiently soured to make it difficult for a person to work or continue working for an employer financial compensation is likely to be the most suitable solution, however inadequate this may seem.

The laws on these aspects are intended to influence social attitudes as much as to protect individuals. Apart from the social injustice of discrimination employers who do not give equal opportunities to people of any race and sex are cutting themselves off from a vast store of ability and skill. They also risk giving offence to valuable customers. Business self-interest alone would suggest that any form of illogical discrimination against any group of people is self-destructive.

Pay

In most cases pay is regarded as a matter solely for negotiation between workers or groups of workers (unions) and employers. There are some exceptions. Trades where workers are known to be relatively weakly organised and where pay rates are regarded as low may have pay set by Wages Councils. The Councils contain representatives of the employers and the workers and an independent member who is normally the chairperson. Their decisions on pay and working conditions take on the force of law after acceptance by the appropriate government minister. In 1985 the Government proposed to abolish the Councils but after representations by employers organisations it did not go as far as this but introduced legislation to remove their authority over young people under the age of 21 and limited their remaining authority to setting a single minimum wage and set of working conditions for an industry.

Another exception is that of equal pay for men and women doing the same or broadly similar work. This is a requirement of the Equal Pay Act 1970. This has subsequently been strengthened in the light of representations that the requirements of the European Community were rather more favourable to women in cases where work was so dominated by female workers that it was difficult to find closely comparable 'male' work. The intention of the broader provisions is that such work should be paid according to rates prevailing for work of equivalent value. There are still many difficulties in this area and, for a number of reasons, the average pay of women workers is still below the average for males.

From time to time the Government may try to control pay rises in an effort to prevent general price increases. Controls may be introduced by law or be 'voluntary' and dependent on agreements with employers' organisations and trade unions. They are, however, very difficult to keep in force for very long.

Working conditions

Outside the trades where there are Wages Councils there are no legal requirements concerning holidays other than the statutory public holidays, still often called bank holidays. Other holidays, along with pay, are considered to be matters to be settled by agreement between employers and worker groups. In some occupations there may be legal provisions relating to the number of hours a person is permitted to work without a break. The main considerations here are those of public safety and the need to protect the public from overtired drivers of goods or passenger carrying vehicles.

Attempts to improve health and safety at work have a long history beginning with the nineteenth-century Acts designed to reduce accidents in mines and from dangerous machines in factories. In 1974 around 30 different statutes dealing with different trades, premises and conditions were replaced by the general Health and Safety at Work Act. This imposed on employers responsibilities to provide and maintain:

- safe machinery and equipment
- a safe and healthy working environment
- a safe working system, taking into account the movement and storage of goods
- safe entry and exit arrangements, including adequate arrangements for
- evacuation of premises in case of fire

There are also very many detailed provisions for various kinds of premises and occupations. These relate to issues such as working space, the provision of seats and rest periods, washing facilities, lighting, eating and drinking arrangements and the availability of first aid equipment.

The Act imposes on the employer the duty to consult with union or worker representatives and to ensure that these people are given time and facilities for training and for carrying out their functions as safety representatives.

Employees who are safety representatives have no special legal obligations to ensure safe working conditions. This liability rests firmly with the employer. Nevertheless all workers do have a legal responsibility to take reasonable care:

a   To avoid injuring themselves and others.
b   Not to interfere with or misuse safety equipment (including fire extinguishers) or, indeed, anything provided to protect their health, safety and welfare.
c   To co-operate with their employers and others to maintain safety regulations as required by the Act.

Enforcement of the law is in the hands of area Health and Safety Executives who investigate complaints and reports made by workers, unions or members of the public but who rely chiefly on the force of Her Majesty's Factory Inspectorate. The Executive, through its officers and inspectors, seeks to educate employers and co-operate with them to raise standards and reduce accidents and work-related illness. Where it meets wilful refusal to conform to the law or criminal negligence it can, and does, prosecute employers and even employees. Employers have to remember, however, that they are still legally responsible for any damage or injury caused to another worker or member of the public as a result of the negligence or carelessness of one of their workers.

Redundancy and dismissal

Rights of workers to receive compensation on becoming redundant through no fault of their own date only from 1964 and legal protection from dismissal at the whim of an employer is even more recent. Today, however, employers have to contribute to a redundancy fund through their national insurance contributions and they may be called upon to justify a dismissal before an industrial tribunal and obliged to pay compensation if the dismissal is judged to be unfair. Consequently employers generally find it necessary to keep records of a worker's misdeeds and to give written warning if behaviour is likely to lead to dismissal. Union representatives are also likely to be informed when a worker is in danger of dismissal.

A worker who is fairly dismissed has no right to compensation beyond anything stipulated in the contract of employment. A worker who is made redundant, however, is entitled to compensation, the amount depending on earnings and period of continuous employment with the employer. Many firms have agreements which are more generous than the minimum legal provisions but they all tend to observe the same general principles that the amount of compensation should depend on previous pay and length of service. There are special provisions for the protection of female workers who require leave of absence because of pregnancy and workers who have been employed for at least two years usually have the right to return to work subject to certain procedures and conditions.

These and other rights are contained in employment protection legislation but very small employers are released from some of the requirements of the law.

Industrial tribunals

References have been made in this chapter to **industrial tribunals** and these clearly have an important influence on the law relating to employment. They are defined as statutory bodies, similar to courts, which have powers to make legally enforceable decisions on many issues arising out of employment law. The majority of cases brought before the tribunals concern cases of redundancy or unfair dismissal. Dismissal thought to be 'unfair' within the meaning of the employment protection laws should be distinguished from 'wrongful dismissal' where an employer is accused of breaking a contract of employment and thus exposed to action for damages or compensation through the normal civil law courts.

Tribunals are intended to be much less formal and less expensive than the normal law courts. Either side can be represented by a lawyer but this is not essential and many workers choose to be represented by a trade union official or conduct their own cases. A tribunal has three members. The Chairman is legally qualified and appointed by the Lord Chancellor's Office, the Lord Chancellor being the head of the legal system. One of the members is nominated by employers' organisations and the other by the trade unions. The awards that can be made by a tribunal are subject to limits established by Parliament. Either side has the right of appeal against a decision to the Employment Appeal Tribunal but an appeal must be based on an issue of law, not of fact.

Tribunals try to be consistent in their decisions so that, over the years, a body of case histories has been built up and these can guide employers and workers in predicting how disputes are likely to be decided. Reference to previous decisions, therefore, can help employers to avoid damaging and public disputes.

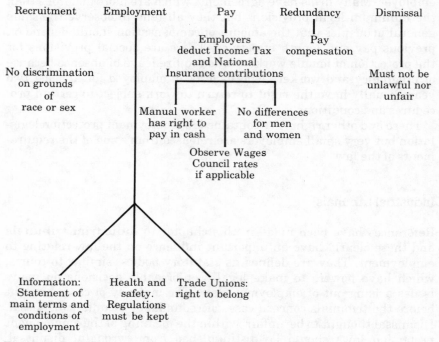

Fig 11.1   Some aspects of law and employment

Rapid review

1   What change in attitude to employment was represented by the Contracts of Employment Act of 1963?
2   What kinds of discrimination should not be practised by employers when they employ workers?
3   Name two statutes that have a bearing on employment discrimination.
4   What are Wages Councils?
5   List the main general duties of an employer imposed by the Health and Safety at Work Act of 1974.
6   State three obligations of employees under the Health and Safety at Work Act, 1974.
7   Name the body responsible for enforcing the Health and Safety at Work Act.

8   **What is the difference between redundancy and dismissal?**
9   **Distinguish between 'unfair' and 'wrongful' dismissal.**
10   **What is an industrial tribunal and what are its main functions?**

Payment for work

Time payments

The main reward for working is, of course, the money wage or salary. Payment contracted as an amount per year, whether paid monthly or weekly is usually called a **salary**. Payment calculated on some other basis is usually called a **wage**. Wages are normally based on a rate per period of time, or on a unit of production or on some mixture of time and production. Although any payment where there is a standard payment per week, month or year is strictly a time rate the term is usually used where the rate is expressed as an amount per hour or per day. When time rates apply there is usually a standard rate for time up to an agreed number of hours in one week and higher rates are payable for additional hours above this – or for hours worked at 'unsocial times' such as at night or at weekends. Overtime paid at higher rates for time worked above an agreed limit also often applies to salaried workers up to a particular level. Managers and other staff above this level may be expected to do additional work when necessary without further payment.

Payments by results

This is a general term for any payment system which seeks to relate the amount a worker earns to the amount he or she produces. A wide range of schemes have been developed to meet the needs of many different types of work. The simplest scheme is to pay 'by the piece', i.e. an amount per article produced. Variations include calculating a standard amount of production per hour and making extra payments on output achieved above this standard. Sometimes it is difficult to relate the individual worker to a particular volume of output because the final product is the result of many tasks carried out by different people. In these cases it is sometimes possible to relate output to a particular team or department and to base additional payments on the combined work of the team. The payments are then shared according to an agreed pattern.

Payments by results schemes are easiest to devise for manufacturing industry where there is a definite end product which can be counted and where the contribution of workers or groups of workers can also be seen and counted. Services are more difficult to reward in this way. A common method, however, is to allow a standard time for particular tasks such as collecting refuse or repairing vehicles and to make additional payments to workers or teams who can complete the tasks in a shorter period of time.

Non-manual work is also often difficult to put on a payment by results system. Some offices have been known to pay typists according to the quantity of work typed but this tends to increase the volume of paperwork whereas the firm would often be more profitable and efficient if there were less. Selling is the most common activity to be rewarded according to results. Most sales staff receive some form of sales bonus or commission and many shop assistants also share in schemes designed to encourage them to make a greater effort to complete sales.

The advantages of payments by results schemes

The basic idea of payment by results always seems fair both to the employer and the worker. The employer is chiefly interested in the product achieved from work and his or her costs are directly related to the amount of production achieved. The employer is able to pay more to the more efficient workers and workers who cannot reach a level of efficiency sufficient to provide the desired level of earnings usually leave of their own accord. The system tends to encourage workers to produce more output and raise their skill level in order to increase income.

For the worker it can be argued that the system gives him or her a degree of control over earnings. The worker who prefers to work more slowly or to take breaks sacrifices earnings but does so as a matter of choice. The worker who desires high income can achieve this through personal effort.

Employers' problems with payments by results

On the other hand the fact that so many different schemes have been devised suggests that they present problems both to employers and workers. Employers can find that they can be costly to operate as each worker's pay has to be individually calculated each week from work records. The amount of administration involved can be considerable. Although computers can reduce the manual work involved they rely on fairly rigid schemes and errors or deliberate falsification of records can be difficult and costly to detect. In practice employers also find that payment by results schemes are a frequent source of labour disputes. Workers tend to misunderstand schemes or make their own calculations which then differ from the employer's. Some workers or groups of workers may feel that others are being treated more generously. It nearly always happens that some types of work produce higher earnings than others. Workers prefer to continue with existing production and production methods on which they may have developed special skills or short-cuts and resist any change which is likely to reduce their earnings for a period during which they have to learn new processes.

A further problem arises from the increased need to impose strict quality control and inspection. In efforts to increase output some workers will let standards fall. Rejected work represents a serious loss to the employer as faulty parts usually have to be scrapped. There can also be disputes with inspectors and accusations that some inspectors are stricter than others.

Perhaps the most important problem for the employer is that paying workers by results assumes that the firm can always sell everything that it can produce. This is by no means always true. If the firm faces difficult market conditions when sales become more difficult it may wish to reduce production for a time but it will find it hard to obtain co-operation from workers who do not wish to see a reduction in their earnings. It was widely believed by workers in the motor industry in the 1960s and 70s that employers provoked strikes from time to time as the easiest way to halt production during a period of falling sales. The alternative would have been to slow down production in the knowledge that workers would have claimed that their earnings ought to be maintained because the cut back in production was no fault of theirs.

Employers who believe that some form of piece rate scheme will always lead to increased production are sometimes disappointed. Once a worker has achieved a desired income level there is a tendency to choose leisure, the freedom to go and chat with a friend, or leave the workshop for a smoke. Workers have been known to work extremely hard for the first three days of the week until they have 'made their pay' and then take life much more easily for the rest of the week. The assumption that workers will always want to maximise their earnings is not correct.

Some modern methods of production give workers little or no choice in their speed of work and they cannot control their output. There are cases where machines have to be operated at a particular speed and any change from this can damage metal parts. In these cases any form of payment by results could be damaging.

Worker attitudes to payments by results

It might be thought that workers would dislike any form of payments by results scheme and see it as a form of exploitation by the employer. The contrary is often the case. In manufacturing industry there is a very long tradition of piece rate payments dating from the days when workers produced goods at home and sold them 'by the piece' to the factory owner. A certain amount of social prestige is attached to piece work in some industries where time rates are associated with unskilled work and piece rates with skilled work. Pride is often taken in mastering particular tasks or sets of tasks, in getting to know a machine so well that it can be adapted to perform more quickly or in organising work so that the desired level of earnings can be achieved with minimum effort.

The ability to control earnings to some extent and even the challenge to set their skill and experience against the skill of the work study officer in order to secure a favourable time or quantity allowance for a new or revised process can be attractive to workers.

Nevertheless workers can also experience their own problems. They can suffer from machine breakdowns or delays in supply over which they have no control. An efficient department can feel that its earnings are being threatened by less efficient workers in other parts of the factory and there is often suspicion that their earnings are not always correctly calculated. There is a natural suspicion of any scheme which is complicated and whose results cannot be checked by the worker or union representative.

Trade union attitudes to payments by results schemes vary. Many union representatives welcome them because they know that they provide sources of disputes between individuals and managers and an alert shop steward can use these to extend his or her influence. Whenever there is a change of work process new rates or allowances have to be calculated and these give bargaining opportunities for the trade union representatives. On the other hand union policy may be to ensure that workers have a more stable income which is not tied directly to production and which is not subject to reductions if the employer no longer needs to increase production. Whenever an employer wishes to change from one system to another, however, the union will naturally seek to ensure that co-operation with the change has to be paid for by some form of wage incentive.

Sharing in profit

Another approach to the wage problem is to try to give workers an incentive to make the firm more profitable by giving them a share in the profits of the enterprise. A profit-sharing scheme does not, in itself, turn the firm into a worker co-operative. To achieve this requires giving workers a share in management and a share in the decision-making functions of management. Relatively few firms have taken this step in the United Kingdom but there are many that have offered participation in profits in some form or other. Profit sharing has featured in some political programmes as a means of trying to reduce the hostility and social division said to exist between employers and workers.

The simplest schemes provide some form of bonus payable in relation to profits. This is common among firms of stockbrokers but is also found in manufacturing and in the service industries. If the distribution of the bonus is entirely at the discretion of the employer it is not strictly a profit-sharing scheme which assumes a definite system which is known to the employees in advance and which is agreeable to them either by custom and practice or formal agreement with unions.

A variation is to distribute company shares according to the size of company profits. There is usually a provision that the shares have to be held for a minimum period, usually a year. The shares may not carry the usual right to vote at shareholder meetings. The attraction of share participation is that the worker not only receives a dividend on the shares but also gains the benefit of any rise in their value as the company's prosperity increases.

Distribution of profit in any form is normally made in proportion to the employees' earnings but may also depend on length of service with the company.

Those who object to profit sharing frequently point out that the practice rewards all workers for what is essentially the result of good management. Similarly workers can also be made to suffer reduced earnings as a consequence of bad management. The argument is thus that workers have no direct influence on profits and, therefore, their pay should not be dependent in any degree on profit. There is also suspicion that employers will seek to keep ordinary wage levels artificially low in order to make the profit-sharing element in earnings as attractive as possible and reduce the bargaining power of unions and workers.

A rather special form of profit-sharing scheme is the tendency to reward senior managers and directors with share option schemes. The purpose is to make the most senior decision makers in the company more aware of their duty to make profits and to reward them in accordance with their success in making profits. Schemes are seen as ways to turn the senior managers into shareholders and so to have the interests of shareholders more clearly in their minds. Business managers of large companies have sometimes been accused of pursuing their own objectives such as the pursuit of power or the growth in size of the company, at the expense of profits.

Payments in kind

A payment in kind takes place when the employee is rewarded with goods or services rather than with money. Such payments cannot replace the main money wage or salary but can form a valuable addition to it. There are many examples of these payments. They include concessionary coal provided to miners, free or very cheap travel provided for certain workers in the transport industries, meals or meal vouchers, awards of 'scholarships' to employees' children in higher education, free or partially paid telephones at home, use of company credit cards and, one of the best known, the company car.

These payments serve a number of purposes. To some extent they can be a visible symbol of status within the organisation. For example as an employee climbs the company ladder he or she receives a larger and more expensive car. It has been argued that they are largely the result of high rates of personal income tax. Some payments have indeed been a way to reduce the liability of the more highly paid managers to tax. This has been recognised by the Inland Revenue which regards payments in kind to the more highly paid as a part of income and as such liable to tax. Company cars are taxed according to a published scale. Another explanation for their spread has been the artificial limit on salary increases imposed by the various attempts to control incomes between 1966 and 1978. A payment in kind was one way to evade pay controls.

Nevertheless these payments remain despite substantial reductions in tax and the removal of pay controls. It seems likely that employers like to keep them because they are a means of keeping control over employees and of making their salaries more flexible. It is very difficult to reduce an existing salary. It is easier to reduce the rate of car mileage allowance or the grade of car allowed to various levels of staff or to increase an employee's contribution to a telephone bill.

The wider term 'fringe benefits' is sometimes used and this more conveniently includes payments of 'expenses' or 'expense allowances' whether or not these are actually incurred by the worker.

Stored payments

The payment to a worker may be seen as being in two parts. One part is paid immediately as wage or salary. The other is stored on behalf of the worker against the day when he or she can no longer work and is retired.

Pension schemes spread widely among firms in the 1950s and 60s during a period of full employment when they were seen as a possible way to discourage workers from leaving. Subsequently governments began to assume that a pension was a social right that every worker ought to have and it became compulsory for employers to contribute to a general State scheme or to provide benefits of a minimum standard under a separate scheme.

More recently pensions have become something of a political problem as governments have tried to increase labour mobility and as the proportion of old and retired people in the population has risen. Taxation reliefs related to pensions have also become a political issue. Some people argue that provision for old age should be a matter for the State rather than a consequence of employment. Others believe that the State should encourage and assist individuals to make their own arrangements for pensions and retirement. It can be argued that present arrangements give too much power to employers, to pension funds and the life assurance offices which have accumulated massive financial empires from pension contributions.

This has now become an issue very much open to public discussion.

Rapid review

1   What is meant by 'payments by results'?
2   List three problems associated with payments by results schemes.
3   State one advantage and one objection to profit-sharing schemes.
4   Explain, using two examples, the term 'payment in kind'.
5   What is meant by a 'stored payment'?

Training for work

One of the great arguments in education is whether or to what extent education should be vocational, i.e. a preparation for particular vocation, career or job. At one extreme a long education may result in a person gaining a lot of knowledge, none of which has any relevance to work, and habits of mind that make him or her unsuited to practical employment. At the other extreme a person may be trained to a high level of skill in one form of employment and if this is no longer required by the economy the person is unsuited to any other job. Each extreme produces a person likely to become a liability to the community. Somehow the education and training system has to steer a course between these extremes and produce people who can bring skills and qualities that are useful in any occupation, who are able to train for a wide range of occupations, and who are able and prepared to re-train should they find themselves in an occupation that is no longer required by society. At the same time many would add that people should be prepared to play a useful and intelligent part in the general life of the community and enjoy their leisure constructively.

Clearly these objectives raise issues that are far beyond the scope of this section which is chiefly concerned with training for work. However, we have to remember that we live in a rapidly changing society and training for work received at the age of 18 may have very little relevance to that same person's needs at the age of 38. At the same time it seems probable that competition for work is likely to remain at a high level for some years and those who are best prepared for work are the ones most likely to find satisfying and rewarding jobs. It also appears to be the case that even when unemployment is very severe there are still shortages of workers in some highly skilled occupations, so that one of the functions of education and training services must be to ensure that there are enough skilled workers to meet the needs of the economy for it to continue to grow and provide rising standards of living for everyone.

In these conditions, therefore, most people recognise that there has to be some training for work during the years of compulsory education at school. Consequently many schools are offering an increasing number of vocational courses or courses that are likely to provide useful preparation for work. Before you try to divide school subjects into vocational and non-vocational, however, it is as well to remember that for many years the development of English Language teaching was moulded by the requirements of the Civil Service and that modern developments in mathematics and computer studies have been influenced by discussions with employers in industry. Vocational influences on school education are much stronger than is often realised.

One trend that has emerged since the 1960s has been that of making the transition between school and work much less sharp and clearly defined. More and more people are introduced to work while still in full-time education and large numbers of full-time workers are able to continue with their education and training. Colleges of Further Education or of Technology assist in this as courses are usually more closely related to work and work skills. There are often close links with local employers and full- and part-time courses exist side by side.

In 1964 the Industrial Training Act made an ambitious attempt to provide for further education and training for large numbers of people at work and set up Industrial Training Boards in many sectors of industry and commerce. Some of the objectives of the Act may have been too ambitious and too wide and the general system of an industrial training levy administered by the Boards has been abandoned. Nevertheless some of the ideas introduced as a result of the Act have survived and there is still a significant amount of training and re-training carried on in sectors where very little was practised before 1964.

The 1980s have brought additional problems not foreseen in the 1960s. By 1985 there were over three million people registered as unemployed and probably more not registered who would work if suitable employment could be found. In this situation it is understandable that many employers prefer to employ only those who have specific skills or work experience to offer and who can contribute to the organisation's revenues immediately. The prospects for those without the required qualities, skills or experience appeared to be bleak. In attempts to provide this experience, if necessary by subsidising employers or by providing for special pay rates below those of fully employed workers, the Government has introduced a number of schemes. The general agency to administer schemes and to co-ordinate the efforts of government, employers and the colleges and schools in the education system has usually been the Manpower Services Commission (MSC).

The precise details of schemes and their names are likely to change from time to time and you will see that one of the exercises in this chapter gives you an opportunity to discover the position as it exists at the current time.

The MSC also has responsibilities for industrial re-training but in a rapidly changing economy there is always a danger that it will produce an additional flow of workers with skills that are already in oversupply. Some people consider that re-training is best carried out within working organisations rather than in separate 'skill centres' operated by the Commission, so that the schemes for re-training are also likely to be changed or modified from time to time. Discovering the current position is the subject of another exercise.

Where to train

Employers are often divided over the question of where to train workers. Some argue that the best place is within the firm 'on the job'. This, it is argued, is cheaper because the 'teachers' can be themselves working employees and the trainee is given knowledge and skills directly related to the work he or she is required to do. No time is wasted in acquiring skills and knowledge not relevant to the firm. Employers may also believe that this kind of training makes it less likely that the trained worker will quickly leave and go to another firm.

In contrast to this view it can be argued that:

a On-the-job training is less effective than skilled training carried out by specialist teachers/training officers.

b Training outside the firm is more likely to stimulate new approaches and introduce new techniques into the firm.

c Outside training is more highly regarded and is likely to motivate the worker more successfully.

d The cost is often less, especially for small firms, because they do not have to take people off work to train others, or suffer the wasted material used in training.

Rapid review

1   What is meant by 'vocational education'?
2   State one function of the Manpower Services Commission.
3   State the arguments for and against 'on-the-job' training.

Exercises

1   Explain the legal obligations on an employer to avoid discrimination against particular groups of workers.
2   Why are there wages councils in some trades? What are the functions of these councils?
3   What precautions should an employer take to try and avoid being taken to an industrial tribunal by a worker who has been dismissed?
4   What is meant by 'payments by results'? Choose one method of payment by results and describe its advantages and disadvantages from the point of view of the *employer*.
5   Why are not all workers paid by results?
6   Discuss the case for and against profit-sharing schemes, from the point of view of the *employer*.
7   A high proportion of all new car sales are to companies which provide cars for certain of their employees. Discuss this widespread practice.
8   Prepare a short talk arguing either for or against the proposition that 'education in school should be more vocational'.
9   Discuss the case for making some form of youth training compulsory for all school leavers.
10   Bearing in mind that when a firm recruits a new worker it requires:
   a a person with the abilities and skills required for the job to be done or the capacity to acquire the necessary skills,
   b a person who will work consistently and reliably and
   c someone who will fit smoothly into the existing work team, describe how you would expect a firm to recruit, select and, if necessary, train a new worker.

12 People at work II

Trade unions

The union and its organisation

The need for unions

In Chapter 11 we described the various legal rights possessed by employees and the obligations of the workers to their employers. However, a worker cannot run to a lawyer every time they suspect that they are not being treated fairly by their boss. On the other hand, if there were no unions, the worker on the shop floor or at the office desk would not really be in a position of equality with the employer. In most cases the worker needs their job more than the employer needs the worker, and in any serious dispute the employer can call on experts beyond the scope or pocket of the average employee.

As an isolated individual then, the worker is much weaker than the employer. If, however, workers can join together and act together they become much stronger. One person alone can be ignored; a hundred acting together – or refusing to act together – cannot.

This basic fact explains why trade unions exist and why unions set such store on loyalty and solidarity. Only by sticking together as an organised group can workers exchange individual weakness for collective strength. Of course, if unions become so strong that employers lose the freedom to operate their businesses in a normal commercial manner, completely new problems arise and society must then decide whether and to what extent union power should be controlled.

Types of unions

Section 28 of the Trade Union and Labour Relations Act 1974 provides a definition of a trade union; this definition refers to an organisation which '... consists wholly or mainly of workers of one or more descriptions ...'. The description of the group of workers or of the union can take almost any form. It may apply to workers in a particular occupation such as plumbers or teachers, to an industry such as mining or railways or to workers in general. Consequently there are craft unions, formed mainly of workers in a particular skilled occupation or group of skilled occupations such as electronics, electrical and plumbing trades. There are industrial unions containing all kinds of workers in the same industry or group of industries such as the distributive trades, including retailing and wholesaling and the boot and shoe manufacturing industries. There are also general unions containing workers across a range of different occupations and industries. The Transport and General Workers Union and the General and Municipal Workers Union are examples of general unions.

Another way to classify unions is by occupational status. They are sometimes referred to as manual, also called blue collar and white collar, containing office and other non-manual workers including the teachers.

Union membership

By no means all workers belong to unions. At the end of 1983 about 11 338 thousand people or just over 42 per cent of the working population were members of trade unions. The official definition of working population includes the self-employed and the unemployed though many of these are likely to have retained union membership.

A higher proportion of men than of women appear to join trade unions. Not all unions report separate figures for male and female workers but of those that do, and these have about 83 per cent of total membership, only 28 per cent of members were females.

In 1983 the 11 338 000 trade unionists belonged to 393 unions defined according to the 1974 Act. The number of separate unions has been declining. In 1973 the total had been 519. Many unions are still very small, In 1983 there were 215 with under 1000 members and these accounted for only around 55 000 workers, about 0.4 per cent of union membership. In contrast the 22 largest unions with 100 000 or more members shared just under 80 per cent of total membership with over 63 per cent belonging to the 11 very large unions having 250 000 or more members. Nearly 91 per cent of unions had fewer than 50 000 members but these accounted for less than 12 per cent of total membership. This extreme concentration poses massive problems of representation and communication. There can be as much diversity of opinion within one of the largest unions as among large numbers of small ones. It is easy to see why union leaders can be accused of not representing the views of members.

The Trades Union Congress

Each union is an independent organisation and is free to pursue its own objectives in its own way. Most of the large unions, however, are

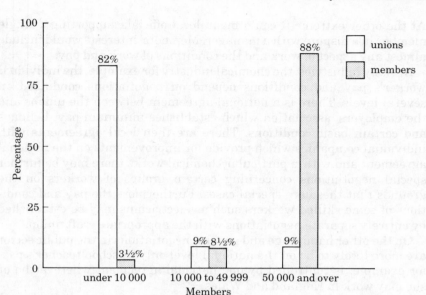

Fig 12.1   The concentration of trade union membership in the largest unions

affiliated to the central body representing the union movement as a whole, the Trades Union Congress (TUC).

This body does have a permanent organisation. It undertakes research and formulates policies which it can recommend to its members and it can seek to influence the government and public opinion. It has the machinery to resolve disputes between unions but its only real disciplinary power is that of expelling a member union – so its leaders have to work mostly by persuasion, negotiation and compromise. They have difficulty in comprehending opponents who do not share or admire these skills. The TUC provides a public platform for the general political objectives of unions which most would describe as seeking to create a political and social framework in which workers can improve and control their living standards and conditions. Individual union leaders, however, would interpret this general aim in many very different ways.

Union bargaining

Unions exist to further the interests of their members and one of their main functions must always be that of 'negotiating with employers with the object of regulating the conditions of work of their members'. This negotiation can take place at several levels. At one extreme this could mean some very broad bargaining between the national officers of the union and a group of employers or with one powerful employer.

At the other extreme it could mean local officials supporting a single member in a dispute with a manager. Members' interests would include almost any aspect of work and the conditions of work and pay.

In many industries, the chemical industry for example, the individual worker's pay and conditions depend on negotiations conducted on several levels. There is a national agreement between the unions and the employers' association which establishes minimum pay, holidays and certain basic conditions. There are then local agreements with individual companies which provide for improvements on the national agreement and within particular chemical works there may be further special negotiations concerning certain groups of workers on the grounds that these are special cases. Furthermore the pay and conditions of some skilled workers such as electricians may be established by entirely separate negotiations with the appropriate craft union.

On the other hand wage and general negotiations in the public sector are more likely to be on the national level only. A schoolteacher's pay, for example, is controlled by one national agreement wherever he or she may work in England and Wales.

All the various types of negotiation described above would be included in the general term collective bargaining. At one time this was used to refer only to formal negotiations between unions and an employer or group of employers in contrast to purely local negotiations within a particular workplace. Today, however, there is a wider recognition of the complexity and variety of worker–employer relations and collective bargaining can describe almost any negotiation where workers negotiate as an organised group rather than as individuals.

The structure of unions

The larger unions have a national network of district and area offices staffed by full-time union employees some of whom will specialise in the affairs of particular localities or of certain trades or industries. The national headquarters of the large union (and sometimes the larger regional offices) will employ legal and other specialists. These assist members in the more complex disputes and with the serious cases of industrial injury where the real battle for compensation is likely to be fought between the union and the employer's insurance company. Smaller unions are likely to have arrangements with one or more of the large unions for assistance with legal and other specialist services.

Unions in the workplace

In recent years a great deal of attention and interest has been shown in unionisation within the workplace. To some extent this has conflicted with older union practices. The large engineering unions, for example,

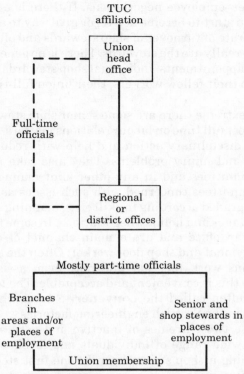

Fig 12.2   The structure of trade unions

still have a local branch network that is based on geographical localities rather than on workplaces and a single branch contains members from a number of local firms and may even retain individual members who have moved away from the area. A particular branch, however, may be dominated by the local big employer, sometimes to the annoyance of workers in other firms. Other unions, including most of the general and white-collar unions have branches based on the workplace so that the branch chairman and secretary will be the two most senior union representatives within the workplace.

Workplace unionism relies almost exclusively on part-time union officials who remain paid employees of the firm. These are the **shop stewards** or **workplace representatives**. The general term shop steward covers many different types of representative with varying degrees of commitment to the union. At one extreme there are people who have been nominated by other union representatives or by their workmates, or even, on occasion, by managers, to be the official steward for a particular group of workers. This person may have little interest in unions or in representing workers' problems and takes little active part in employer–employee negotiations. If there is a dispute such a person may then start to become active, or give way to another worker. There is a high rate of turnover of shop stewards and often some uncertainty as to who really are the stewards. There is no general rule regarding elections or appointments. Individual shop stewards must, however, be acceptable to their fellow workers, their union full-time officers and to the employer.

At the other extreme there are some senior shop stewards who work full time or almost full time on labour relations matters. They represent workers facing disciplinary action and help with redundancy, retirement, sickness and injury problems. They also take part on Health and Safety Committees and in any other joint management–worker negotiating committees concerned with such issues as job evaluation (where jobs are graded according to skill etc.), manning levels, training and, of course, wages and holiday negotiations. In some firms the senior stewards have an office and are a main channel of communication between management and shop floor worker. Often the senior stewards of several unions work together and may even assist each other's members where this is convenient and acceptable. The leading steward in a factory is often called the **convener**, a term which appears to have originated in the Scottish engineering factories.

Between these two extremes of inactive and very active stewards there can be a wide range of individuals and levels of commitment. To some, becoming a shop steward can be the first step in a life-long interest, involving union study courses, committee work and negotiation, part-time study and, frequently, close involvement with one of the political parties, usually the Labour party, and participation in local voluntary work, perhaps in local government. A few become full-time union officers but most gain heightened interest in the social side of what is often boring and routine work and active participation in the life of the local community.

The development of active workplace unionism has sometimes been seen as a direct challenge to the traditional pattern of collective bargaining between organised management and official or formal union structures with their area offices and full-time officers. It has also been seen as a threat to the 'right to manage' of the managers and supervisors within the workplace. This relationship between union representatives and managers and their interaction through joint committees is examined later in this chapter.

The power of trade unions

To some extent unions have common interests with employers. Unions want their members to be prosperous and the more prosperous the workers the more they can afford to buy the goods and services produced by firms. On the other hand union pressure to increase wages and improve working conditions must, in the short run, reduce business profits and the incomes of business owners.

The ultimate action that a union can take to defend its members or to pursue members' interests is to withdraw labour. Legally this is a breach of the agreement made between worker and employer and must cause financial loss to the employer. If the normal law relating to agreements (contracts) were to apply this would expose the union to the risk of having to pay crippling damages to the employer. In effect the union would be powerless. It has long been understood, therefore, that effective trade unions must be given some special privileges to permit them to take action. This is just as much in the social interest of protecting workers as human beings as limited liability is in the economic interests of the community.

However, as with the company privilege of limited liability the real question is how far should this special treatment and immunity from the normal pressures of the law go. This becomes increasingly important in the modern, highly interdependent economy where a stoppage in one activity can damage very many others and where it is often ordinary members of the public rather than the employers who suffer.

This problem has been controversial for most of this century. The division between immunity from the law and the control by law has moved several times, reflecting changes in political power and the relative strength and bargaining power of employers and unions. The position existing in 1985 depended largely on the Employment Acts of 1980 and 1982 and the Trade Union Act of 1984. Very broadly the Acts preserve union immunity for action taken by groups of workers against their own employer (subject to the balloting provisions outlined below), but forbid action against other firms. There are also codes of practice which attempt to draw the distinction between lawful picketing designed to persuade workers to support a dispute and unlawful and criminal attempts at violent intimidation and incitement to commit acts of violence.

The 1984 Act provides that:

a The principal executive committee members of unions and those having votes at executive meetings must be elected by secret ballot at least once every five years.

b Unions must compile and maintain registers of members' names and addresses.

c Unions lose their immunities from legal action if they do not hold a ballot not more than four weeks before authorising or confirming a call for a strike or other action that breaks the contract of employment between members and their employer.

d   A union's political funds must be approved by ballot of members at least once every ten years.

In practice, of course, it is often extremely difficult to define clearly and precisely where these divisions actually come. It is also sometimes hard to know whether action taken by particular groups of workers does have the authority of the union. The powers and responsibilities of shop stewards are not always too clear. This is an area of worker–employer relations which is likely to remain controversial for some time to come.

Rapid review

1   Name three types of trade union.
2   How is union membership distributed between the unions?
3   State two functions of the TUC.
4   What is meant by the term 'collective bargaining'?
5   What is a shop steward?
6   List four provisions of the Trade Union Act 1984.
7   What is meant by 'secondary picketing'?

Employer organisations

Employers and managers co-operate at several levels both nationally and locally. Although firms compete with each other they also have many common interests and problems. As groups they can be more effective in negotiation with government, in influencing public attitudes and in relations with trade unions.

Bodies representing employers

The Confederation of British Industry

The best known national organisation representing employer interests is the Confederation of British Industry (CBI). This represents business as a whole, including the nationalised industries, the service sectors as well as manufacturing and construction. It operates as a constant pressure group seeking to influence government policy but it is also an important channel of communications whereby government and the community are able to influence employers and managers. The CBI is one channel of 'education' through which employers and managers become aware of public opinion and expectations over such issues as social and environmental responsibility and 'good' practices in industrial training and in the conduct of labour relations.

Employers' and trade associations

The CBI is too large to represent adequately the special interests of firms in particular trades and industries. For this purpose the employers' and trade associations are more appropriate. Although the distinction between these two kinds of bodies is not always clear cut, an employers' association has the function of representing members over common problems of production, including the negotiation of wages and working conditions with trade unions and with any appropriate government departments. An example would be the West Midlands Engineering Employers Federation.

Trade associations are concerned with matters of trade and distribution for a particular industry. Well-known examples include the Society of Motor Manufacturers and Traders, the National Federation of Building Trades Employers, the Electrical Contractors' Association and the Road Haulage Association. The original object of many of the industrial trade associations was to fix prices and negotiate wages with trade unions. Product price fixing has been mostly illegal for many years but negotiation with unions remains part of the work of some associations. Most represent their industries in negotiations with government departments such as with the Office of Fair Trading over matters concerning consumer protection and the establishment of quality standards. Associations may also deal with the Department of Trade over foreign trade problems connected with imports or exports.

Chambers of commerce

These are local associations of business organisations. They provide many useful services for their members and sometimes help to administer the smaller trade associations. Their services include the provisions of some certificates required for exports to a number of countries, translations into and from foreign languages, making contacts with foreign firms and chambers of commerce and arranging visits of foreign buyers and putting foreign buyers in touch with local firms. Some of the larger local bodies provide help in settling labour disputes, arranging arbitration (settlement by a neutral person or persons) or even just providing a neutral place where union officers and employers can meet in a peaceful atmosphere.

Most of all, perhaps, the chambers of commerce provide a further channel of communication between business organisations and the government. They also help to put local and regional business viewpoints and problems to the notice of appropriate parts of the government machine. On the other hand they can help to explain government policy and legislation to business firms, to educate members in matters of public relations and good labour relations. Most local associations are keen to promote exports and they maintain libraries containing information essential to exporters and they help to put members with problems into contact with other members who know how to solve them.

Rapid review

1   Name one organisation which represents the interests of employers as a whole.
2   Distinguish between 'employers' associations' and 'trade associations'.
3   List two functions of a chamber of commerce.

The management of people

The personnel department

The growth of the large business organisation has made personnel management into a specialised branch of business management. The origin of the personnel department lies in early efforts to promote the welfare of workers in the belief that a workforce which was cared for by a benevolent employer would produce more than one which regarded the employer with hostility. This 'contented cow' approach to worker management has not entirely died out but most modern personnel specialists recognise that the human beings who make up the workforce form a complex society subject to many influences, objectives and pressures. The skilled management of people – the human capital employed in production – is as important to the success of the firm as the management of financial capital – money.

The need to have a specialised personnel department has been much increased by the legislation outlined in the previous chapter. There are now firm rules concerned with advertising for staff, with recruiting, with training and discipline, with redundancies, dismissals and with retirement. One of the most important functions of the department is to ensure that the firm keeps within the law over all these issues. A worker may no longer be dismissed at the whim of a foreman and a conflict of personalities between a worker and supervisor can sometimes lead to situations requiring many management skills.

When disputes do occur and are referred to industrial tribunals the personnel department is likely to have to arrange the employer's case. Except in very large companies with separate labour relations departments the personnel department is responsible for labour relations within the workplace, although it must be careful not to appear to challenge the authority of managers within their own departments. The personnel department is essentially providing a skilled service to the firm. It cannot directly interfere with the decisions made by managers in other departments though it may hope to influence their attitudes and the way they manage the people under their control. Personnel officers can find themselves helping to solve all sorts of problems concerned with pay and working conditions and working relationships. This work brings them into constant contact with the senior shop stewards. The union workplace organisation of stewards often provides a useful communications link between the personnel department and the workers on the shop floor.

Joint worker-management committees

These are bodies made up of representatives of management and of workers. The committee chairperson is usually the managing director or another senior manager of the company. The worker representatives would normally be chosen from the shop stewards and would include the convener and other senior stewards from all the unions recognised as having negotiating rights within the company. In multi-plant companies there are likely to be committees at each main factory or place of production. There are often separate committees for manual and for supervisory, clerical and similar staff.

Regular meetings are held, usually monthly, and these are administered by the personnel department which may also assume some responsibility for arranging prior meetings of shop stewards, where the works convener will be the chairperson, so that matters of concern to the workers will be brought up at the meeting of the joint committee.

Practices vary considerably from company to company, even from workplace to workplace. Attitudes of managers and shop stewards to these committees also vary greatly, especially as there is rarely a very clear agreement as to their exact powers and functions. At one extreme managers may regard them as convenient channels whereby workers can be informed of managerial decisions and given some idea of the background (market demand, competition, production costs etc.) against which the decisions have been taken. On the other hand the committees may be seen as a formal part of the management–trade union negotiating process in which management presents relevant information and seeks to secure worker approval and co-operation for the measures to be taken. Sometimes alternative strategies may be presented in an effort to solve problems and worker views sought before any one particular course of action is chosen. Most managers tend to see the committees as a way of communicating information to workers and of obtaining information from them concerning conditions on the shop floor. It is clearly preferable to find out what grievances are developing and be able to do something about them before they cause disruption to production.

Worker representatives also have varying views. Some are suspicious of management plots to win over shop stewards to the management side and so to deprive the workers of effective leadership. Some believe that the committees offer a chance to influence managerial decisions and to secure an increased share of profit and better working conditions and relationships for union members.

In a large works the main committee may also contain a number of sub-committees to deal with such issues as health and safety, job evaluation (sorting and grading different jobs in an effort to produce a logical pay structure) and training.

Styles of management

You will have realised by now that employer–employee relationships, or in the larger public companies, manager–worker relationships, can be seen as being on two levels. There is a set of formal, legal relationships where the boundaries of employers' powers and responsibilities and workers' rights and responsibilities are established by laws. These were examined in Chapter 11. At the same time there is a pattern of informal relationships which are intensely individual to the firm or even to a particular workplace. The larger the firm and the more workers there are, the more likely are these to be institutionalised into recognised committees, officials, unions and so on. Nevertheless how these work, or fail to work, and the nature of the relationship between people at work, depend very much on the attitudes of the people involved and especially on the attitudes of the people with the greatest decision-making authority.

Managerial attitudes are important whatever the size of the firm. It is sometimes suggested that the quality of labour relations gets worse as the size of the working group gets larger. There is some evidence that the amount of 'labour disruption' (strikes, go-slows, overtime bans etc.) recorded by the Department of Employment rises with the size of the workplace. However, we should be very careful before jumping to the conclusion that work in a small firm is always more pleasant than in a large company. Individual workers often have little power or influence in small firms and are not often unionised. The only effective response to unpleasant working relationships with employer–managers is to leave the firm. There are good and bad labour relations in all sizes and types of firms. If managers or employers see their workers only as labour units required to produce as many units of production at the smallest possible cost, if workers see employment only as an unavoidable means of earning money to be earned with as little effort as possible, then there will be conflict. If, on the other hand, employers and managers recognise that workers are also human beings with a range of human needs, desires and emotions and if workers recognise that the firm can only survive and provide employment if it can produce goods and services that people want to buy at prices they are able and prepared to pay, then it is probable that satisfying working relationships can be achieved.

To say that there are two styles of management is to over-simplify. There are as many styles of management as there are managers. However, simplifying complicated issues is one way to start to understand them. Many social scientists have studied people at work and you should be aware of the contribution that some of these have made to our knowledge. Macgregor, for example, suggested that managers could be influenced by two conflicting theories of worker attitudes to work. Theory X assumed that people disliked work and only worked because they had to earn money. Workers had to be very closely ordered and controlled. They had to be motivated by a mixture of 'stick and carrot'. Managers had to exercise strict discipline and give detailed instructions which had to be obeyed without question. In contrast to this view, theory Y suggested that work was a natural part of life and that people had a basic motivation to be creative in their jobs and were best left to control their own ways of doing things as much as was possible. If they were given realistic targets they could devise their own ways of achieving them. Other observers have pointed to the fact that unpleasant working conditions could destroy worker motivation and reduce the quality of worker performance. Yet other researchers, notably Elton Mayo, have shown that workers respond to changes in their working conditions and are stimulated when they feel that what they are doing is of genuine interest to others, especially to their managers.

The need to work

Clearly managers should have some understanding of human behaviour and of what people are looking for when they are at work. Here again there are conflicting views and some apparent conflict of evidence. One famous study of assembly line car workers indicated that these worked purely for money which they used to build good homes and satisfying lives outside the workplace. They went to work only to 'earn a living'. Other studies have shown that many workers, including many married women, do not actually need to go to work to earn money but do so to satisfy other needs which, they feel, can only be met by belonging to a work group. Attempts have been made to identify and classify these needs. One of the best known of these is Maslow's 'hierarchy of needs'. This suggests that there is a kind of pyramid with the basic needs at the base. When these have been satisfied then people move up to try and achieve a higher level of satisfaction. Once this level has been achieved they move up further and so on. The levels suggested are the following.

1 *Basic needs* of food, clothing and shelter which, in an industrial society, are provided by the money earned from work.
2 *Safety needs* which consist of protection from the insecurity of unemployment and the various misfortunes of life such as accident and sickness. Money can purchase some degree of security but workers also value a 'secure job'.
3 *Social needs* of human companionship and communication. These are satisfied through membership of a group. People appear to have a need to belong to a recognisable group.
4 *Ego needs*. Ego means I and this set of needs refers to the self-esteem and social importance that goes with having a job and a recognised place in the working community.
5 *Self-fulfilment*. This is the highest level at the top of the pyramid and it relates to the need to achieve and to 'do something with one's life'. Earlier in this chapter we noted how some workers in rather routine jobs were able to find considerable satisfaction in trade union work.

If people seek satisfaction for such a wide range of needs in their work then it is difficult not to agree that work is an essential part of life. It then becomes clear that unemployment is a very serious social and human problem. We may question whether early retirement is an entirely desirable way to reduce unemployment. Nevertheless it could be argued that people have been conditioned to rely on work to satisfy their needs because this is in the interests of the owners of wealth who increase their wealth through the labours of others. As society changes then people's attitudes will also change. Work is always likely to remain an important part of life but there is room to organise it better and, perhaps, to provide more benefits for those who do the work.

Rapid review

1 **In what ways has legislation since 1963 extended the functions of personnel departments?**
2 **What is a joint worker–management committee?**

3   **Outline two contrasting theories that managers could hold concerning worker attitudes to work.**
4   **List five possible 'human needs' that may be satisfied by working.**

Exercises

1   Identify six of the largest trade unions. Classify these as skilled, general or white collar.
2   Choose an industrial dispute that has received prominence in either the national or your local press and other news media. Identify the cause of the dispute. Discuss this and its outcome. To what extent do you think that the dispute received 'fair and unbiased' reporting in the various media channels you have examined?
3   Visit a union district office and interview a union district full-time officer. Write an account of either (a) the services provided by the district officer or (b) the work of the district officer.
4   In what ways do trade unions and labour relations in the public sector of the economy differ from those in the private sector?

Before attempting Questions 5–9 you would find it helpful to arrange (through a company personnel office) to interview a convener or senior shop steward or arrange a talk to your class by a senior shop steward.

5   Discuss the view that shop stewards should be brought more closely under the control of the full-time union organisation.
6   A shop steward represents the members and the union. What problems do you think might arise as a result of this double duty?
7   Discuss the statement that 'employers need shop stewards as much as do trade unions'.
8   'The rule of law requires that no person or group of people should be above the law.' Discuss the implications of this statement in relation to the functions of trade unions.
9   Should all workers have the right to strike or should this be limited in the case of certain groups of workers in the public services? If so which groups?

In order to answer Questions 10 and 11 you should write to the body concerned and ask for any relevant leaflets or booklets. You may also be able to arrange an interview or a talk by a visiting speaker.

10   Write a report on the work and services provided by either a trade association or your local chamber of commerce.
11   Write a report on the work and services provided by either the CBI or ACAS.
12   'Management is the government of a business company and the trade union is the official opposition.' Explain and critically discuss this statement.
13   Discuss the statement that 'every manager is a personnel manager'.
14   The term 'alienation' has been used to describe the attitudes of workers who get no satisfaction from work and who are hostile to their employers. Discuss possible causes of alienation and the kinds of work and firm in which it is most likely to be found.

15 Interview ten working adults of different ages and in different occupations. In the light of these interviews write an account of 'why people work'.

16 'Pay them well enough and you have no labour relations problems.' Discuss this statement made by an employer in a manufacturing industry.

17 Choose an occupation that you think you would find satisfying. Explain the reasons for your choice. Find out and discuss the qualifications required to enter and progress in that occupation.

18 The figures relating to trade unions and trade union membership in this chapter, were derived from the *Employment Gazette* (January 1985) published monthly by the Department of Employment. Visit your local reference library and obtain the latest available figures. Prepare suitable diagrams to illustrate these. To what extent do they continue the trends identified in this chapter?

Questions from examination papers

Short answer questions

1 Outline briefly *two* general duties imposed on employees by the 1974 Health and Safety at Work Act. AEB 0(A) 1982

2 Give *three* examples of fringe benefits. AEB 0(A) 1983

3 Name *three* advantages to an employer of on-the-job training compared with off-the-job training. AEB 0(A) 1983

4 Outline briefly *three* advantages to a firm of using a system of piece rates for paying production workers. AEB 0(A) 1984

5 Explain the term 'discounted cash flow' as used in accounting terminology. AEB A Level 1985

6 A business receives an order for £100 000 worth of components. The direct material costs are estimated at £20 000, the direct labour costs at £40 000 and general overhead costs apportioned to this job at £25 000.

Calculate the contribution to fixed costs to be expected from accepting this order. AEB A Level 1985

Essay questions

1 'The major problems faced by small firms involve shortages of finance and specialist management services.'

 a What is meant by the term 'small firm' and why do these difficulties affect them in particular?

 b Examine the reasons for the existence of so many small firms in the United Kingdom. AEB 0(A) 1982

2 *a* Distinguish between on-the-job training and off-the-job training, mentioning the main advantages of each.

 b Examine the reasons why most firms have given emphasis to staff training in recent years. AEB 0(A) 1982

3 A public limited company which produces electrical components for motor vehicles plans to expand its output by opening a new factory in the United Kingdom.

  a Outline briefly *four* separate factors which might influence the location of such an organisation.

  b Compare at least *four* suitable methods of financing such a project.

  AEB 0(A) 1983

4 *a* What are the essential elements of a good system of stock control?

  b Explain how such a system affects a firm's costs, sales and profits.

  AEB 0(A) 1983

5 Helen Cooper has been the sole owner and manager of a health and beauty salon for the past five years. She now wishes to expand the salon and has invited Linda Farleigh, a close friend, to become a partner in the business. Linda has accepted the invitation.

  a Apart from providing additional finance for expansion, what advantages and disadvantages may be associated with the formation of a partnership?

  b The two partners require £20 000 to enlarge the premises and £10 500 to obtain new equipment. Outline *four* external methods of finance available to them and comment on the suitability of each for the partners' requirements. AEB 0(A) 1984

Case study

The following case study shows how a firm can face a major crisis affecting all aspects of management. In this situation an important decision has to be made involving a choice between various possible options. The decision made by this firm is explained in the study. Would you have made the same choice?

At the end of the case outline there are some questions for you to discuss. You may well think of others. If you do, raise them with your teacher.

Freezewell Electrics Ltd

Freezewell was set up by Mr Andrews and Mr Bastin in 1959. The firm originally had a paid-up capital of £2000 of which £1500 was put up by Mr Andrews and the rest by Mr Bastin. Mr Andrews had been trained as a electrician but had many years' experience as a salesman. Mr Bastin was a refrigeration engineer. With the firm from the start was Mr Clifford, a domestic appliance repairer with Mr Andrews' previous employers.

Ambitiously, Freezewell took on a double shop showroom in an industrial area on the North West side of the Birmingham–Wolverhampton conurbation. One shop could be devoted to appliances from the local Gas Board. The advantage of this was that Freezewell simply acted as agents for the sales of these appliances and did not have to tie up capital to buy them. The two shops together gave, at the rear, plenty of office and stores space and, in addition, a yard area for further storage.

In the early 1960s the firm did well both in terms of commission sales, other sales of domestic appliances, repair work on commission and other domestic repairs. In addition, Mr Bastin started to develop work in the commercial field, both for installations of equipment and for repairs. Sales in the commercial area tended to involve considerable outlay on equipment and customers required credit, on average, of about two months. In addition, in order to obtain repair work, maintenance contracts had to be entered into to provide customers with a guarantee of speedy service for equipment breakdowns. Maintenance contracts, however, require customers to pay a certain amount of money 'up front' (at the start of or on renewal of the contract) each year.

In 1964 Freezewell was threatened by two developments. Firstly the Gas Board concession was withdrawn. Secondly the abolition of Resale Price Maintenance (a system whereby manufacturers could insist that all retailers charged the same price when selling their products) meant that large chain stores could cut the retail prices of domestic appliances well below those charged by Freezewell. However, worries about being able to let small shop premises following the abolition of Resale Price Maintenance, led the landlords of the premises to negotiate a favourable 21 year lease, on condition that Freezewell continued to rent both shops. After much deliberation, Messrs Andrews and Bastin decided that they could build up the service, repairs and commercial side of the business rapidly enough to make renting the shops a reasonable gamble, especially as one of the shops, converted to offices and stores, would enable the company to undertake more commercial business.

The terms of the lease were that the initial rental would be £750 per year, with reviews at the end of 7 and 14 years, at which times the rent could be increased by up to 20 per cent. The full increases were invoked in 1971 and 1978.

In the 1960s and 1970s Freezewell was successful in building up the domestic repairs and commercial business. The increasing dominance of large chains in the domestic appliance market actually led to a demand for stores to supply specialist spare parts and Freezewell successfully exploited this market. On the commercial side the company served a wide range of customers, including supermarkets, restaurants, specialist warehouses, food coldstores, public houses and morgues. In 1977 the firm was offered a large contract to provide a programme of installations, with back-up services and maintenance, to a supermarket chain. After much discussion this offer was turned down as it would have meant too much of the firm's business being dependent on just one customer.

The decision to turn down the supermarket contract was taken jointly by Mr Andrews and Mr Bastin although Mr Bastin was strongly tempted. All important decisions have been taken in agreement by the two of them, although Mr Andrews is still the major shareholder. They have also taken equal incomes and benefits over the years.

In the 1970s Mr Andrews became interested in the new video industry but eventually decided not to pursue this because, by this time, he was reluctant to become involved with something novel.

The recession of the early 1980s when most business firms were experiencing falling sales and profits, caused some difficulties for the commercial side of the business as firms cut back their investment plans. Freezewell had to shed some staff at this time but did not have to make any compulsory redundancies because some left the firm in the natural course of things. By 1983 the personnel of Freezewell Electrics Ltd was as follows:

Joint Managing Directors
Mr Andrews Aged 63, widower, with two married daughters, Iris and Joan. Joan expects shortly to qualify as an accountant.
Mr Bastin Aged 55, married with two sons, one at university reading Geography and the other, aged 30, working for a large electrical engineering firm.

Company Secretary
Mrs Bastin Aged 54, assists with routine office work on a part-time basis.

Other Managerial Personnel
Mr Eldridge Aged 36, with Freezewell since 1975, assistant sales manager (commercial). Qualifications: Ordinary National Certificate (Engineering), married with three young children.
Mr Dobbs Aged 60, with Freezewell since 1977, assistant manager for domestic sales and repairs. Over 40 years' experience in retailing and repairs of domestic electrical appliances. Oversees the work of the shop and stores for both parts of the business.
Mr Clifford Aged 53, with Freezewell from the start. Promoted from engineering to service supervisor in 1970. His work involves co-ordinating the activities of the various service engineers on a day-to-day basis and dealing with the routine paperwork relating to this. Married with two grown-up children he is really happiest 'getting his hands dirty' and is only too pleased with any opportunities to do some repair work himself.
Mrs Frisby Aged 47 with 14 years' service, has the title of 'Office Manager' but in reality acts as secretary to the Managing Directors and supervises the general office work apart from certain jobs such as wages and invoicing which are shared by Mr Andrews and Mr Bastin. She has three children, one still at school and she lives round the corner from the firm.
All managerial staff except Mrs Frisby have a company car which they may use for private purposes.

Office Staff
Clerk/typist (female) aged 27, married with 3 years' service.
Clerk (male) aged 19, 1 year's service. He joined Freezewell after failing A levels. Interested in computers.
Part-time typist (female) aged 32, married.
Bookkeeper (male) aged 67, semi-retired.

Shop Assistant
One male aged 26 with 2 years' service

Engineers
There are 12 engineers, all male, with ages ranging from 25 to 42 and with length of service ranging from 3 to 12 years. Six are members of the Amalgamated Engineering Union (AEU), having retained their union membership since their time

with various larger engineering firms. The union workplace representative is Mr Gibbons, a 38-year-old married man who has been with Freezewell for 10 years.

Of the engineers, three, all union members, are specialists in domestic appliance repairs. Of the others, two specialise in commercial installation and the remainder spend most of their time on commercial service and repair work although they do spend some time on domestic work. There are two apprentices, one of whom works full time with the installation team and the other divides his time between domestic service and helping Mr Dobbs.

Each engineer (but not the apprentices) drives a van which, because of lack of space at the work premises, they are allowed to garage at home. Unofficially this means that they can use their vans in their spare time although this does sometimes cause concern about high mileage, unfortunate accidents and heavier insurance charges.

In 1983 Freezewell were informed by the landlord for the shop that he intended to raise the rent from £1080 to £9000 for both shops or £5000 for either from 1985, on the expiry of the lease arranged in 1964.

Messrs Andrews and Bastin carried out an urgent review of the company's position and arrived at certain preliminary conclusions.

1 The new rent was reasonably typical for the type of premises in the local area.
2 Purpose-built industrial units with much more storage and parking space were available at a rent of £8000 per year or for purchase at a price of £80 000 on the south east side of Birmingham.

Mr Bastin was keen to move the whole business to a new site. Existing commercial customers could continue to be served and new ones more easily found in this new location which was in a developing area close to the National Exhibition Centre, Birmingham International Airport, the centre of the national motorway network and a proposed Freeport. The domestic side of the business would, however, have to be abandoned. In addition, the site would be much more convenient both for himself and Mr Andrews who were now living in the prosperous residential area of Solihull.

Furthermore, Mr Bastin's elder son, Henry, had expressed an interest in coming into the business. He had received a substantial financial offer of voluntary redundancy from his present firm and could put this money into the company in return for an appropriate shareholding. He could also bring some useful business contacts and had suggested that Freezewell might diversify into air conditioning. Moving to a new site offered the opportunity to rethink the whole 'market orientation' of the business and also to overhaul its operations. Henry believed that the firm might be carrying some 'dead wood' among the personnel. He would not be prepared to join the business in its present form.

Mr Andrews was more reluctant to move. Any of the options seemed about as expensive as the others. All concerned seemed able to make a living from the business as it was currently being conducted and he felt that the increased costs could be absorbed by some moderation in wages. He felt sure that with careful explanation to all staff they would see this. There was probably also scope for some modest increases in prices. Domestic customers rarely had a clear idea about the price they should expect for a repair and the amount of repeat business being done with commercial customers suggested that they valued reliability and quality as much as low prices.

Mr Andrews was also reluctant to let down any existing staff, in particular Mrs Frisby, Mr Dobbs and Mr Clifford, all of whom he felt were threatened by the proposed changes. As far as bringing Henry into the business was concerned, he was quite prepared to let him have a shareholding sufficient to equalise the Andrews and Bastin 'family' interests as he felt that this would simply regularise a situation which, in practice, already existed. However, he was worried about some of Henry's ideas and wondered if they were not more appropriate to a larger firm.

In the end, Mr Andrews was persuaded by two considerations.

Firstly, his daughter Joan, newly qualified as an accountant, argued that the firm was currently in danger of 'overtrading' on its working capital and it badly needed an injection of new capital such as Henry was prepared to provide in order to reduce its dependence on trade credit. In addition, concentration on a narrower range of business could reduce the amount of stock being carried. Trade might also be more price-sensitive than Mr Andrews supposed. Staying at the same site might only produce a new crisis in the future as the firm would have no opportunity to expand. Mr Andrews did suggest retaining one of the shops in order not to lose the valuable retail business but Joan argued that the shop could only afford its essential element, an expert like Mr Dobbs, as long as he was also contributing to the commercial side. She, like Henry, stressed the value of this opportunity for reorganisation and rationalisation.

Secondly, although discussions had been kept to the Andrews and Bastin family, rumours circulated among the other members of the firm. At last Mr Gibbons brought matters to a head by insisting on negotiations. He was sympathetic to the firm's problems and offered full co-operation in any decision, but only as long as there were no compulsory redundancies.

In the end, Freezewell moved to a rented, purpose-built industrial unit on the east side of Birmingham. All but one of the engineers moved with the firm but the apprentices, the shop assistant and all the female office staff, including Mrs Frisby, left. Total severance costs, including ex-gratia payments, were £4000.

Henry, now with 1000 shares and the title of Sales Director, reorganised the office personnel. As he knew the commercial side of the business, Mr Eldridge was put in charge of the office with the former clerk as his assistant with responsibility for scheduling service calls, and one full-time secretary-typist. Joan Andrews agreed to help on a part-time basis with financial matters. Mr Dobbs became storeman, full-time. The Bastins themselves concentrated on marketing the firm's services. Mr Clifford was given the title 'service co-ordinator' but, in effect, went back to being an engineer although it was doubtful whether his health would permit him to continue with this work. Henry started taking Mr Gibbons with him on site visits with a view to promoting him to a sales position.

Mr Andrews announced his intention to go into semi-retirement.

This case study raises many issues. Notice that the crisis that faced the firm between 1983 and 1985 was not its first. In earlier years it had turned problems into opportunities but on one occasion it had turned down an opportunity to change direction and grow larger. Perhaps both controlling families were influenced by this memory when major decisions had to be taken in 1983. You should give some thought to the realities of 'risk taking' which many people suggest is the true function of the business owner – the **entrepreneur**.

Here are some further questions for you to discuss.

1   Do you think that the directors overlooked any important issues?

2   Why do you think the company decided to rent rather than buy the new premises?

3   If Freezewell had decided to buy how might it have raised the necessary finance?

4   What lesson in communications is illustrated in this study?

5   Do you think that the labour relations side of this problem could have been better handled? If so what suggestions would you make?

6   Why did Mr Andrews think that Henry's ideas were more suited to a larger firm?

7   Suggest some financial savings that could result from the move. Why were these savings not made earlier?

8   Do you think Freezewell could have continued the domestic side of the business? How might it have done this?

9   Critically discuss the office reorganisations introduced by Henry indicating possible problems and advantages.

10   How might the company take advantage of the new assistant office manager's interest in computers?

11   Study the accounts of Freezewell. Identify those entries which led Joan to argue that the firm needed fresh capital.

12   Describe the previous crises faced by Freezewell Ltd. Comment on the way these were handled.

13   How would you expect the requirements of domestic and commercial customers to differ?

14   Assume that the company decides not to take its office equipment to the new site but to sell it for any price it will fetch and to re-equip the new office completely. What options are likely to be open to the firm in financing this re-equipment? What opportunities might arise out of this decision?

15   What transport and communication advantages are offered by the move from one side of the large West Midlands industrial conurbation to the other? Why are these important for a service organisation such as Freezewell Electrics Ltd?

Freezewell Electrics Ltd
Trading and Profit and Loss Account for year ending 30 April 1983

	£		£
Materials used	285 000	Sales	560 000
Add Wages	146 000		
	431 000		
Gross profit	129 000		
Office overheads (salaries etc)	35 000		
Directors' remuneration and pension	30 000		
Rent	1 080		
Rates	600		
Light and heat	800		
Insurance	3 500		
Postage, stationery etc.	3 000		
Telephone	2 000		
Motor vehicle running expenses	32 000		
Bank charges	100		
General repairs	500		
Advertising	500		
Depreciation	11 000		
Legal and audit charges	400		
Sundries	5 000		
Net Profit	3 520		
Total	129 000		

Freezewell Electrics Ltd
Balance Sheet as at 30 April 1983

	Cost	Depreciation	Balance
	£	£	£
Fixed Assets			
Fixtures and fittings	6 000	4 000	2 000
Motor vehicles	85 000	44 000	41 000
Current Assets	£		£
Stock: 30 April 1983	28 000		
Debtors and prepayments	96 000		
Cash at bank	4 700		
Bank deposit	5 000		
Cash in hand	300		
		134 000	
Less *Current Liabilities*			
Creditors and accruals	124 000		
Hire purchase payments due	8 000		
		132 000	
Net working capital			2 000
Total net assets			45 000
Financed by			
Authorised capital			
5000 Ordinary shares at £1 each			
of which issued and fully paid			
2000 shares at £1 each			2 000
Retained profit carried forward			19 000
			21 000
Directors' loans			
Mr A Andrews			19 000
Mr B Bastin			5 000
			45 000

13 Management and integration

Nothing makes itself, nor sells itself. Every business ultimately depends on the people involved in it, on its workers, managers, shareholders, suppliers and customers. It is the responsibility of managers to co-ordinate all these people in order to make the business as effective as possible. In this chapter we take a closer look at the practical problems of managing a business. We look at ways of managing people effectively; at the firm's responsibility to all the various individuals and groups involved in it. We also look at some further aspects of the 'principles of management' and finally at what we really mean by an effective business.

In the previous chapters we have examined the various specialised areas of management. In order to explain them clearly we have had to deal with each separately. In practice, as you have seen in the case study of Freezewell Electrics Ltd, all these separate functions become involved in any major decision and anything that affects one inevitably affects the others. At this stage of study you should now be able to appreciate more clearly this inevitable integration in business management.

Managing people

Attitudes and incentives

At the end of Chapter 12 we saw that the attitude of management to workers could be quite different according to the view that was taken of people's attitudes to work. In the nineteenth century there was a widespread belief that, on the whole, people were lazy, unimaginative and unambitious. To get the best work out of them, therefore, managers had to provide, on the one hand strict controls and punishments for unsatisfactory work, and on the other hand, simple financial incentives. They thought that people would work only for money or to avoid punishment.

Fig 13.1   What makes people tick?

In the twentieth century we have come to realise that this approach to motivating people is, in many cases, far too over-simplified. It has become clear that people will respond to all sorts of motivations, not just financial ones. This has led to many innovations in the way work is organised. Here are some examples.

1 *People may regard goals as a challenge* This is especially so if they have participated in setting the goals for themselves. This, for example, has led to the popularity of systems of 'Management by Objectives' (MBO) in which superiors and subordinates discuss targets for the latter and ways in which these can be achieved. Once these objectives are agreed, subordinates should be strongly motivated to achieve them without the need for close supervision.

2 *People may prefer working in teams* This is often impossible if work is designed as a series of self-contained separate operations as on an assembly line. Work may have to be redesigned to be carried out by groups rather than individually.

3 *People may work better if the work is more satisfying* However big the financial incentive, if work is repetitive and stifling people are likely to get bored and inefficient. This has led to the introduction of programmes, for example, of *job enrichment* in which the work is made more challenging and interesting, or of *job enlargement*, where the worker is given a wider range of tasks to perform.

4 *People tend to respond to an interest taken in them as people*   Strangely enough a manager who concentrates on 'getting on with the job in hand' and who takes little interest in his or her worker's individual problems may get poor results. Very often, the best results are born out of good 'human relations' between workers and management.

Look again at the last idea (**4**). It may seem obvious that people will respond better to better treatment, but there is an important point there which is often overlooked. Many business managers pride themselves on operating all kinds of schemes designed to improve human relations. They seek to make jobs more satisfying, to encourage worker self-improvement and so on, only to abandon all these when times are hard. They then return to a system of crude 'sticks and carrots', of punishments and simple financial incentives.

A management which takes this course of action may justify it by saying it would like to carry on with the other schemes but 'cannot afford them'. However, in so doing it is showing that it does not really believe that they work. Remember that the justification for schemes such as MBO, job enlargement and so on, is not simply that they make people happier. This may or may not be true but it is irrelevant. The point is the belief that they *lead people to be more efficient and productive*. If this is true it is precisely when times are tough for the business that it needs the schemes. It is then that it needs an efficient work force.

The problem of control

If it is really true that emphasis on human relations, job enrichment and so on can make workers more effective why do firms sometimes abandon these incentives?

The problem is that schemes like these can sometimes conflict with other objectives that the firm is trying to achieve. Sometimes the conflict is imaginary rather than real but a manager may still feel that it is important. For example:

1 *Organising work in teams raises problems of accountability*   If you wish to check the performance of individual workers, perhaps to measure the amount of production achieved by each worker or to arrange bonus payments, this is more difficult when work is carried out by a collective group. In addition, there is the fear that some people will not 'carry their weight' or will have to be 'carried by the others'. However, it is also true that very often the disapproval of workmates is the most effective way to correct this kind of behaviour.

2 *More complex work increases the problems and costs of supervision* If people are given more responsibilities or more complex work it may be argued that this will lead to difficulties in monitoring and checking performance so that supervisory costs are increased. Once again this is only partly true. An alternative would be to maintain the same level of supervision or even reduce it. This would, of course, mean placing more reliance on the workers' own initiative and judgement. Some managers are reluctant to 'let go' in this way.

3 *Reorganising work along the lines that have been suggested can be costly* For example, to reorganise a factory from assembly line operation to a system of teams in the way that has been adopted in some car plants in Sweden, involves much redesign and changes in layout of plant and machinery. However, supporters of such changes say that they are likely to pay for themselves in the long run through increases and improvements in the work produced. If the firm looks only at short run costs it may decide that it cannot afford the changes.

Rapid review

1 State and briefly explain four innovations in the organisation of work following realisation that people do not work simply to earn money or to avoid punishment.
2 Suggest three reasons why the 'human relations approach' to work organisation may be abandoned by business managers.

The personnel of the modern firm

So far we have concentrated on one very important group of people in the firm: the workers. We have already mentioned other important groups: the shareholders, suppliers and customers. In law, a company belongs to its shareholders, a partnership to its partners and a sole proprietorship to its single owner. There is still a view of the firm which says that the interests of every other group of people involved in the firm are subordinate to those of the owners. However, this is today a rather difficult line to take, whether in legal, moral or practical terms.

Legal obligations

We have already seen (in Chapters 7 and 11) that a firm owes obligations to customers, creditors and employees that can override those to its owners. For example, if the firm is wound up, financial obligations to all these others must be met before the owners are entitled to any claim on the assets of the firm. Again, the law now recognises the importance of a job and of the employer's obligations to the individual worker by giving the force of law to certain of the employee's rights under the Employment Protection Act. Customer rights have also been greatly increased since the early 1960s by a series of Acts of Parliament including the Trade Descriptions and the Sale of Goods Acts and by the activities of bodies such as the Office of Fair Trading.

Moral obligations

'Responsible business is good business.' Many firms make a point of going beyond their legal obligations towards customers, suppliers and employees and society in general. For example, a point may be made of meeting claims from customers and suppliers without resort to legal wrangling. Enlightened and benevolent attitudes may be fostered towards employees, and the firm may pursue socially desirable policies such as safety and protection of the environment or the sponsorship of community activities.

Supporters of such programmes claim that, quite apart from being morally worthwhile in their own right, they often 'pay off' for the firm in the form of more custom and better industrial relations. This has led cynics to claim that firms only pursue morally responsible attitudes because it is profitable to do so. However, this is a point that need not detain us here. The question whether it is only moral to do things that do not have the possibility of reward is a philosophical point outside the scope of this book.

Practical considerations

Ways in which 'responsible business' may turn out to be 'good business' include the following:

a *Increased sales* Existing customers are encouraged to do business again and new customers are attracted by the firm's reputation. Marks and Spencer have built up an enviable reputation among the buying public partly as a result of their reputation for quality and fair dealing.

b *Stability and commitment of managers and employees* The legalistic idea that the most important people in a business are the owners alone looks weakest in a public limited company. Individual shareholders may dispose of their shares quite easily through the stock market and in addition are likely to have only a small part of their savings tied up in one firm. Contrast this with employees, managers or workers, who have much greater difficulty in leaving the firm – they have to find another job – and whose financial 'stake' in the company is in one sense greater because their jobs are likely to be their main sources of income.

The firm may experience a major turnover of shareholders without being fundamentally affected. On the other hand, a major loss of managers or skilled, experienced employees can be very damaging.

Putting these points together we see that on the one hand the wellbeing of the firm is critically dependent on the commitment of key workers and on the other, such workers will be looking to the firm to show a commitment towards them. Hence a responsible attitude towards employees can be crucial. In Japan, the leading firms pride themselves on offering lifetime employment to their workers along with prospects for personal improvement, in return for a very high degree of loyalty and involvement from the workers. In the UK many firms prefer to try to hold on to employees during a period of depressed business even if this does not appear to be justified in the short run.

c *Possible legal developments* A firm will often have an eye not only to immediate legal obligations but also to likely developments. For example, business practices that appear to wriggle through a legal loophole today may attract such public outrage that legislation follows swiftly and firms that have been engaging in them may gain a reputation for being 'cowboy' or 'fly by night' operations. A legal tightening up of this kind occurred in the UK when 'pyramid selling' was outlawed.

In addition, one can anticipate that practices already compulsory under the law in other countries might be introduced into this country. For example, in all large West German companies, workers are entitled to representation on the firms' supervisory boards which oversee company policy. A firm might decide to anticipate such changes voluntarily rather than appear later on to be only accepting them rather grudgingly when compelled by law to do so.

Rapid review

1 List all the groups of people to whom a business firm is likely to have legal obligations.
2 Explain with at least one example, what is meant by 'the moral obligations of business'.
3 List three practical ways in which 'responsible business can turn out to be good business'.

Structure and management of the firm

The firm as a 'coalition'

It has been suggested for the reasons we have discussed that the modern firm could be best regarded as a coalition of interested groups such as shareholders and employees rather than as serving the interests of one group only. This helps us to understand the role of management which has to keep the various members of this coalition satisfied. Once again, we see the role of business management as a sort of balancing act, trying to keep various important groups of people happy, while pursuing the overall goals of the firm. We shall return to these 'goals' in the last section of this chapter.

Control and management

Throughout this chapter we have talked about the role of management rather than of the entrepreneur or of the owners of the firm. In a small firm, of course, the only manager may be the major shareholder or sole proprietor of the firm. However, in a large organisation it is unlikely that one individual will be responsible for all of its activities. In a large public limited company, the shareholders elect a *board of directors* who have overall control of the business. A broad outline of the powers and responsibilities of directors in one very large company, Unilever, is shown in Fig 13.2.

However, in a large firm it is unlikely that the board will be able to concern itself with more than matters of general policy and strategy. Matters of greater detail must be attended to by others on their behalf.

Some directors will be *non-executive directors*, that is to say they do not have a management role in the company other than as members of the board. Others will be *executive directors* with specific responsibilities for particular functions. There may be a sales or marketing director, personnel director, finance director and so on, each with substantial departments to supervise. The senior executive director is usually the *managing director* who co-ordinates the work of the other executive directors. The *chairman* of the board is usually non-executive.

Within each of the departments there may be a further hierarchy of managers. As one goes lower in this hierarchy the responsibility of each manager is likely to become more and more specific. A possible structure of management is illustrated in Fig 13.3.

There is one consequence of this which should be realised by managers. For example, in Fig 13.3 it is quite likely that the area

Powers and responsibilities of the board of directors

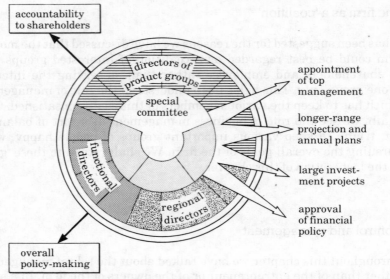

Fig 13.2   Powers and responsibilities of the board of directors. Reproduced from 'Unilever's management and organisation' by permission of Unilever plc

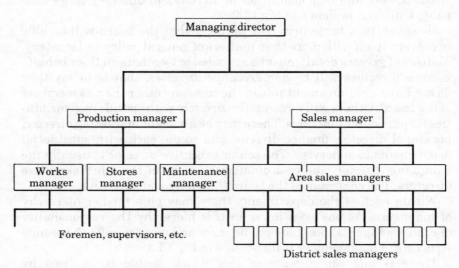

Fig 13.3   Organisation chart

managers will have been promoted on the basis of competence as branch managers and that the sales director himself (or herself) was once a very good area manager. It is almost inevitable that each superior could do the work of the subordinate at least as well as that person and often better.

This means that there is a great temptation for managers to carry their supervision to the point of interference or even to the extent of doing the subordinate's job for them. Not only does this lead to the latter being frustrated and their time being wasted but the manager fails to devote proper attention to his or her own work. Much of the point of *delegating* work to others is to allow more time to do one's own job properly. In senior positions in the firm that job is less to do with matters of technical detail and much more to do with the management activities explained in Chapter 1, of co-ordination, planning and decision making.

Rapid review

1 Why would it be inaccurate to refer to the 'entrepreneur' in connection with the large public company?
2 Explain the differences between executive directors, non-executive directors, the managing director.
3 What is meant by the 'delegation of work'?
4 What is meant by the 'hierarchy of management'?

More about efficiency and objectives

Which is the more efficient: a Mini or a Grand Prix racing car?

If you answered, 'A Mini', you might be told, 'Then try entering a Mini in the next Grand Prix!' If you answered, 'The racing car', you might get the response, 'But a Mini will go many times further on a gallon of petrol'.

The point is, of course, that you cannot measure the efficiency of anything unless you have an idea of what it is trying to do. This is as true of firms as it is of cars. You need to know, for example whether the firm is trying to increase profit, increase sales or provide more employment.

We saw in Chapter 1 that there are a number of objectives that business organisations might try to pursue. Organisations in the public sector may have even more. Before judging how efficiently a business is being run you need to know what its objectives really are. For example, if a sole proprietor feels it is very important to keep control of the business it is not inefficient to refuse to expand the business to the point where other shareholders and managers have to be brought in. The proprietor is pursuing the objective by keeping the firm small. If a public corporation has a major objective of 'public service' it is not possible to judge its efficiency by looking at its profits or losses. This explains why British nationalised industries now have other *performance indicators*.

Objectives and decision making

Another reason why it is important for an organisation to have objectives is that they help in planning and decision making.

The purpose of planning is very often misunderstood. It is not an attempt to 'mastermind the future' – to set out in detail everything one hopes to do in the future and then stick to this regardless of what actually happens. Planning is supposed to help us to decide what to do *now* in order that we may achieve our objectives.

Suppose, for example, a firm has a target in terms of profits that it wishes to earn over the next five years. We can show this as a graph such as Fig 13.4.

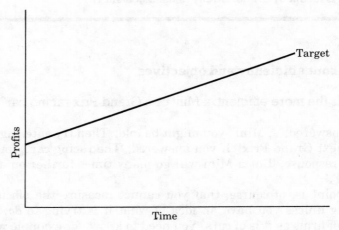

Fig 13.4

If the managers of the firms then look at the present and likely trends of, for instance, output and sales, they may produce a forecast of likely profits such as Fig 13.5.

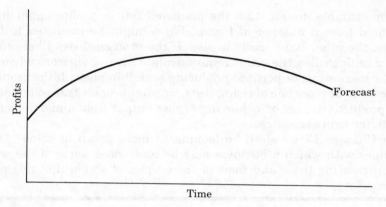

Fig 13.5

Putting Fig 13.4 and Fig 13.5 together we get a picture such as Fig 13.6. This shows us that in the near future profits are likely to exceed the target but later they are likely to fall short.

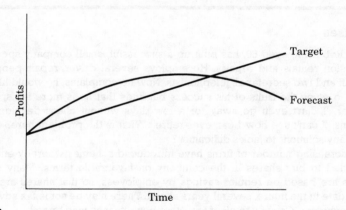

Fig 13.6

Action will be required if the targets are to be achieved and maintained. More detailed analysis along the same lines may show what sort of action is required, when it is required and whether any action is required now.

This knowing whether or not a decision is required is an important part of decision making. Sometimes people feel they are confronted by so many things that are happening and may require attention that, in the end, they do nothing. A systematic approach, comparing forecasts and objectives can help us to see whether action is needed, when it is needed and even what kind of action.

For example, in Fig 13.5 the predicted fall in profits might have resulted from a number of trends. Sales might be predicted to fall, or, on the other hand, costs to rise. If the problem looks likely to be one of falling sales, the action required might involve vigorous advertising or marketing, or perhaps producing something new. If the problem appears to be more one of rising costs, we might concentrate on improving productivity, i.e. on achieving higher output from a more efficient use of the firm's resources.

In Chapter 17 we shall be looking in more detail at some of the changes with which a business may be confronted, some of the ways of anticipating these and some of the courses of action that might be appropriate.

Rapid review

1 What should be the first step in the measurement of efficiency?
2 What is meant by the term 'performance indicator'?
3 Is profit always a reliable measure of efficiency?

Exercises

1 Jack Robinson, aged 60, has built up a successful, small company specialising in television rentals and repairs. He employs several driver/repair people, two shop staff and two secretarial/telephonists. Now he complains, he would like more time off to enjoy the fruits of his success but finds that he is more indispensable than ever. 'I can't even go away for a few days without chaos developing,' he complains. 'I can't see how I can ever retire.' What is the problem here? Can you suggest any solutions to Jack's difficulties?

2 An increasing number of firms have introduced schemes whereby employers are entitled to buy shares in the company on favourable terms. Many of these schemes are based on regular savings by employees, so that shares are bought at some date in the future, several years ahead. There may be some tax advantages in these schemes. Can you think of any other benefits they may bring?

3 A firm with a high proportion of skilled workers is aware of a radical new technology which would require different working methods, the employment of people with new skills and the fading out of existing skills. Rumours are rife in the firm and already there have been several unofficial strikes. Can you suggest constructive action that the firm could take?

4 You are the managing director of a company which operates a local chain of High Street supermarkets. Sparks & Co, a firm of management consultants, have prepared a list of suggestions which, they claim, will increase your firm's profits by 50 per cent within five years. These include closing the High Street shops and opening a small number of out-of-town hypermarkets or superstores. This change, together with other proposals, would involve reducing the work force by 30 per cent and introducing a strong element of payments by results into the wages of most workers. Comment on and discuss these suggestions.

14 Business communications

The importance of communications

The general need for communication

In the previous chapter we noted that the firm is sometimes looked on as a form of coalition between various groups, each with an interest in its continued survival and success. We can identify the shareholders, the directors and managers, workers, customers who want its products, the government which wants it as a source of taxation and even members of the public generally who may wish to become customers or workers in the organisation or who share the same environment.

If all these groups have an interest in the firm then all, to some extent, need to know what it is doing and how it is performing. They also need to be able to judge how its activities are likely to affect them. Of course the firm itself cannot communicate anything. Although it may exist as a separate entity in law this is only a 'legal fiction'. The company seal cannot write a letter or pick up a telephone. What does happen is that one group communicates with, and receives communications from, the others. Notice that in examining communications we immediately tend to think in terms of communications in the large organisation. This is not to imply that communications for the small-firm are not important. Clearly they are and some aspects are clearly defined by law but in general there are fewer barriers to the flow of information in small firms than there are in large. The village storekeeper is in constant contact with his or her customers and assistants, and is unlikely to stay in business very long if he or she is a poor communicator. The managing director of a chain of hypermarkets cannot meet the customers and the staff at the stores' checkouts every day but, unless he or she understands their feelings and aspirations and their changing attitudes, is also unlikely to be successful. The managing director and his or her managers have to overcome the communication barriers which arise as a business grows.

Some of the communication channels and pressures likely to be experienced by a large retail organisation are illustrated in Fig 14.1.

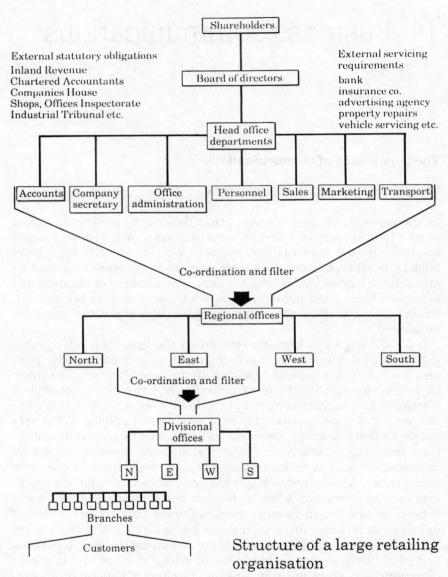

External statutory obligations

Inland Revenue
Chartered Accountants
Companies House
Shops, Offices Inspectorate
Industrial Tribunal etc.

External servicing requirements

bank
insurance co.
advertising agency
property repairs
vehicle servicing etc.

Shareholders

Board of directors

Head office departments

Accounts | Company secretary | Office administration | Personnel | Sales | Marketing | Transport

Co-ordination and filter

Regional offices

North | East | West | South

Co-ordination and filter

Divisional offices

N | E | W | S

Branches

Customers

Structure of a large retailing organisation

Communications tend to be filtered and co-ordinated via board — head office department — regional office — divisional office — branch retail store. Sometimes these stages are by-passed in cases of importance or urgency.

Trade union representation

Negotiations with trade unions often are channeled through the personnel manager. Trade union employee representatives are selected from staff, usually by ballot.

Fig 14.1   Communications in Organisations. Reproduced from *People and Communication* by Desmond W Evans

Formal and informal communications

One thing we have to realise is that it is impossible not to communicate. If the village shop is untidy, windows dirty, floor unswept and the shopkeeper in scruffy clothes, anyone entering the shop gets an immediate message that the business is badly run. The customer would suspect that stock is old and quality poor. It would be wise to count the change carefully. In much the same way we get an impression of the quality of the management as soon as we enter a hypermarket. If checkout queues are long, staff surly, shelves untidy and half filled and car parks untidy we know that management is losing control. On the other hand clean premises, shelves constantly being refilled, friendly staff and no undue waiting at checkouts all suggest an efficient management and a well-run business.

It is not even necessary to visit a firm to get an impression of the way it is run. The way a telephone call is answered tells us a great deal. The appearance of a letter opens a window on the organisation. The customer who receives a letter from a bank with several alterations and a spelling mistake tends to wonder whether the accounts are being handled carefully and whether mistakes are also being made with standing orders.

No firm can ignore communications. It must pay as much attention to the informal system of messages that are being transmitted through its normal day-to-day activities as to the formal system which it creates for the deliberate collection and transfer of information between the various groups that make up the total coalition of the continuing business organisation. Both communication systems are taken into account as we examine some of the important links between these groups.

Rapid review

1 What is meant by informal communications?
2 Why should firms pay attention to informal communications?

Communications in practice

Information and management

Business management has been described as a process of 'taking decisions under conditions of uncertainty'. This is because the manager has to prepare today for what is expected to happen tomorrow. We know what happened yesterday – though no decision taken today can alter that – but what is decided today will affect what happens tomorrow and how successfully the firm copes with tomorrow's events. Wrong decisions may mean that customers cannot find the goods they want on the shelves of the hypermarket and they have to wait to pay for the goods that they have found because not enough staff are on the checkouts.

Good decisions can only be made if the decision maker receives reliable information. In a large company decisions are often made by teams or groups of people who have to consider and discuss the information available, arrive at their decision and then ensure that it is carried out and the results fed back to the group. All this is communication. The more important the decision and its implications for the future of the company and its workforce the more important it becomes to ensure that communications are effective.

Suppose, for example, that a manufacturing company is considering whether to produce a new product. Let us give a little thought to the range of information needed by the senior executives who have to make the final decision. They must have information about:

a The market conditions for the product, i.e. estimates of how much is likely to be sold at a range of possible prices, taking into account the probable reactions of competitors.

b The supply conditions for the materials, machines and labour required to produce the product so that costs can be estimated and a time schedule prepared showing the quantities that can be produced within a given time period.

c The cost of setting up new production plant, including any new building required and the time this is likely to take and also the cost of acquiring the necessary finance to meet these *start-up* costs.

On the basis of all the available information concerning the costs and possible gains to the company from producing the new product the managers must decide whether the gains are sufficient to justify the risks involved. They are likely to have to give some thought to possible events outside their control that could affect demand for the product and the production costs. For example, the Government might decide to 'squeeze' the economy, to make money more costly and difficult to borrow, to make wage rises more difficult to obtain or imported materials more costly. Modern managers have to take a broad view of economic and political events because these can often have a big impact on a company's fortunes. It is not difficult to see that a company's communications systems have to be carefully organised if the people who have decisions to make are to obtain the information they need when and where they need it and in the form in which it can be most useful.

Management and shareholders

If managers have to seek information from many sources they must also provide information to the groups interested in their decisions. They need the support of shareholders, people and organisations with money to invest and who may become shareholders and the banks and other financial institutions which advise investors if they are to obtain the finance they need to expand their operations or even to keep their equipment and production methods up-to-date. If the company's existing shareholders are not satisfied with the performance of the management they are likely to sell their shares and this will force down the price and make the company unpopular among financial advisers. Most senior managers of public companies keep a constant watch on the price of their company's shares and they often go to a great deal of trouble to persuade those with influence on finance markets that the company is well managed and worth supporting.

The need to communicate with the main centres of finance is one reason why most large companies have their Head Office or a major office in London. Most employ public relations officers who try to make sure that the company obtains favourable publicity, that senior managers and directors meet influential people and that news to the credit of the company becomes widely known.

This kind of activity may be as concerned to conceal information as to publish it and because it is so important that shareholders, possible shareholders and the public generally should be provided with balanced and accurate information, companies are legally required to prepare annual accounts containing certain facts about their activities and finances. These accounts must be audited (carefully checked, inspected and approved) by accountants who are members of professional bodies approved by the Department of Trade and Industry. In the case of private companies the accounts must be lodged with the Registrar of Companies and are available for inspection by anyone. A copy must also be sent to each shareholder. Public companies are subject to similar rules but, in addition, any company whose shares are traded on a stock exchange must observe the rules of the exchange regarding the publication of information. The London Exchange, for example, requires companies to publish summary accounts at half-yearly intervals and these must be sent to all shareholders. It also expects companies to make their published accounts readily available to anyone who wishes to see them.

Company accounts

The purpose of obliging companies to publish accounts is to ensure that people can obtain essential information about the company's activities and the state of its finances. This purpose is only achieved if those who receive the accounts can understand them. Clearly the more skilled and advanced your knowledge of accounting the more information you are likely to gain; but as a student of business studies you should be aware of some basic facts and techniques.

Published accounts are really in two parts. Some very large companies such as Unilever extracts from whose report and accounts are used in this chapter, publish two booklets but usually they form part of one document. The first part is the Directors' Report which should contain an outline of the company's activities and results for the year, any significant developments such as major sales or acquisitions and the names of directors and their holding of the company's shares. By far the best way for you to find out the contents of the Directors' Report is to examine some published examples, and the exercises at the end of this chapter make some suggestions which should help you to do this.

The second part of the annual publication is the actual set of accounts made up of the Profit and Loss Account and the Balance Sheet and certain information which the Companies Acts require the company to disclose, including the 'emoluments' (payments from all sources including salary, fees, bonuses etc.) to all directors and to 'highly paid' employees.

The Profit and Loss Account summarises the company's performance during the year and shows the total sales turnover, total costs, the resulting **gross profit**, any other income producing an **operating profit** and the way that the profit is distributed to shareholders (in dividends), to the State (in company taxation) and in 'retentions' (the amount kept back for further use in the company's activities). The accounts of large companies will supplement this summary account with further notes. Some of the notes to the Unilever turnover and costs are shown in Fig 14.5. Notice that published accounts always show figures for the preceding as well as the current year so that comparisons can be made. Profit, of course, represents the difference between revenue and cost and is explained more fully at the end of Chapter 15.

The balance sheet shows the value of the company's assets (items of value which it owns) and its liabilities (obligations to make payments) as at the close of the company's financial year. Take note of the terms **fixed assets** and **current assets**.

Fixed assets in the Unilever accounts are made up of **tangible assets** and **fixed investments**. Tangible or physical assets are items owned

CHAIRMEN'S FOREWORD

There was good progress in 1985 towards strengthening the key areas of the business. Investment continued in the restructuring and expansion of our European operations, and we are pleased to tell you that the measures taken in the last few years have resulted in a substantial increase in operating profit. This is crucial to the health of the Concern because Europe is and will remain the heartland of Unilever.

1985 was a year of major investment in our brands in the United States, mainly in detergents. Several new products had been successful in test market and we were determined to invest in this success. We knew this would decrease profitability in 1985 but we wanted to increase our volume and market share. Our targets have been achieved in spite of sustained resistance from our competitors.

Our reported results in 1985 were bedevilled by fluctuating exchange rates especially in the last quarter. This was particularly marked because of the decline in the dollar and other overseas currencies against both sterling and the guilder. Our earnings at comparable rates increased by 15 per cent, but at closing rates in sterling they rose by only 3 per cent whereas in guilders they fell by 1 per cent. On the other hand profit attributable expressed in U.S. dollars rose by 28 per cent.

A major continuing strategic aim is to strengthen our market position by selective acquisitions and in 1985 companies were acquired which support our core activities in a number of countries including the United States. We also made an offer for Richardson-Vicks, a large American toiletry company which would have been an extremely good strategic fit, but we were not prepared to pay more than our assessment of its worth and were overbid. It remains our intention to be more strongly represented in the United States; this will be achieved by investment in internal growth as in 1985, and by way of further acquisitions – but at the right price.

The acquisition of Brooke Bond has been a great success. The major parts of the group have settled well and remarkably quickly into our Food & Drinks business, whilst Baxters (Butchers) and the Mallinson-Denny timber operations have been sold. Good progress has also been made in selling other companies which no longer form part of our strategic thrust, and the end of our disposal programme is now in sight.

The overall direction of UAC International has been reviewed and steps have already been taken to implement its agreed targets. Its profits have improved despite difficult trading conditions in many of its territories.

Although we cannot report a dramatic increase in results because of the effect of exchange rate movements, there has been real progress. Unilever is well placed to take advantage of the opportunities ahead. Our companies are more efficient than ever and are applying the most modern technologies. Our attention is clearly focused on businesses and markets in which we have a proven track record. But we are not complacent and will continue to improve our skills in all aspects of our business. We are resolved to increase the momentum of innovation and to bring our new products to the market place more quickly.

Sir Kenneth Durham
Chairman Unilever PLC
Vice-Chairman Unilever N.V.

F.A. Maljers
Chairman Unilever N.V.
Vice-Chairman Unilever PLC

Fig 14.2   The Chairmen's Foreword to the 1985 Report and Accounts of a major multinational company. What business objectives are implied in this Foreword?

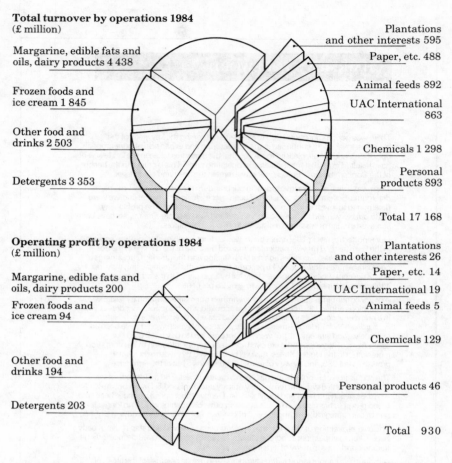

Fig 14.3   A pie chart (see Chapter 15) showing the operation of Unilever in 1984. Reproduced from *Unilever in 1984* by permission of Unilever plc

by the company and which enable it to conduct its business. They include land, buildings, plant and machinery. Fixed investments include shares and loans in other companies not legally owned by Unilever but which have very close connections with it. These investments are held on a long-term basis.

Current assets are those which are intended to be held only for a short time. The Unilever accounts show four main groups of current assets. These are: **stocks** (raw materials, to be used in production, work in progress, i.e. items in the course of being produced and finished goods and goods held for re-sale); **debtors** (payments due to be made by trade customers and others); **current investments** (shares and loans

CONSOLIDATED PROFIT AND LOSS ACCOUNTS

for the year ended 31st December

£ million

1983	1984	Combined (British and Dutch Organisations)
13 386	16 172	**Turnover** (1)
(9 036)	(11 029)	Cost of sales (2)
4 350	5 143	**Gross profit**
(1 973)	(2 542)	Distribution and selling costs (2)
(1 652)	(1 700)	Administrative expenses (2)
23	29	Other operating income
748	930	**Operating profit** (3)
60	70	Income from fixed investments (4)
111	111	Other interest receivable and similar income (5)
(150)	(186)	Interest payable and similar charges (6)
21	(5)	**Financial items**
769	925	**Profit on ordinary activities before taxation**
(353)	(388)	Taxation on profit on ordinary activities (7)
416	537	**Profit on ordinary activities after taxation**
(31)	(34)	Outside interests in group companies
385	503	**Profit on ordinary activities attributable to shareholders**
–	(26)	Extraordinary items (8)
385	477	**Profit after extraordinary items attributable to shareholders**
(3)	(4)	Preference dividends
(143)	(165)	Dividends on ordinary capital
239	308	**Profit of the year retained**
		Movements in profit retained
239	308	Profit of the year retained
(12)	(236)	Goodwill
29	76	Effect of exchange rate changes
(54)	93	Sterling/guilder realignment
202	241	Net additions to profit retained
2 683	2 885	Profit retained – 1st January
2 885	3 126	Profit retained – 31st December

Fig 14.4a   The profit and loss account of a large multinational group.
Reproduced from the Annual Accounts of Unilever 1984

CONSOLIDATED BALANCE SHEETS

as at 31st December
£ million

1983	1984	Combined (British and Dutch Organisations)
		Fixed assets
2 502	3 127	Tangible assets (9)
328	394	Fixed investments (10)
2 830	3 521	
		Current assets
2 087	2 784	Stocks (11)
1 878	2 266	Debtors (12)
393	450	Current investments (13)
540	666	Cash at bank and in hand (14)
4 898	6 166	
		Less:
		Creditors due within one year
458	1 038	Borrowings (15)
1 883	2 459	Trade and other creditors (16)
214	253	Taxation on profits
97	116	Dividends
2 246	2 300	**Net current assets**
5 076	5 821	**Total assets less current liabilities**
		Creditors due after more than one year
617	793	Borrowings (15)
47	46	Trade and other creditors (16)
49	60	Taxation on profits
		Provisions for liabilities and charges
569	710	Pensions and similar obligations (17)
498	617	Deferred taxation and other provisions (18)
–	–	Inter-group – N.V. / PLC
135	178	**Outside interests in group companies**
		Capital and reserves
164	162	Called up share capital (19)
21	21	Share premium account
91	108	Other reserves (20)
2 885	3 126	Profit retained (21)
3 161	3 417	
5 076	5 821	**Total capital employed**

Fig 14.4b   The balance sheet of a large multinational group. Reproduced from the Annual Accounts of Unilever 1984. These summary accounts are supplemented by more detailed notes as in Fig 14.5

NOTES TO THE CONSOLIDATED ACCOUNTS

£ million

Combined

1983	1984	
		(1) Turnover
		Analysis by geographical areas:
7 677	8 776	European Community countries
868	1 041	Other European countries
2 151	3 109	North America
365	439	Central and South America
940	1 016	Africa
1 385	1 791	Asia, Australia, New Zealand
13 386	**16 172**	
		Analysis by operations:
3 345	4 438	Margarine, other fats and oils, dairy products
3 596	4 348	Other foods
2 780	3 353	Detergents
722	893	Personal products
991	1 298	Chemicals
432	488	Paper, plastics, packaging
977	892	Animal feeds
813	863	UAC International
550	595	Plantations, transport and other
14 206	17 168	Total turnover
(820)	(996)	Less internal turnover
13 386	**16 172**	
		(2) Costs
(9 036)	**(11 029)**	Cost of sales
(1 973)	**(2 542)**	Distribution and selling costs
(1 652)	**(1 700)**	Administrative expenses
(12 661)	(15 271)	
		These comprise:
(2 052)	(2 269)	Remuneration of employees
(3)	(3)	Emoluments of Directors as managers
(260)	(249)	Unilever pension schemes
(95)	(111)	State pension costs
(176)	(199)	Other social security costs
(2)	(2)	Superannuation of Directors
(2 588)	(2 833)	Total staff costs
(7 184)	(9 003)	Raw materials and packaging
(297)	(338)	Depreciation
(63)	(72)	Hire of plant and machinery
(5)	(6)	Auditors' remuneration
(48)	(60)	Exceptional items (eg disposals and reorganisations)
(2 476)	(2 959)	Other costs
(12 661)	(15 271)	

Fig 14.5   Two of the notes which supplement the summary accounts of a large multinational group. See Fig 14.4. Reproduced from the Annual Accounts of Unilever 1984

stocks held for investment rather than for trade purposes and which can be sold at short notice without affecting the activities of the company; **cash at bank and held by the company**.

Another way to look at current assets is to see them either as cash or items which can be turned into cash in a short period of time.

Just as the company has assets which can quickly be turned into cash it also has obligations to make payments in the short term. These are termed **current liabilities**. Our company example shows four groups of current liabilities of payments to be made within one year. They are: **borrowings** including loans which were originally long term but which are now due to be repaid during the coming year; **trade and other creditors**, trade credit being the term usually used to describe the amounts due to be paid for items purchased on credit account terms; **taxation on profits**, most taxes being due on 1 January following the end of the company's financial year; **dividends**, i.e. the share (division) of profits due to be paid to the shareholders.

The Unilever accounts show the amount by which the current assets exceed the current liabilities as **net current assets**. Another term traditionally used for this net amount is **working capital**.

Some simple ratios and calculations based on these important elements in the published accounts are examined in Chapter 15.

Management and workers

The idea that employers should provide information for their employees is a relatively new one. Of course employees and their representatives can always obtain or inspect the company's published accounts. Some of the larger trade unions have made effective use of this right for bargaining purposes. In addition, however, there has been a growing feeling in recent years that employees who have invested a large part of their lives in working for an organisation should also have some legal rights in that organisation alongside those of the shareholders who have invested some of their money. The right to information is a necessary step towards any fuller recognition of worker rights.

The law now requires that employees should have access to certain information. In industrial premises, for example, an abstract of the Factories Act should be posted and the addresses of Safety Inspectors and a Medical Adviser must be displayed. There must also be notices of meal intervals and the clock used to determine these. In certain industries further information has to be displayed.

New workers must be given details of their employment contract as outlined later in this chapter.

Some senior managers, while accepting that reasonable safety and welfare standards must be maintained, may oppose measures to provide fuller information on the grounds that it threatens the management's right and duty to manage the enterprise in the interests of the shareholders who are still the legal owners of the company. Others, however, believe that more efforts should be made to disclose and discuss information with workers. They argue that:

a Many workers obtain some information in the course of their normal work but this is likely to be distorted in the absence of full facts and to lead to damaging rumours and speculation. It is better to have a formal system of disclosing information than to be subject to 'leaks' and rumours.

b Communication is a two-way process. If employees have a better understanding of company objectives and policies and of the problems the company faces they are more likely to be able to contribute information that leads to a better understanding of 'factory floor problems' on the part of management.

c Sharing information and a willingness to discuss problems and seek contributions can help to encourage co-operation and overcome damaging management–worker conflicts.

d Where workers share in bonus or other payments that depend on company profits and success in the market place then they have a clear right to information relating to the calculation of sales and profits figures.

At the same time there has to be proper recognition that the disclosure of some information would help competitors and damage the company. However, if the company has a good reputation about information disclosure, workers are more likely to preserve important secrets than they are when all information, however trivial, is regarded as being 'strictly confidential'.

Formal management–worker communication channels

Many firms have joint management–trade union committees often with sub-committees for specialist issues such as pensions, safety (where there is a legal requirement for employee participation under the 1974 Health and Safety at Work Act), or job evaluation (which determines pay scales for particular jobs). Sometimes there are separate committees for manual and for non-manual workers. Committees meet regularly and are usually chaired by senior managers. Worker representatives are usually selected through the normal trade union machinery.

In non-union firms similar committees are likely to exist with worker representatives elected according to agreed procedures. In such firms there may be even greater emphasis on worker–management communications precisely because the employers wish to keep out trade unions.

Large companies often have 'in-house' journals or even regular newspapers prepared by professional editorial staff. They contain contributions from employees, items of news and also market and sales information supplied by management. Such journals are intended to foster a feeling of belonging to a common organisation and to provide a channel for communicating management policies to workers. There is, however, a very thin line between conveying news and supplying propaganda and often only items favourable to management are included. The in-house journal is not normally seen as a method of airing criticisms of management or even of admitting to past managerial failures.

A number of companies have adopted a policy of circulating published accounts with illustrations and explanations to workers or their representatives as well as to shareholders. Sometimes these are discussed at joint management–trade union meetings.

A common problem in large companies is that experienced workers often develop short cuts in working practices and keep these to themselves in order to make their own lives easier. Managements would prefer a full disclosure of these changes. This is partly because they can cause problems which the individual worker does not appreciate unless they can be explained to him or her. For example, speeding up a machine can change the physical structure of metal parts and lead to later cracking. On the other hand a genuine improvement in a work practice can lead to considerable savings if it is more widely adopted. From time to time companies set up **suggestion schemes** which encourage worker disclosure of any ideas they may have to improve efficiency or reduce cost in return for a significant share of any financial savings that are made. Managers may also hope that the offer of a financial reward will stimulate new ideas.

These schemes seem to have a mixed response. Some companies report major savings from quite simple ideas. Others find that there is little to justify the administrative cost of the scheme. It could be argued that an efficient management that fostered continuous communications and was alive to conditions at every level of work does not need a suggestion scheme.

Some companies recognise that management in a changing world with changing technology requires continuous updating of skills and knowledge so that managers at all levels from supervisor to senior manager benefit from periodic exposure to training sessions. Quite apart from spreading knowledge of new technology and management techniques such sessions enable managers to take a fresh look at their own jobs, to meet others with similar problems but perhaps, with different attitudes and solutions and generally to re-awaken interest and stimulate fresh thinking. It is less common to give similar opportunities to workers below management grades.

Within any organisation there is always a need to convey routine information on such matters as holiday arrangements, safety precautions, canteen or other facilities. It is costly to circulate notes to all workers although this is sometimes necessary. Notice boards are usually required but, in time, become invisible because familiar and, if neglected, become so cluttered with out-of-date material that no one looks at them. Notice boards require thought and attention and some system of regular maintenance and revision – like any other system of communication.

New workers and information

Since the passing of the Contracts of Employment Act, 1963 employers have been under a legal obligation to make known to new employees the terms and conditions under which they are employed. Workers employed for at least 16 hours per week must be provided with a written statement of the main terms and conditions of their employment within 13 weeks of their employment. The statement should include details of pay, holidays, notice needed to terminate the contract and disciplinary procedures. Workers employed less than 16 hours but at least 8 hours per week must receive a similar statement within five years of employment.

In addition most employers wish to ensure that new workers are aware of company policy towards trade unions, their obligation, if any, to join a trade union or a particular trade union, or their rights not to join a union. New workers should also know their rights and obligations if they fall sick or have an accident at work. Any pensions rights and obligations should also be made known and the procedures to be followed if they wish the employer to deduct from their wages their trade union contributions, payments under a Save As You Earn scheme or any other agreed payment.

Most employers will be anxious to ensure that new workers fit into the general company way of doing things as quickly as possible. The employer will want them to feel that they are part of the company and have a degree of loyalty to it. There is thus a great deal to communicate in a short space of time.

Procedures for communicating this information to new workers vary with the size of the company. A small firm may simply give a typed letter to the new worker setting out the essential details of the employment contract such as period of notice required on either side for termination, amount and method of wage payment and, perhaps the procedure for reporting sick. In a very small firm the employer or a senior manager or long-serving worker will have a general talk about the firm and simply tell the new worker who to approach with any difficulties or questions. Large company procedures will be much more formal. The worker will probably be given a rule booklet setting out the kind of information outlined above and stating company policy and procedures on most of the matters likely to arise. There is also likely to be some kind of induction period operated by the personnel or training department. This will include talks by managers, possibly talks by senior shop stewards or union officials, and question and answer sessions, and the worker will be shown round the main parts of the factory and shown how his or her particular department or work-shop fits into the total pattern of production in the organisation. The larger the firm the more elaborate the induction process is likely to be. Some firms have films or videos showing the history of the company and its main activities. Some have printed notes giving similar information. A number do surprisingly little to make sure that new employees know something about the organisation they have joined.

Companies and the public

Most large companies are aware that they cannot avoid having a public image. It is, therefore, in their interests to pay attention to that image and try to ensure that it is as favourable as possible. This involves maintaining a public relations or similar department (e.g. external affairs). This will try to secure favourable publicity in the news media, to maintain contacts with government ministers, appropriate Members of Parliament and civil servants, and to negotiate and maintain contact with environmental and other pressure groups such as those concerned with sex and race equality. It will generally ensure that outside interests are aware of the company's viewpoint and activities and also that the company management is aware of how it may be affected by sensitive public issues.

This can be a most important aspect of communications for multi-national companies operating in many countries. Most companies were taken by surprise by the scale of the oil price rises of 1973–4 and by the Iranian revolution. They cannot afford many such surprises and most are now better organised to obtain early warning of events likely to affect world production and trade.

Routine communication and standardisation

It will be apparent by now that large companies regularly have to communicate a great deal of information both internally and externally. It is helpful in many ways to standardise the form in which

Typical company internal documentation flow.

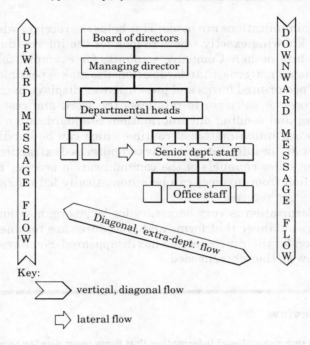

Key:

⊳ vertical, diagonal flow

⊳ lateral flow

Internal documentation flow in an inter-office context

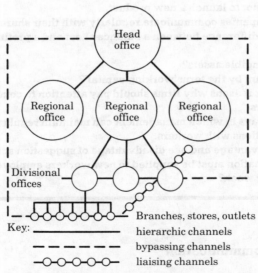

Fig 14.6 Typical communication channels for a large company. Reproduced from *People and Communication* by Desmond W Evans

these communications are made. This helps the receiver who then saves time by knowing exactly where to look for the information most relevant to him or her. Company accounts, for example, follow certain conventional patterns. Standardisation also makes possible the preparation of pre-printed forms and pre-formatted displays in computer and word processor software to minimise the work and cost involved in collecting and sending out information. Standardisation turns much of this work into a matter of routine which can be handled by semi-skilled staff – or fully automated by computerised extraction of information from other channels of the communication process. For example information from invoices can be automatically fed into stock control or accounting records.

Standardisation is very necessary for large organisations but there is always a danger that forms and procedures are retained long after the reason for their introduction has disappeared. Some system of regular review is, therefore, needed.

Rapid review

1 Give two examples of information that firms must display to meet the requirements of health and safety legislation.
2 List three kinds of information necessary to managers when they consider whether or not to launch a new product.
3 How do companies communicate regularly with their shareholders?
4 What is the difference between a balance sheet and a profit and loss account?
5 What are tangible assets?
6 What is meant by the term 'working capital'?
7 Suggest four reasons why firms should pay attention to communication with workers.
8 List three ways in which management can maintain regular communications with workers.
9 State one advantage and one disadvantage of suggestion schemes.
10 What information must be supplied to new workers employed for at least 16 hours per week?

Methods of communication

Most of these will become apparent during the development of this chapter but it is useful to summarise the main communication methods and to comment generally about their main advantages and difficulties.

Face-to-face meetings

Actually meeting people is still usually the most effective means of communication where ideas are to be exchanged, problems discussed and decisions made. In spite of all the advances in communications technology modern business managers spend far more time in meetings and conferences than did their predecessors. This is probably because of the increasing complexity of business and the constant need for co-ordination of different managerial specialisms in order to achieve almost anything.

The better the preparation, the more specific the issues to be discussed and the more efficiently the actual meeting is organised and controlled, the more likely it is to make successful decisions. The most dangerous meeting is the one that has no real purpose. A communication system that is based on regular meetings sometimes fails because there is not enough work to justify the number of meetings arranged. Discussion then becomes trivial. Senior members stop attending and the system collapses.

The advantages of any face-to-face meeting are immediate feedback, the stimulation of ideas and discussion and the general interaction of personalities. There is also the implication that having taken some trouble to attend the meeting the people involved consider it to be important. This is why information that is particularly important for an individual or which may be hurtful in some way should normally be conveyed by a face-to-face meeting. To inform an employee in writing that he or she is not being considered for promotion without giving that person a chance to discuss the situation is not likely to lead to good management–employee relations.

There are disadvantages to face-to-face communications. A dominant personality can stifle discussion and ideas. Personalities can clash and build communication barriers and meetings can be costly in time and travel costs. An attempt to give some of the benefits of meetings at less cost, the telephone services offer 'telephone conference' facilities. These can also be linked to video screens to provide 'confravision'. These techniques have their uses but can be frustrating and expensive.

The telephone

This is probably the most popular form of business communication. It is swift and there is immediate feedback. On the other hand it can be very expensive, especially when misused. Time can be wasted searching for people or passing from one office to another. Offence can be taken if the impression is given that the person requested is doing something else considered to be more important or if a long wait is experienced. Some managers seem to enjoy the expensive game of ensuring that the other person always has to wait for them. Some time is always taken in 'preliminary chat' and it is always dangerously easy to forget to take notes of calls and so to forget promises made. The lack of an automatic permanent record of the conversation is a major disadvantage and can lead to later disagreement and conflict.

Telephone use has become such a heavy cost for the large business organisation with many separate branches and offices that some very big companies are setting up their own closed systems for internal communications. British Telecom also now faces competition for the business of large-scale users from Mercury, a privately owned company.

Checklist for using the telephone

Knowing how to make and to receive telephone calls: greetings, identifications, message-taking, obtaining confirmation, providing feedback, closing the call, passing messages on.

Using the spoken voice effectively: articulation, clarity, warmth, friendliness, courtesy, charm, persuasiveness.

Employing telephone reception techniques: routing, filtering, message-taking, appointment-making, relaying information.

Planning telephone calls: organising the message, having supportive documents to hand, being aware of time and costs, synthesising essential information, ensuring the transmission and receipt of all required information.

Being fully conversant with the equipment and systems in use within the organisation: use of internal and external telephone directories, switchboard facilities etc.

(Reproduced from *People and Communication* by Desmond W Evans)

The teleprinter

Telex overcomes many of the shortcomings of the telephone while being as swift and often less expensive. It makes use of the national and international telephone networks to send signals which become written messages.

Modern teleprinters now combine the telex system with the services of electronic typewriting and word processing. Messages can be typed into the system's memory for transmission at a pre-set time more convenient for the receiver – an advantage in international communications when lines can become blocked at busy times or if advantage can be taken of differential charges. The machine can make several attempts to obtain a line and can transmit the same message to many different destinations.

Messages can be altered and checked before transmission in much the same way as on a word processor. The modern teleprinter is also quiet and attractive in appearance so that it is moving back to the heart of the office. The telex–teleprinter also provides a permanent written record for sender and receiver.

Electronic communication

The modern teleprinter, of course, relies on electronics and developments in electronic communication are taking place so rapidly that you need to keep constantly alert for new advances. Some of the more interesting developments involve the transmission of diagrams and photographs and links between computers so that information fed into or produced by one computer in one place can be transmitted to other computers elsewhere.

Most long-distance transmission systems, however, are dependent on the national and international telephone networks and as technology advances these are in danger of becoming overloaded. Communication satellites have expanded transmission capacities but these have not completely replaced cable, largely because of the time lags between signals over the very long distances involved in satellite communication. A mixture of satellite and cable is found to be necessary in many cases. Further developments are becoming necessary in the actual transmission of electric signals.

The electronic office

An important part of communication is the storage and retrieval of information. Sometimes this is called communication over time. An efficient information storage system must:

a   use as few resources of space, equipment and labour as possible;
b   enable information to be located quickly and easily;
c   provide easy and inexpensive methods of up-dating, amending and destroying stored information;
d   be simple to use;
e   be reliable, easy and inexpensive to service and maintain;
f   be accessible to all authorised users;
g   be secure from unauthorised use.

Convenience and versatility

Message preparation

Your telex messages are typed directly into Cheetah's electronic memory. Cheetah remembers the messages for as long as you want – an in-built battery protects the memory in the event of loss of power to the machine. Messages can be retrieved at the touch of a key for transmission or editing.

Text editing

Cheetah incorporates a word-processing facility which gives fast and efficient message editing. Letters, words or even whole lines can be deleted at the touch of a key, and new text inserted wherever you wish. Cheetah automatically closes up the text after deletions to prevent gaps, and moves letters from one line to the next to avoid word splitting at line ends.

Quiet operation

With the Cheetah, message transmission and reception is almost silent, and the printer is little noisier than a normal typewriter. Cheetah brings telex back to its rightful place, at the centre of the modern office.

Simultaneous functions

Cheetah can transmit or receive messages completely automatically, whilst the operator is preparing another message on the display. Incoming messages can be stored in Cheetah's memory until the printer is free, or the operator can give priority to the incoming message by pressing the Attend Call key.

Abbreviated calling codes

Up to 16 frequently called telex numbers can be stored in Cheetah's memory against single character codes. When a code is typed Cheetah automatically calls the number, saving time and avoiding mistakes.

Fig 14.7   The advantages claimed by British Telecom for one type of teleprinter

Automatic calling and clear-down

Cheetah can automatically transmit a message stored in its memory at a pre-set time. If the line is busy Cheetah normally makes up to 5 further attempts to get through – and it can transmit the same message to many different destinations. Cheetah will also clear manual calls automatically, freeing the operator for other tasks.

Fault finding

Cheetah is largely electronic in operation and has few moving parts. It is highly reliable and its central processor runs continual fault finding checks.

Keyboard, screen and printer

Cheetah's keyboard has a conventional typewriter layout, with colour coded function and control keys. It is electronically buffered, enabling it to keep up with the fastest typist. The non-glare screen is adjustable for angle and brightness, and the text display rolls smoothly up and down – there are no jerks and jumps to distract the eye. If permanent copies of messages are required Cheetah's printer will produce them clearly, quickly and quietly, and in A4 or A5 page sizes ready for filing.

Private circuit use

The Cheetah teleprinters 85 and 87 can be used on private telegraph circuits, either point to point or as a network terminal via message switchers. The teleprinters operate at speeds up to 60 characters per second in local and are offered with transmission speeds of 50, 75 or 100 baud when working to line.

Modern electronic technology enables firms to come closer to achieving these ideals than could any purely paper-based system. The automated office combines computing, microfilming (see Chapter 8), two-way links with other data sources and offices, printing and copying to enable information to be stored, amended, retrieved and distributed with an ease and economy of space and labour – and increasingly with financial savings – never before thought possible.

You should make every effort to see and handle for yourself as much modern equipment as possible and try to keep up with fast-moving developments. Figure 14.8 illustrates some of the services of an 'electronic

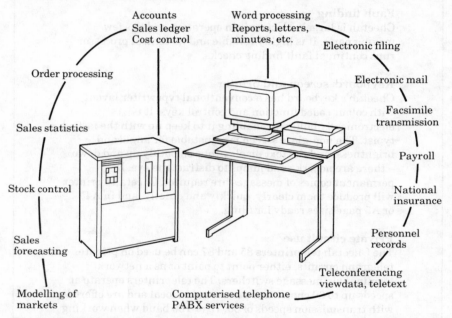

Fig 14.8   What does information technology do in the office? Adapted from *People and Communication* by Desmond W Evans

office'. Your should notice how many of the developments in computing, printing, copying and microfilming have made equipment simple to use with ordinary, familiar materials and brought machines out of specialised rooms into the heart of the working office. Managers who were terrified of 'banda machines' are quite happy to use a plain paper copier!

Paper-based communication

New technology rarely destroys old methods. Normally it modifies them and changes roles while opening up new opportunities and services.

We are unlikely to see a paperless office and, in fact, modern storage and copying techniques have given fresh life to paper-based communication. The word processor linked to a copier combines the advantages of the microchip and paper, as, of course, does the teleprinter.

Electronic communication has the advantage of speed but speed is not always essential and does not always justify its expense. It is also necessary to communicate with those who do not have advanced receiver technology. Business offices, therefore, still produce vast numbers of letters and internally circulated memos. The memo is less formal than the letter, does not contain addresses, salutations etc., and is usually produced on cheaper paper. Office customs vary between signing and initialling memos.

The great advantage of traditional paper communication is that it is a relatively cheap form of permanent record. The disadvantages stem from the ease of production as they are not always produced with sufficient care. Work is increased by inadequate preparation leading to the transmission of unclear or incomplete information. The message received is not always the same as the one intended to be given. A witty comment made on a Friday afternoon can look very different to the reader on a Monday morning and what is written and posted cannot easily be erased.

The business practice of sending dictated and typed letters and memos has also produced a sex-based class system in the business office with most letters dictated by men and typed by women. This form of class structure is changing and it will be interesting to see the effect of changing technology on the social structure of the office.

Rapid review

1 State one advantage of face-to-face communications.
2 State two reasons for the popularity of telephone communication in business and two problems likely to arise from encouraging the use of the telephone.
3 List three advantages of using teleprinters for business communications.
4 Explain the difference between a memo and a letter.
5 What is meant by the term 'automated office'?
6 State eight qualities desirable in an information storage (filing) system.

Barriers to communication

Many people have noted that improved communications technology does not always improve communications if by communication we mean the effective transfer of information from one person or group to another person or group. Television has not increased the mutual understanding between Americans and Russians, for example. Human attitudes and prejudices do not change as rapidly as electronic technology. Too much communication can leave people in as much ignorance as too little.

Increasing attention, therefore, is now being given to the management and use of communication or information technology. If the communication process is not better understood then advances in technology will cause more problems than they solve.

This is a very large subject and in this chapter we can only mention just a few of the issues affecting communications in business.

Distortion and bias

This can arise in many ways, quite apart from deliberate attempts to mislead. *Noise*, for instance, is a general term applied to any form of distraction that prevents the receiver of a communication from assimilating its message. A person may be talking on the telephone and be interrupted by a caller to the office with the result that neither is heard effectively.

The sheer weight of communications can produce a similar result. If twenty memos of instructions arrive together the receiver is unlikely to read any one thoroughly. The danger of the copying machine is evident! Word processors may have the effect of lengthening documents so that they are not read fully: if a document has to be retyped each time it is altered there is an incentive to remove unnecessary material. If new material can simply be inserted into the old document which is then printed automatically it is much more likely to grow longer at each revision.

Filtering is another form of unintentional distortion of information. As information passes from one person to another each is likely to omit anything that might be seen as putting the sender in an unfavourable light. The supervisor responsible for machine maintenance is likely to underestimate the number of breakdowns in case this is taken to be evidence of bad maintenance. Sales people will not report unfavourable reaction to a product which it is their job to sell. Subordinates may avoid reporting incidents that might be taken as reflecting badly on a superior. These may not be deliberate omissions. Most of us tend to put unpleasant things out of our minds but the result is that managers who have to take decisions make these decisions on the basis of inaccurate information. Badly designed machines are re-ordered. Resources are put into promoting products that are not going to be accepted by the market and so on. The human machine is the one whose technology has not changed over the centuries.

Threats from communication

The ease of recording and transmitting information poses new dangers. Data stored on one computer can quickly be made available for another. Lists of people who share a common interest, e.g. investment, or a sport, have a commercial value. For example, a person who orders a book on golf from a mail order company may then receive a letter advertising golf equipment. A computer list has been sold. This can be irritating but does no real harm. More dangerous is the transfer of information, often in an incomplete or distorted form, that governs the attitudes of government departments or important commercial services towards individuals or even families.

A person may refuse to pay a bill because of suspected overcharging or genuine misunderstanding. That person's name may be placed on a blacklist kept by a credit reference company and lead to future refusals of credit. A person's name may appear on a blacklist by error. There are many cases of similar names and initials as you can see from a telephone directory. The error may only be suspected years later when it can cause very great embarrassment or actual damage to a career.

Errors are much easier to spot on manual records. Experienced users often notice suspicious anomalies. Computers accept information without question and do not see anomalies they have not been programmed to see. People still have a dangerous faith in the accuracy of the printed word. It can be even more dangerous to believe that 'it must be right because it has come from the computer'.

This problem has been recognised. The Data Protection Act came into force in 1985 and gives people rights to inspect records and also sets limits and controls over the use of computer lists. As of May 1986 anyone storing personal information about other people in a databank has to be registered. However, it remains an area where continued vigilance is necessary. A great deal of harm and suffering may be caused before it is suspected that an error has been made.

Rapid review

1 What is meant by 'noise' in relation to communication?
2 How and why is communication 'filtered' in a business organisation?
3 What new dangers are associated with the development of electronic communication?

Exercises

1   Visit three local shops and write a report on each to show what is communicated by the appearance and stock display and the attitude of the staff.

2   You are asked to plan six training and education sessions to improve the standard of communications for the staff of a private vehicle sales, service and repair garage. Outline the topics you would include in each lesson and suggest the methods you would use to emphasise the importance of good communications to the success of the business.

3   Discuss the view that 'the better the communications between management and workers the better the relationship between workers and the public'.

4   Draw a diagram to show the lines of communication involved when a manufacturing company is considering whether to produce a new product.

5   Obtain a copy of the published reports and accounts of a public company whose shares are traded on the London Stock Exchange. List the information these provide on the following: employees; wages of employees; activities of the company; areas in which the company operates; number of shareholders and size of average shareholding; the capital of the company; profits and dividends. Has the information been presented in a helpful or a confusing way? Are the Report and Accounts difficult or easy to understand (e.g. are terms or technical words used without explanation)? If difficult, suggest ways in which they could be improved; if easy, list the techniques used to assist the reader.

6   Write to six former students of your school or college who have left in the past two years to start full-time employment and find out from them:

  a   what induction arrangements were made when they started work

  b   what written information they received regarding the terms and conditions of their employment.

To what extent have the employers carried out or exceeded their legal obligations?

7   Obtain a brochure describing a teleprinter. With its help describe the contribution of the teleprinter to business communications.

8   Discuss the view that 'the greater the efficiency of the communication techniques available, the more difficult the task of maintaining efficient communications'.

15 Statistical interpretation and presentation

Throughout this book much of the information has been given to you in the form of figures and diagrams. These have included tables of numbers, numerical examples and graphs of various types. In business, too, communication and presentation of information often uses numbers and diagrams in preference to words. Corporate plans, company reports, presentations to clients and so on, all present information in this way. Why?

The purpose is to present information clearly and concisely. A well prepared set of numbers or diagrams will often convey much more meaning than many paragraphs of words. A set of precise and clearly presented data also allows people to refer to what they are interested in and ignore what is irrelevant to them – whether this be stock market prices, football results or the weather forecast!

Numerical data, properly used, are less ambiguous than words. For example, 'The ABC Company has made a profit of £200 000, which is 42 per cent greater than last year,' is more precise than 'The ABC Company has shown a big increase in profits this year'. One reason for this is that words such as 'big' have only a relative rather than a precise meaning. One of the reasons for using standard forms of communication in business is to cut down on vagueness and ambiguity and reduce misunderstanding. The proper use of numbers helps to achieve this end.

A further advantage of presenting information in numerical form is that it allows us to work out such things as trends, forecasts and averages.

In this chapter we look at the use of diagrams and numbers in more detail. Throughout the chapter keep asking yourself such questions as:

'Do these numbers or diagrams convey a clearer or more precise meaning than words?'

'Can we extract further information from this presentation of the data, e.g. can we make comparisons or detect trends?'

and also, unfortunately:

'Is the information presented in this way at all misleading?'

Handling numbers

Averages

Everyone knows about averages. We talk about the 'average customer', 'average rainfall', 'an average programme', 'up to average', 'cricket averages' and so on. What is usually meant here is what is more accurately called the **arithmetic mean**.

The arithmetic mean is the sum total of all items in a series, divided by the number of items in the series.

Example 1 The temperature reached on the seven days of one week was as follows: (in °C) 23, 20, 19, 18, 25, 25, 24.

$$\text{Arithmetic mean} = \frac{23 + 20 + 19 + 18 + 25 + 25 + 24}{7} = \frac{154}{7} = 22°C$$

Example 2 The sales of a firm in the first three months of the year were as follows: month 1 £40 000; month 2 £48 000; month 3 £44 000

$$\text{Arithmetic mean} = \frac{£40\,000 + 48\,000 + 44\,000}{3} = \frac{£132\,000}{3} = £44\,000$$

In these two examples, the arithmetic mean has given a reasonable impression of 'typical' temperatures or sales, although you might have noticed that the average in Example 1 was a temperature which was not actually recorded on any one day of the week. But now look at Example 3.

Examples 3 A group of 17-year-old students is being taught by a 56-year-old teacher. There are 12 students. What is the arithmetic mean of the ages of all the people in the classroom?

$$\text{Arithmetic mean} = \frac{(17 \times 12) + 56}{13} = \frac{260}{13} = 20$$

So the 'average' is greater than the age of all but one of the people involved! In no sense can 20 be regarded as the 'typical' age of these people.

We need some other way of showing the 'average'. One such method is the **median**.

The median is the midpoint value of a series, ranked in size from smallest to largest.

Let us look at our previous examples again.

Example 1 (temperatures). Ranking the temperatures in size gives us:
 18 19 20 *23* 24 25 25
 Median temperature = 23°C

Example 2 (sales). Ranking as in Example 1:
 £40 000 *£44 000* £48 000
 Median sales = £44 000

Example 3 (ages)
 17 17 17 17 17 17 *17* 17 17 17 17 17 56
 Median age = 17

Clearly, in some cases the median may be very similar to the arithmetic mean, whereas in others it may be very different. In the latter case it will be found that some very high or very low values will be significantly affecting the arithmetic mean, as in the ages in Example 3. In these circumstances the median probably gives a better idea of the typical case. However, it must be said that the arithmetic mean itself has many advantages. One of these is that it lends itself much more readily to further numerical and algebraic manipulation than does the median.

You may have noticed that in all the examples we have used the total number of values in the series was an odd number. If it had been an even number there would, of course, be no midpoint but two items in the middle of the series. In such a case the median is the *arithmetic mean of the two items in the middle of the series*.

Example 4 Six employees earn wages (per week) of:
 £50 £80 *£90* *£100* £100 £180

$$\text{Median wage} = \frac{£90 + 100}{2} = £95$$

As an exercise work out the arithmetic mean of this series (the answer is given on page 284).

One further way of showing the 'typical' case is to find the observation which occurs most frequently. For example, suppose we need to know the frequency with which machines tend to break down so that we can budget for spares and maintenance. Out of 100 machines we may find that some never seem to break down, a few break down very frequently but most are out of action for two, three or four times a year. We can show this on a graph showing the distributions. This **distribution curve** is illustrated in Fig 15.1. You can see that the curve peaks at a frequency of three breakdowns. This figure of 3 is known as the **mode** of the distribution.

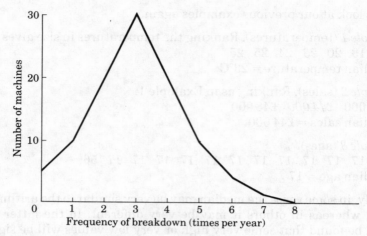

Fig 15.1   The distribution curve

The mode, or modal value, is the value of the most frequently occurring item in a series.

The mode is a useful way of comparing the typical figures in different series but can be misleading if the shapes of distribution curves being compared are very different as in Fig 15.2.

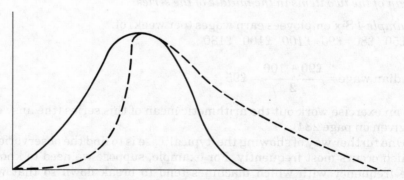

Fig 15.2   Distribution curves may have similar modes but very different shapes

Ideally we would only directly compare the modes of two series with exactly similar distributions. If we have rather different distributions then the mode can only be used with careful reservations.

Range and variations

The averages that we have just been looking at give only limited information about the series to which they refer. Often, as we have seen, this information can be misleading. Before we regard any average, whether mean, median or mode, as being a typical figure it would be useful to know how representative it really is. How much, for example, do other observations differ from the average? Look at the following example:

Example 5 Compare the following group with the class and teacher group of Example 3:

  Grandmother aged 60
  Children and their partners aged 36, 32, 30, 28, 22 and 17
  Grandchildren aged 11, 9, 7, 4, 3 and 1.

The arithmetic mean of this group is 20 and the median 17, just as in Example 3. The **dispersion** of ages, however, is clearly very different.

One way of showing this is by drawing the sort of distribution curve shown in Figs 15.1 and 15.2. This gives a good visual impression but unfortunately it would be rather unwieldy if every average had to be accompanied by a picture. We need to reduce the information to a single statistic.

Firstly we could simply give the **range** of observations.

The range is the difference in value between the highest and the lowest items

So, in our earlier examples:

Example 1 (temperatures)
Highest value 25°C, lowest 18°C   Range = 7°C

Example 2 (sales)
Highest value £48 000, lowest £40 000   Range = £8000

Example 3 (ages)
Highest value 56, lowest 17   Range = 39

Example 4 (wages)
Highest value £180, lowest £50   Range = £130

Example 5 (family)
Highest value 60, lowest 1   Range = 59

We would probably feel that in Examples 3 and 4 the ranges given are rather misleading. One or two items such as the age of 56 or the wage of £180, are so different from the other numbers that they are stretching the ranges.

An alternative is to obtain a measure of the extent to which individual items deviate from the arithmetic mean. We cannot simply add up all the deviations because, by definition, they would add up to zero. For instance, in the sales example the mean = £44 000 and the deviations are +£4000 and −£4000.

What we can do is to square all the deviations and total these. Squaring the deviations has two effects:

1 All the results will be positive (squaring a negative produces a positive).
2 The total will be affected strongly by the squares of large deviations but only slightly by the squares of the small ones.

From this result we can obtain the **variance** and **standard deviation**.

The variance is the total of the squared deviations divided by the total number of items in the series
The standard deviation is the square root of the variance

In *Example 1* (temperature), remembering that the arithmetic mean was 22°C.

Observations	Deviations	Squared deviations
23	+1	1
20	−2	4
19	−3	9
18	−4	16
25	+3	9
25	+3	9
24	+2	4
		52

Variance = $\dfrac{52}{7}$ = 7.43

Standard deviation = $\sqrt{7.43}$ = 2.43

In *Example 2* (sales) the arithmetic mean was £44 000.

Observations	Deviations	Squared deviations
£40 000	−£4000	£16 000 000
£44 000	0	0
£48 000	+£4000	£16 000 000
	Total	£32 000 000

Variance = $\dfrac{£32\,000\,000}{3}$ = £10 666 667

Standard deviation $= \sqrt{10\,666\,667} = £3266$

You should work out the variance and the standard deviation for examples 3, 4 and 5. The answers are given on page 284.

Ratios and percentages

When we discussed the mode a little earlier we talked about comparing the mode of one series of numbers with that of another. This reminds us that one of the main points of us using numbers is to be able to make precise comparisons between one piece of information and another. For example, how large is one number relative to another, or how much of a total is accounted for by a sub-group. One way of showing this is by the use of **ratios**.

A ratio is the relation of the size of one number to another and is usually found by dividing the larger by the smaller

Example 6 In the company referred to in Example 2 it is found that total sales for the quarter to trade customers are £99 000, and sales to private customers are £33 000. The ratio of trade to private sales is thus, £99 000:£33 000, or 3:1, found by dividing £99 000 by £33 000.

Example 7 Suppose that the same level of sales is maintained throughout the year so that total sales are £528 000. The average level of working capital over the period is £33 000. The ratio of sales to gross working capital (per year) is thus £528 000:£33 000, or 16:1, found by dividing £528 000 by £33 000.

Example 8 Suppose that the level of gross working capital (current assets) of the firm is, in fact, £33 000 when the balance sheet is drawn up while the level of current liabilities is £26 400. The ratio of current assets to current liabilities is thus £33 000:£26 400, or 1.25:1.

In all these examples you might ask, 'Is this good or bad? Is it high or low?' There is no answer to such questions unless we have some sort of standard or target to refer to. For example, other firms in the industry might be achieving a sales:working capital ratio of 20:1. If so then the result for Example 7 suggests that sales for this firm are rather sluggish, given the amount of capital the firm is using. The firm in this position can be said to be 'under-trading' on its working capital.

We shall be looking again at the interpretation of this type of ratio in the final sections of the chapter.

Another way of handling this kind of information is through **percentages**.

A percentage is a fraction expressed as a rate per hundred

Example 9 Look again at Example 6. Trade sales account for £99 000/£132 000 = 3/4 of all sales. As a percentage this is 3/4 × £100 = 75%. Similarly, private sales account for (£33 000/£132 000) × 100 = 25% of total sales.

A percentage is thus little more than a decimal fraction expressed another way. However, people often find it easier to appreciate what is meant by, for example, 40% rather than by 0.4 or two-fifths.

Rapid review

1 **List three kinds of averages.**
2 **Give each average for the following: 2, 4, 4, 6, 7, 8, 8, 9, 10, 11, 11, 11, 12, 18, 45, 74.**
3 **State what is meant by the variance and the standard deviation.**
4 **Which would you expect to have the smaller standard deviation – the figures of Question 2 or the following: 4, 6, 8, 9, 10, 10, 10, 11, 13, 13, 15, 16, 23, 28, 29, 35?**
5 **Check your answer to Question 4 by calculating the standard deviation for each set of figures.**
6 **Express the following ratios as percentages: 1:2, 1:3, 1:4, 1:5, 1:8, 1:12.5, 1:10.**

(Answers on page 284)

Presenting data visually

Pictures and diagrams are often the clearest and quickest way of conveying and receiving information. We have already used a type of **graph**, the distribution curve, earlier in this chapter and other types of diagrams have been used throughout the book.

One of the most valuable uses of diagrams is to allow us to make comparisons between figures, or to appreciate the relative sizes of different quantities. A business department responsible for ensuring that monthly supplies of certain products conformed to expected seasonal variations found that more accurate predictions could be made with the help of a large graph. A temporary attempt to remove the graph resulted in errors.

There is often a choice between different kinds of diagrams. When making a choice we need to make sure we use the method which:

a   Shows the relevant data and excludes the irrelevant
b   Highlights the most important information
c   Avoids unnecessary clutter

d Gives the best visual impressions of the message we are trying to convey

Some types of charts and diagrams

Pie graphs (pie charts)

These are an attractive way of showing how a total is divided into its constituent parts. For example, Fig 15.3 shows the proportions of the United Kingdom working population engaged in different types of work.

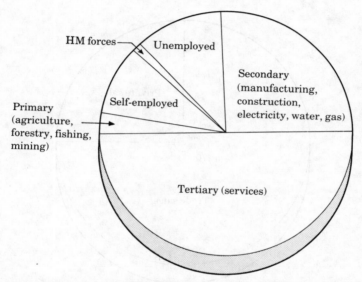

Fig 15.3   Distribution of the working population, UK 1984. Source: Monthly Digest of Statistics

Figure 15.3 gives an immediate visual impression of the importance of the service trades and the relative unimportance of primary industry as large scale sources of employment.

How is such a graph compiled?

Remember that a circle represents 360° so that half a circle is 180° (360 × 0.5), one-fifth of a circle by 72° (360 × 0.2), one-tenth by 36° (360 × 0.1) and so on.

Turn back to Example 6. Total sales are £132 000. Trade sales are £99 000 and private sales, £33 000. To show the proportion of sales going to trade customers, calculate 99 000/132 000 as a fraction and multiply this by 360°.

This gives:

$$\frac{99\,000}{132\,000} \times 360 = \frac{3}{4} \times 360 = 270°$$

Similarly the proportion going to private customers:

$$\frac{33\,000}{132\,000} \times 360 = 90°$$

We use these results to draw the angles at the centre of the pie graph to show the trade and private segments. This is shown in Fig 15.4.

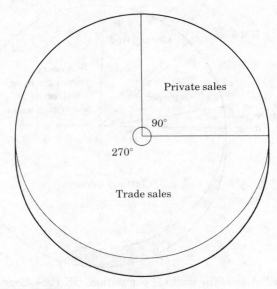

Fig 15.4   Sample pie chart

Bar charts

Bar charts can be used for much the same purpose. A bar chart is made up of vertical columns divided according to their components using the scale chosen for the vertical axis as shown in Fig 15.5 where the right hand bar represents the same information as the pie chart of Fig 15.4. The bars to the left represent the company's sales in total and by class of customer, for the same quarter in previous years. It is a merit of bar charts that changes over time in the composition of a total and in the total itself can be represented in the same diagram.

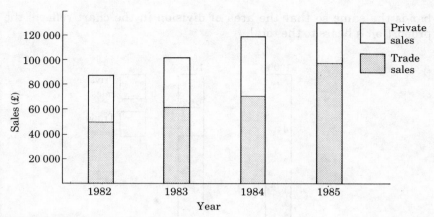

Fig 15.5   Sample bar chart

This chart illustrates the rise in the relative importance of trade sales
in a period when total sales were also rising.

If we wish to emphasise the change in composition and are not concerned with the change in total we can make each bar the same size
to represent 100 per cent and then divide the bars in the same proportions as the divisions in the data. We can do this simply by multiplying
the length of the bar we wish to use by the fraction formed when each
division is divided by the total. For example, using the sales figures
for 1982 and 1985 from Fig 15.5 and choosing a bar length of 10 cm
we calculate divisions of:

$$\frac{50\,000}{89\,000} \times 10\,\text{cm} = 5.6\,\text{cm for trade sales (1982)}$$

$$\frac{39\,000}{89\,000} \times 10\,\text{cm} = 4.4\,\text{cm for private sales (1982)}$$

   Total length = 10.0 cm

$$\frac{99\,000}{132\,000} \times 10\,\text{cm} = 7.5\,\text{cm for trade sales (1985)}$$

$$\frac{33\,000}{132\,000} \times 10\,\text{cm} = 2.5\,\text{cm for private sales (1985)}$$

   Total length = 10.0 cm

This is shown in Fig 15.6. This also shows the divisions in percentages
and the shift from private sales to trade sales is illustrated more accurately when the total change is omitted. Notice that the width of each

bar is the same so that the area of division in the chart reflects the proportion it bears to the total.

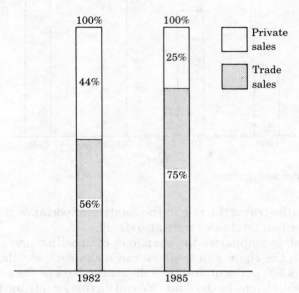

Fig 15.6   Sample bar chart

Frequency distribution curves and histograms

Look back at Fig 15.1. This showed the number of machines that tended to break down three times, four times and so on. The curve showed that the most frequently encountered number of breakdowns was three and 30 machines broke down this often. Only five never broke down and only one had as many as seven breakdowns.

This information might be clearer if we constructed a **histogram** from the data. Very much the same information would be plotted but we would now construct a series of columns to represent the number of machines experiencing each number of breakdowns. This is shown in Fig 15.7.

The histogram is the series of columns, the length and area of each showing the number of machines experiencing a given number of breakdowns. For comparison the original distribution curve of Fig 15.1 is shown as a broken line. You may consider the histogram gives a much clearer idea of the number of machines involved at each level of breakdown. In addition, the construction of a continuous curve may be thought to give a false impression if we try to read it like a graph.

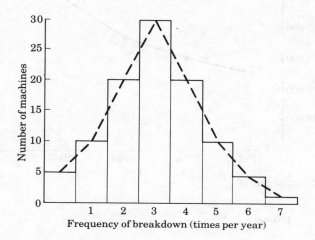

Fig 15.7   Sample histogram

For example it is simply not true that 15 machines break down 2.5 times each year, as might wrongly be inferred from Fig 15.1.

Graphs

Once again, we could show the information contained in Fig 15.5 in another way, this time in the form of one or more graphs in which the sales information is plotted against time.

When we are interested in two **variables** (data that varies in response to some definite influence), one of which is thought to be influenced by changes in the other, we term the first the **dependent** and the second the **independent** variable. We then measure the dependent variable vertically and the independent variable horizontally. Here, trade sales vary with time so the sales are measured vertically as shown in Fig 15.8.

Sometimes, in order to show changes more clearly still, we might omit some of the vertical axis and so amplify the changes. For example, we might omit most of the first £50 000 of sales from the vertical axis of Fig 15.8 and redraw it as in Fig 15.9.

The rise in trade sales is now made very clear.

However, there is a danger in redrawing graphs in this way. The change in trade sales shown in Fig 15.9 may be much clearer but it is also exaggerated and it may be misleading. This might simply be unfortunate but it could also be deliberate and with the intention to deceive.

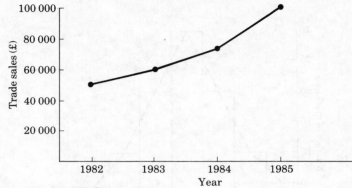

Fig 15.8   Sample graph

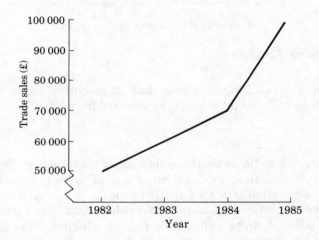

Fig 15.9

Rapid review

1   **List three considerations which should influence the choice of diagram to illustrate data.**
2   **List the main kinds of diagrams used to illustrate data.**
3   **Explain the terms 'dependent variable' and 'independent variable'.**

Misleading and deceptive presentation

We have just shown how graphs can be misleading. The same can be said of all other forms of statistical and pictorial presentation. This is unavoidable because they all simplify and reduce information so that in doing so it is possible that they omit something important and over-stress something of fairly trivial significance.

We have already pointed to some of the drawbacks of the different methods as we have gone along but let us look at a few more examples.

Averages

Newspapers sometimes quote figures supposedly showing 'average incomes'. In fact the majority of people earn less than the average (measured by the arithmetic mean). This is because the range of incomes has a minimum of zero but no maximum, and the average is increased by very large incomes earned by some industrialists, lawyers, pop stars and so on.

Ratios and percentages

These can sometimes be used to give a spurious impression, by selecting figures which really have no connection with each other. For example, 69 per cent of a company's sales might have been secured by bald-headed salesmen, but this statistic might or might not be totally meaningless.

Graphs

Graphs can be used to show relationships that might be totally meaningless. If we have two sets of numbers we can always draw a graph which seems to relate them. For example, suppose we find that, in the course of a week, the sales of some articles fluctuate. We also notice that some days are sunnier than others. We could then draw a graph, as Fig 15.10, relating sales to hours of sunshine. This may look impressive but of itself it proves nothing. The sales of some things, such as ice cream, might well be related to sunshine. The sales of others, say Do-It-Yourself goods, are less obviously connected although some relationship is a possibility. An apparent relationship might be much more to do with heavy sales at the weekend. If those days also have plenty of sunshine, we could get the kind of graph shown in Fig 15.10.

Pie graphs, bar charts and other devices

Figure 15.11 purports to show unemployment rates in different parts of the United Kingdom. The height of the figure in each area depicts the relative size of unemployment. This gives a good visual impression

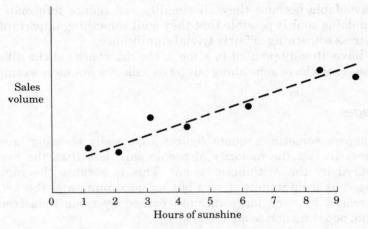

Fig 15.10   Notice that this graph has been constructed as a 'line of best fit'. This means it is a line drawn through all the observations in a way that minimises the scatter of actual observations away from the graph

and makes it easy to measure the differences, if this is what is wanted. But in fact there is a subtle exaggeration. A figure that has twice the height also has twice the width and thus four times the area. The figure is thus not twice but four times the size and conveys a hidden message about disparities in unemployment rates that is not really true.

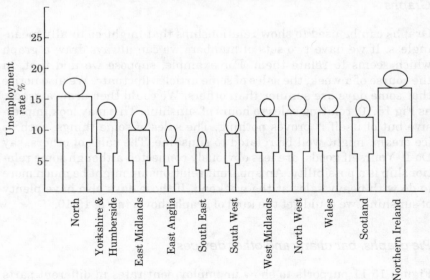

Fig 15.11   Unemployment rates in regions of the UK, May 1985. Source: *Monthly Digest of Statistics*

This effect has to be watched for whenever devices such as pie graphs or bar charts are being presented in order to ensure that what is apparently being done for visual effect is not conveying an extra, distorted meaning.

Rapid review

1 Why would it be misleading to say that the sets of figures in Rapid review Questions 2 and 4 (p. 272) were similar because they both had 'averages' of 15?
2 How can a simple graph be made to exaggerate a movement in a variable?
3 Why do figure diagrams sometimes convey a distorted meaning?

Presenting and using accounts

Some accounting concepts

Few of us are accountants or bookkeepers and this is not an accountancy text book. To many people the terms and methods used by accountants are a mystery which they fear they cannot understand. However, many of these are really derived from one or two straightforward and logical ideas.

Firstly you have to realise that *accountancy and bookkeeping are fundamentally exercises in keeping records*. Their primary function is literally to 'keep account' of things. They help to show where the output of firms comes from and where the inputs into the firm went. In money terms, this means where the firm earned its income and what its costs were.

A second fundamental idea is that *nothing comes from nothing*. Any money earned means that something has been sold, and vice versa. Any money spent should mean that something has been bought, and again vice versa. This is the basis of what is called 'double entry bookkeeping'. Every transaction is entered in the accounts twice. For example, the purchase of raw materials leads to a reduction in the firm's cash and an equivalent addition to the firm's stocks of raw materials. The sale of goods means a reduction in the stock of goods and an addition to its cash.

A third point is that the firm's affairs can be looked at either *at a single moment in time* or *over a period*. To follow this point imagine making a list of all the things you own, or are owed at this precise time. Accountants would refer to these as your **assets**. You might think of them as your *wealth*. Of course, you may also owe money to other people. These obligations to make payments to others are your **liabilities** and you can also list these at this particular time. In the next week you may earn some more money – your **income** – and also spend more – your **expenditure**. You could summarise these items of income and expenditure into an account showing your financial activities for the week, and then once again list your assets and liabilities at the end of the week, again at a particular time.

Let us see how these ideas are applied to the accounts of a firm.

Bodgit's Ltd is a small jobbing building firm in which Mr and Mrs Arthur Bodgit are the only two shareholders. Together they put up £1000 in cash to start the business. At the start of trading on 1 January 1985, the *balance sheet*, the statement of assets and liabilities of Bodgit's, looked like this:

	Assets		*Liabilities*
	£		£
Cash	1000	Owners' interest	1000

The first point to notice here is that the firm already has liabilities equal to its assets. How can this be? The logic is clear. If the firm has assets worth £1000 then somebody must have a claim on these assets. In this case the owners of the firm have this claim. A balance sheet must, literally, balance. All the assets must be accounted for by a claim by somebody.

In the course of a month, Bodgit's Ltd carries out a number of transactions and does work for several customers. Jobs worth £3000 are carried out and half of these are paid for in cash before the end of the month. A second-hand truck is bought for a cash payment of £600. Materials worth £500 are obtained on credit and £300 worth of these materials are used. Mr and Mrs Bodgit draw £1000 in wages.

How do we summarise this information?

The accountant will separate the purchase of materials which will be used up in the course of doing the work from the purchase of an asset such as the truck which, it is hoped, will be used during the course of a large number of jobs. In addition, the accountant will attempt to relate the income earned from jobs in the month to the direct costs of doing the work. This information will be shown in the *trading and profit and loss account* as follows:

	£		£
Sales	3000	*Cost of sales*	
		Labour	1000
		Materials	300
		Profit	1700
	3000		3000

Notice that once again the two sides balance. In this case they are brought into balance by the profit. Had payments by the firm (costs) been greater than money received then the difference to make the two sides balance would have been a *loss*.

The balancing profit appears again when we draw up the next balance sheet showing the total of assets and liabilities as at the 1 February – a precise date again.

Assets	£	Liabilities	£
Cash	900	Current (short-term) creditors (for materials)	500
Materials	200	Owners' interest (shares)	1000
Debtors	1500		
Truck	600	Accumulated profit	1700
	3200		3200

Points to notice include:

a The owners are separated from the firm they own. In legal terms the firm is considered to be a completely separate entity.

b Accumulated profit appears as a liability because it is owed to the owners of the firm.

c The profit and the amount of cash held are two different issues. Here, the profit is £1700 but the actual cash in the firm is only £900. This is because the firm owes and is owed money.

d Debtors appear as a major asset and creditors as a liability.

e It is usual to distinguish between assets and liabilities which are *current*, that is due for payment, or to be turned into cash in the near future, and those that are *fixed*, which are not. Cash, materials and debtors are current assets. Trade creditors are current liabilities. The difference between the two is known as the firm's *working capital*.

Analysing the accounts

As Bodgit's continues to trade the accounts will become more complicated but the same basic, careful, principles will apply. For example, plant or buildings may be obtained by credit. It is normally thought to be prudent to distinguish between short-term creditors and debtors of the type shown in our simple balance sheet, from long-term creditors and debtors. This is because it is important for the firm to know what money can be expected to be paid to the firm in the near future and also what debts have to be repaid soon. This is an area where **accountancy ratios** may well be used, for example, to compare current assets with current liabilities. Unless the ratio of current assets to current liabilities is comfortably greater than 1:1 there is a danger that the firm will get into trouble through being unable to meet immediate cash demands on it.

Another key ratio is the amount of capital in the firm represented by share capital, or accumulated profit, compared with the amount borrowed from outsiders (the debt:equity or **gearing ratio**). Too high a ratio of debt to equity can again spell danger for the firm. All of its efforts may go to meeting interest charges on debt, leaving nothing for profit.

Again we can compare the **volume of sales** with the firm's working capital. The ratio we would expect will differ according to the type of industry. In food retailing, stock will turn over much faster than in car or jewellery trading. However, relative to the type of industry in question, too high a ratio of sales:working capital can be dangerous. This is called **overtrading** and the firm may simply not be able to support this level of business in the future. Quite simply, without more liquid assets it might, for example, be unable to purchase stock. Too low a ratio, **undertrading**, is just inefficient and represents a waste as it probably means that productive assets are lying idle.

You can see that even a simple set of accounts can be analysed to reveal important information about how a firm earns its money and how stable it is. They can show how much the firm is really worth to its owners. You should now obtain a copy of the published accounts and report of a major company and see if you can work out these ratios.

Rapid review

1 What is meant by 'double entry bookkeeping'?
2 Why must a firm's total liabilities always equal its total assets?
3 List two important accountancy ratios that can be calculated from the balance sheet.

Answers to example exercises
Example 3. The variance is 108 and the standard deviation is 10.39.
Example 4. The arithmetic mean is 100, the variance 1566.7 and the standard deviation 39.58.
Example 5. The variance is 265.7 and the standard deviation 16.3.
Answers to Rapid review questions
Question 2. Arithmetic mean = 15, median = 9.5, mode = 11.
Question 5. The standard deviation for question 2 = 17.96 and for question 4 it is 8.72.

Question 6. 50%, 33.33%, 25%, 20%, 12.5%, 8%, 10%.

Calculating trends

This section covers a rather more difficult mathematical concept and some students may prefer not to attempt it at this stage of the course.

It is often useful in business to be able to work out a **trend** from information you already have in order to be able to predict what is likely to happen in the future. A trend represents a tendency for events to follow a particular pattern. Using trends to make predictions about the future assumes that certain tendencies that have occurred in the past will be repeated to some degree in the future.

It is really well beyond the scope of this book to explain fully how trends are calculated and some of the difficulties and pitfalls to look out for. If you wish to take this topic further you should consult a good textbook in statistics such as *Statistics for Business* by P & G Whitehead, published by Pitman Publishing Ltd in 1984.

We briefly explain here a standard technique for calculating trends and then point out some of the points that you should take into account.

Calculation

Look at the following table of information.

Michael & Angelo Decorators (M.A.D.) have been placing advertisements in the local newspaper. The advertisements differ in size up to a maximum of six lines. The firm has kept a record of the number of enquiries it has received in different weeks and is now attempting to see if the number of enquiries is **correlated** to the length of advertisements. If we say that they are correlated we mean that a change in the value of one is likely to affect the other. The records show:

Number of advertisement lines	Number of enquiries
1	5
2	8
3	7
4	11
5	16
6	13

We can plot this on a **scatter diagram** as shown in Fig 15.12 to see

Profit

The simplest definition of profit is *the difference between revenue and costs.*
However, there are several different practical definitions of profit. They
are different because they serve different purposes. Take this example.

Chippie Dale runs a small made-to-measure bedroom furniture business.
He employs two workers at £150 per week each (wages and employer's
national insurance payments). He rents an office/workshop at £30 per week
and has a van, machinery and tools, total value £10 000, which need replacing,
on average, about every 5 years. Each job costs about £100 in materials and
is priced at around £400. One job keeps one worker busy for a week.

Profit Measure 1: Gross Profit

To calculate this we deduct from revenue the costs directly incurred in earning
it. These costs are normally reckoned as materials and direct labour. So,
for each job we have:

	£	£	£
Sales			400
Less cost of sales:			
materials		100	
labour		150	
		———	
		250	
Gross profit		150	

£150 for each job! Mr Dale must be a rich man! But we have so far ignored
all the costs which are incurred indirectly. What these have in common is
that they are normally incurred whether or not sales are being made, or
at least they are not easily attributable to any one job.

Profit Measure 2: Net Profit

To calculate this we deduct from the gross profit all the other costs. Let
us do this for a trading period of one week

Costs	£	£		£
			Gross Profit (2 jobs)	300
Rent	30			
Rates	5			
Depreciation	40			
Telephone	5			
Heat & light	5			
Petrol	10			
Other motor vehicle				
(insurance, repairs etc.)	20			
Postage	2			
Sundries	13			
	—			
		130		
Net profit		170		
		—		—
		300		300

At £170 per week, Mr Dale's net profit is little more than the wages he pays his workers and you can calculate for yourself what would happen if he only sold one job in a week rather than two. How could he improve his position? Should he raise his prices? Should he employ more workers and attempt to obtain more jobs? Consider for yourself these possible courses of action.

Also consider the possibility that a customer for a made-to-measure piece of furniture might disappear before taking delivery and before making payment. Mr Dale is left with some furniture but it will not be made-to-measure for anyone else. As scrap the materials are worth only £40.

A friend offers him £100 for the furniture. Should he take this offer?

If you work through the figures you will see that his would leave him with a gross profit of zero and a net loss of £130 per week. Should he reject the offer on the grounds that 'it will lose him money'?

The key test in this situation is to compare revenues with *avoidable costs*. The only avoidable cost here, now that the work has actually been done, is £40, the scrap value of the furniture. If they are the only costs then accepting the revenue represents a profit of £60.

Can all these different measures of profit be correct? Yes, because they are used for different purposes.

The gross profit figure shows how much *contribution* our trading activities made towards covering overheads and towards our final net profit.

Our net profit figure shows whether total revenues have been sufficient to cover total costs and, if so, by how much.

Our final calculation is a device for business decision making. It is always worthwhile asking, 'What is the alternative? If we do something else will we make more or less profit?'

if there appears to be any relationship. As you can see there does seem to be some relationship. It would be useful if we could work out a trend here. This might help us to predict the number of enquiries that would be received in response to, say, a 10- or a 15-line advertisement. We could try to draw such a trend line through the scatter diagram by eye, that is to say to use our judgement as to the trend line which seems to be present. You might try this before reading further.

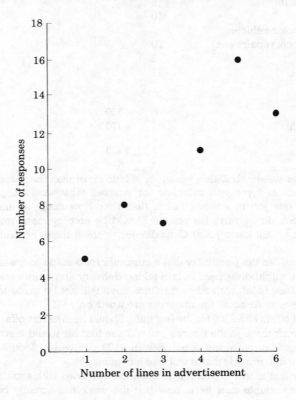

Fig 15.12

Alternatively, we can use statistical techniques. Here we will try to fit a *linear regression line*. This is a 'line of best fit', i.e. the line through the scatter diagram which minimises the total distance between each point and the line. This line has the following features:

a It is represented by a straight line.

b For each value of one variable, such as the number of lines, it will give as accurate a prediction as possible of the actual value of the other. By 'as accurate as possible' we mean that we try to minimise the total amount by which the actual values deviate from predictions. In actual practice we minimise the sum of the *squares* of the deviations. This is so that negative deviations are not simply cancelled out by positive ones. If we square the deviations the squares of negative as well as positive deviations are positive.

c It will pass through the *mean* of the whole scatter diagram.

The equation of the graph we are trying to draw may be given as:
$$y - \bar{y} = \beta(x - \bar{x})$$
where y = the number of responses

    x = the number of lines

    $\bar{y}$ = the arithmetic mean of the variable y

    $\bar{x}$ = the arithmetic mean of the variable x

the formula for $\beta = \dfrac{\frac{1}{n}\Sigma(x-\bar{x})(y-\bar{y})}{\text{variance of } x}$

The top line of this formula is called the **covariance** of x and y. This is the measure of the extent to which changes in one variable are associated with variations in another. If the covariance is small there is little correlation.

Remembering that x represents the number of lines and y the number of responses we can set out all the figures we need for the calculation as follows:

The arithmetic mean of x $(\bar{x})$ = 3.5
The arithmetic mean of y $(\bar{y})$ = 10

x	y	$x - \bar{x}$	$y - \bar{y}$	$(x-\bar{x})(y-\bar{y})$	$(x-\bar{x})^2$
1	5	-2.5	-5	12.5	6.25
2	8	-1.5	-2	3.0	2.25
3	7	-0.5	-3	1.5	0.25
4	11	0.5	1	0.5	0.25
5	16	1.5	6	9.0	2.25
6	13	2.5	3	7.5	6.25
				$\Sigma(x-\bar{x})(y-\bar{y}) = 34.0$	$\Sigma(x-\bar{x})^2 = 17.5$

We can then calculate

$$\beta = \frac{\frac{1}{6} \times 34}{\frac{1}{6} \times 17.5}$$

$$= 1.9429$$

So we can draw our trend line as the graph of the equation
$$y - 10 = 1.9429\,(x - 3.5)$$

rearranging this we have
$$y = 3.1998 + 1.9429x \qquad \text{from which we derive Fig 15.13}$$

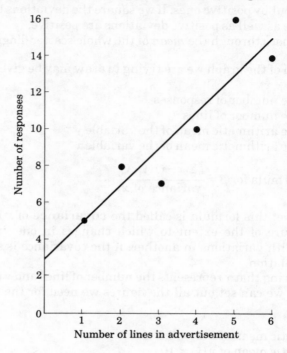

Fig 15.13

An easy-to-use computer program which does these calculations for you is available in the *Introduction to Microeconomics Software Package* by Dave Blight and Tony Shafto (Tutor Software). The program operates on Apple and BBC microcomputers.

We now extend, i.e. *extrapolate* this trend line to read off, for example, how many responses we would expect from a 10-line advertisement (about 23) or how many lines we would need to give us an expected response of 30 (about 14).

Problems and pitfalls

As with any other statistical technique, plotting trends using linear regression analysis has its problems. You should be aware of some of these, even if you do not become familiar with the way they are calculated. Very often people in business are confronted by trends of this kind calculated by computers. It is important to know what to make of these and not to be overawed by such techniques. You should be aware that:

1 It is *always* possible to draw a 'line of best fit' through any scatter diagram even if there is no real correlation. Regression analysis is usually backed up by tests to check if the results are **significant**.
2 There are more complex ways of drawing curved or other non-linear lines of best fit. These might be better representations of the real trend.
3 You should note that even if two or more variables do turn out to be significantly correlated you should be careful how you show this. Does x cause y or y cause x? For example, in the M.A.D. case, responses and size of advertisement are correlated but logically it would be advertisements causing responses and not the other way round. However, we could have done all the calculations regressing advertisements on responses rather than the other way round and get just as good results.

Just as with all the other techniques described in this chapter, regression analysis is only a tool and is no substitute for the application of judgment and common sense.

Exercises

1 The table on page 292 gives details of visible imports and exports into and out of the United Kingdom for the years 1972 and 1982. Draw pie charts to show the changing composition of imports and exports over those years. Comment on the changes.
2 You are considering advertising on local radio. A market research agency tells you that the average listener in your town listens to 1 hour 10 minutes of radio each day. How useful is this information? Set out the sort of statistical information you really want from an audience survey.
3 You are a mail order company offering cuckoo clocks that you buy for cash for £4 each and sell for £8 each. Your advertising, which is obtained on credit, costs you £10 000 per week. Post and package costs per clock are £1.50. Other costs, such as office overheads, are not affected by the volume of sales and average £1000 per week. The only significant item of capital 'tied up' in the business is your stock of clocks which averages 20 000. Average weekly sales are 5000.
    a Calculate, for an ordinary week, your gross and net profits and ratios relating these and your turnover to working capital.
    b Sales may and do fluctuate. Construct a chart showing how your profit figures are affected by a range of sales from zero to 20 000 per week.
4 Choose an appropriate method of statistical representation to illustrate the difference in manufacturing employment in the following countries:

Canada	17.5	Italy	24.7	USA	19.8
Netherlands	20.3	Japan	24.5	Norway	18.2
West Germany	32.5	United Kingdom	24.5		

These figures represent percentages of the country's civilian employment.

Value of UK visible exports (f.o.b.) (£ million)

	1972		1982	
Total	9 602.3	(100.0)	56 538.4	(100.0)
0. Food	346	(3.6)	2 497	(4.4)
1. Beverages and tobacco	314	(3.3)	1 451	(2.6)
2. Crude materials	291	(3.0)	1 295	(2.3)
3. Mineral fuels etc.	242	(2.5)	11 193	(19.8)
4. Animal and vegetable oils etc.	11	(0.1)	47	(0.1)
5. Chemicals etc.	951	(9.9)	6 119	(10.8)
6. Manufacturers classified by material	2 192	(22.8)	7 941	(14.0)
7. Machinery and transport equipment	4 090	(42.6)	18 098	(32.0)
8. Miscellaneous manufactures	881	(9.2)	5 158	(9.1)
Manufactures, 5–8	8 114	(84.5)	37 316	(66.0)
9. Others	285	(3.0)	1 740	(3.1)

Value of UK visible imports (c.i.f.) (£ million)

	1972		1982	
Total	11 072.9	(100.0)	56 940.3	(100.0)
0. Food	2 101	(19.0)	6 414	(11.3)
1. Beverages and tobacco	255	(2.3)	837	(1.5)
2. Crude materials	1 253	(11.3)	3 613	(6.3)
3. Mineral fuels etc.	1 247	(11.3)	7 401	(13.0)
4. Animal and vegetable oils etc.	89	(0.8)	317	(0.6)
5. Chemicals etc.	631	(5.7)	4 181	(7.3)
6. Manufacturers classified by material	2 197	(19.8)	9 861	(17.3)
7. Machinery and transport equipment	2 287	(20.7)	16 358	(28.7)
8. Miscellaneous manufactures	868	(7.8)	6 683	(11.7)
Manufactures, 5–8	5 983	(54.0)	37 083	(65.1)
9. Others	145	(1.3)	1 275	(2.2)

(Figures in brackets indicated percentage of the total)
Source: *Annual Abstract of Statistics*

16 Information processing and technology

Business records

The need for records

This book has shown how the business organisation is constantly communicating and interacting with a wide range of other organisations and people. This is a continuous process. Today, for example, I might place an order with a firm for some goods in response to a price quotation I obtained last week. I shall expect the goods to be delivered to me next week and to pay for them at the end of the month. If I am not satisfied with the goods I shall need to be able to refer to this precise transaction in order to make a complaint. For its part the firm must ensure that the goods that I ordered are in stock and are sent to me and that I pay the correct price.

This is just a simple transaction but it serves to illustrate how many communications take place over a period of time and form part of a continuous series. For the whole process to take place smoothly both I and the firm need to keep a record of each stage of the transaction and to keep it in such a form and way that it is available for reference at each successive stage.

If we again make use of our example of the clothing firm we can identify some of the main types of records that it will need to keep. They are likely to include details of:

a Materials ordered and the terms under which they have been ordered including prices and expected dates of delivery.
b Stocks of materials and equipment held, when purchased, their cost and any maintenance programmes.
c Orders received, prices and terms agreed for orders and dates promised for delivery.
d Present and past customers and their history of purchases and payments.
e Full- and part-time workers, their rates of pay, tax deducted and code, national insurance and pension contributions, history of sickness and absence and any special details such as qualifications, skills and so on.
f Trade union links, agreements made with unions, continuing negotiations etc.

g List of shareholders, transactions of shareholders' meetings, dividend payments.

This list is by no means complete. The firm, for example should keep records of the legal requirements relating to working conditions, dismissals, redundancies and so on. If it imports or exports it will need to have records of the procedures it must follow and the forms it must complete and licences it must obtain.

In fact each department or division of the firm must have its own records. The details in our list relate to such areas of management as purchasing, marketing, production, personnel, finance and company secretarial or administration.

Requirements for a record system

A business record is an account of a communication, transaction, event or series of communications, transactions or events of relevance to the business organisation so that it must exist in some form whereby it can be referred to, as required, in the future by those properly authorised to do so. At the same time many records are confidential to the individual business or to sections of the business so that access should not be possible for those who do not have any legitimate purpose with them. The requirements for an effective business record system are, therefore:

a It must be capable of being kept *without deterioration* for as long as it is likely to be needed by the organisation.
b It must be capable of being located and referred to speedily and simply so that it has to be stored in a systematic manner comprehensible to whoever is likely to need to have legitimate access to it.
c Bearing in mind that all business activities use resources which are then not available for other purposes the setting up and maintenance of the system should make the least possible use of resources subject to any special needs of the business.
d The records should not be accessible to those who do not have any legitimate purpose in referring to them. Confidential personnel records, for example, should not be available to any but senior and trusted staff. Many firms have technical or market information which is valuable to them and would be even more valuable to a competitor, so that security can be an important aspect of the system.
e The record, or selected details from the record, should be capable of being communicated to those needing the information wherever they may be. The ability to transmit information can be an important

aspect for the large organisation operating in many different locations.

f As people often wish to refer to selected parts of a record it is desirable to be able to abstract desired information from a record or set of records.

Record systems

We must first recognise that most firms operate at least two parallel record systems. These are:

1 A system for current and continuing transactions.

2 A system for what may be called dormant or sleeping records, those records not currently required but which may be needed at some time in the future.

At the same time there should be some organised system for ensuring that records are transferred from system 1 to 2 when they are no longer current. Similarly it should be possible to transfer records from 2 to 1 when necessary and if this means a complete physical transfer some record should be retained in the main system that the transfer has taken place.

Although much of the literature on record systems is concerned with permanent records and firms often devote substantial resources to these, in practice it is frequently the case that the greatest problems occur with current systems – or too often the lack of adequate systems. Anyone who has been kept hanging on to a telephone for a long and expensive period only to be told eventually that no one can deal with the query because 'we can't find the file' will realise the amount of wasted time and labour caused by inadequate current record systems.

Another way to classify record systems is by the material on which they are based. Accordingly we would identify paper, film and computerised methods. Often we find some mixture of these methods. For example, current records may be entirely paper based and on transfer to the permanent or 'sleeping' system selected information is retained on microfilm.

Paper records

Paper-based recording has a number of advantages.

a The record is easy to set up and is often formed from the documents actually employed in the transaction, e.g. the proposals form used to apply for insurance can become the main reference record for a customer's current file. The term 'file' is used to describe a set of documents or papers all relating to a particular subject such as a customer or item of equipment. The file will (or should) contain copies of all written communications and notes of verbal communications relating to its subject.

b   Paper records are easy to read and do not necessitate the use of any special equipment.

c   Provided it is kept out of sunlight paper can be kept for long periods without serious deterioration. Business historians are sometimes delighted to discover chests of business records several hundred years old and still easily readable.

d   Paper can easily be transported and is relatively cheap to send by post. Today it is very easy to duplicate by photographic means.

On the other hand handling paper can be time-consuming and postal transfer is often too slow for the needs of modern business. The traditional way to transfer records from the current to the permanent system was to retain a single card abstract of the main information in a readily accessible location, often with an additional index, while the main file record was physically stored in a separate location. Such systems can still be found in some small commercial offices but they are unsuitable for modern large-scale business because they require a great deal of expensive manual labour, are very subject to human errors and use up a great deal of expensive space. City-centre business offices cannot afford to pay thousands of pounds in rent simply to store paper.

Early attempts to streamline paper recording made use of punched cards. These made it possible for machines to sort, locate and select cards. However, expensive equipment was needed to translate printed information into punched holes and back into printed form. Mechanical punched card systems were expensive in space, labour and capital (machines). They were only useful when employed on a larger scale and have now been replaced by computerised methods.

Film-based records

Microfilming was first used to eliminate the expensive storage of paper files and records. The attraction for firms was that full records could be retained in a small fraction of the space formerly occupied by the old paper system. It was, however, expensive and time-consuming to make the film and sometimes difficulties were encountered in locating records on films.

Modern electronic technology has brought the microfilm into the ordinary office and it is becoming an everyday aid to daily office work. The office worker, using a microfilmer, can convert ordinary paper documents into microfilm which can be stored as a roll, cartridge or microfiche as desired. Some systems are linked to computers to produce an index of the stored film for retention on the floppy disks as used in microcomputers. This combination of microfilming and microcomputer enables the user to locate and view any desired record very quickly and easily.

Microfilmed records can be viewed on a screen or can be quickly printed on paper. In fact the modern system combines microfilming, microcomputing, and photographic duplicating/printing to produce an integrated recording service which is simple to use and maintain and relatively cheap to use once the necessary equipment has been obtained.

Fig 16.1 outlines one integrated system of the type described.

Computer systems

Modern business computers are of three main types: mainframe, mini and micro. Business record systems can be based on any one of these or on a mixture of two or all three.

Mainframe is the term often given to a large, high-capacity machine, staffed and programmed by specialists and processing information fed to it through terminals situated at suitable locations in the organisation and linked to the main computer by telephone or cable.

A micro- or desk computer will probably be familiar to you as there are very few educational establishments in Britain without one or more of these. The computer itself will probably have a typewriter-style keyboard, capacity dependent on the chips with which it is fitted, a familiar visual display unit (VDU) or screen, and be linked to one or more printers. Some developments seek to replace the keyboard with other ways to feed the computer with data or to give it instructions. The aim is to produce inexpensive and simple ways of direct reading of printed, typed or written matter and for instructions to be given by voice or by touching the screen. Laser scanners will read specially prepared information in forms such as the bar codes on retail labels but it would clearly be a great advantage to have simple, cheap and reliable methods of reading ordinary paper material without any special preparation.

The term minicomputer is often given to one that is larger and more powerful than a desktop micro but which does not have the capacity and range of the mainframe.

Large organisations sometimes have systems which make use of micros to fulfil many local tasks and provide facilities for local office routines and word processing. The micros are then linked to the main computer network to provide it with the information needed for the main organisational records.

Any computer is as useful and as flexible as the software (the programs or sets of programs) needed to operate it. Most computer manufacturers supply standard software packages to carry out most of the

Canon CAR System

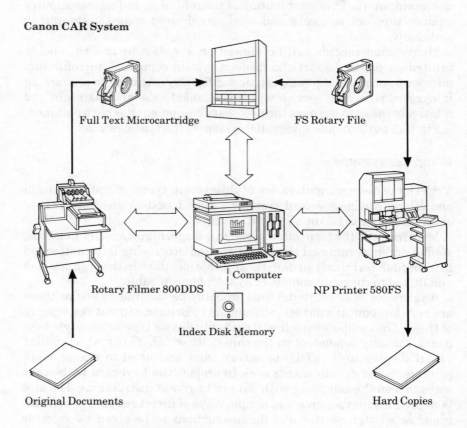

Full Text Microcartridge

FS Rotary File

Rotary Filmer 800DDS

Computer

NP Printer 580FS

Index Disk Memory

Original Documents

Hard Copies

FOR ELECTRONIC FILING SYSTEM — COMPUTER ASSISTED RETRIEVAL —

In this system, full information is stored in compact microfilm cartridges, while the computer data file maintains an index of the microimages.

Assigned to each page or file to extract data, is a film address consisting of cross-referenced keywords together with the cartridge number and page/file number. This address data is simply keyed into the desktop computer to make a random-access index for future reference. The floppy disk is used as an extendible data memory.

In data search for reference, first enter the keyword corresponding to the desired information, into the desktop computer. The computer searches its data file and displays the requested film address on the CRT monitor to locate the film cartridge.

Place the selected film cartridge in NP Printer 580FS, select print mode, and press start key on the computer. Then, NP580FS locates documents on film and delivers prints as required.

Fig 16.1   An integrated recording service. Reproduced courtesy of Canon Inc.

recording and administrative tasks normal in business offices but these are often not suitable for the individual firm. Preparation of individually designed software is a skilled and expensive operation and there is not an oversupply of software engineers with the necessary programming and business skills to prepare these. Look at the claim made for a computer based stock control system illustrated. To install such a system requires a detailed knowledge of business organisation as well as the capabilities of computers.

The more flexible and adaptable the software package the more difficult it often is to operate. A typical business management package allows the operator to design individual records which can then be used for several purposes such as addressing labels, preparation of invoices, keeping customer and staff records and so on. Once prepared the records are stored on floppy or hard disks and individual records can quickly be located and amended. Selected information from records can also be obtained and printed. The user of such a package has to be quite highly skilled and possess qualities of intelligence, initiative, care and accuracy beyond the normal requirements of the old type desk clerk or secretary. The computer is changing the nature of office work. There are fewer people in the modern office but those who are there are doing demanding and interesting work which is a world away from the ledger keeping of forty years ago.

The advantages of a computer-based record system are:

a Once installed and operating the system is less expensive to operate than a manual or mechanical system because it uses less labour and space.
b Access can be gained to selected records very quickly and selected information can be obtained quickly in visual or printed form without calling on typists.
c Information can quickly and easily be transferred from one location to another and from one set of records to another.
d There is often no need to make any distinction between current and 'sleeping' records as access can quickly be gained to information kept on hand on disks.
e Computer held information can very quickly be converted into paper form for such purposes as invoices, accounts or reminder letters by computers linked to printers and/or copiers.
f People can often be trained to use the system without any difficulty even when preparation of the actual records is more complex so that managers and others who only need to refer to records can do so without calling on other staff for assistance.
g Records can be quickly amended and so kept up-to-date with relatively little trouble or expense.

Fast response to customer needs

A customer calls to check a promised ship date, or to price a new order, or to change an order, or to question an invoice.

With the System/36, you can have answers easily available because, with System/36 and online applications, your files are up-to-date, complete, accurate and easy to retrieve.

From display stations, you can quickly add new data, change data, delete data. Mistakes can be identified and corrected as the information is entered.

Data can go directly from keyboard to computer data base. Once there, it can be made available at any display station. With online application support, a few key-strokes and the customer request is answered on the display screen – while the customer is still on the phone.

Having data at your fingertips helps build good will ... and sales. It can also build profits by helping to reduce the cost of responding to customers.

Manage inventory more effectively

By making inventory item information available online at System/36 display stations, you can give a new meaning to inventory management. Your system can help you:

- Monitor item movement
- Plan special promotions
- Evaluate item profitability
- Reduce overall inventory level
- Monitor customer service
- Check vendor performance
- Take advantage of discounts, freight allowances, special pricing
- Simulate new inventory policies and forecast results before taking action.

Forecasting tomorrow's demand

In distribution, past performance guides future planning.

The IBM System/36 can help you keep sales figures and daily operating information current and make them quickly available at work stations.

For planning and forecasting functions, the information you and your staff need is in the computer – and can be easily displayed or printed on demand. As a result, it's easier to spot trends as they develop or to change stocking plans in response to changes in customer demand.

Electronically, you can analyse your inventory more thoroughly and simulate alternate buying strategies.

And the system helps you respond quickly to the future as it evolves. So you can be in better control tomorrow, as well as today.

(Courtesy of Canon Inc.)

The advantages claimed for one computerised record system

On the other hand some of these advantages hold possible dangers for the business. Systems operate only as long as the computers themselves are in operation. Those relying on mainframes operated by a few key staff are very vulnerable to industrial action or sabotage from these staff. Micro systems are usually less centralised and vulnerable but computer breakdowns or damage to software can cause problems. It is desirable to keep back-up data disks but all disk held information is vulnerable to magnetic interference or to natural disasters such as fire.

Some firms that have installed computer systems fear the consequences of system failure so much that they continue to keep parallel manual records. This seems to defeat most of the objectives of setting up computer based systems.

The accessibility and transferability of computer held information gives opportunities for criminals and computer based crime has exploded in recent years. Elaborate security measures tend to destroy some of the most valued benefits of the system.

However, computer technology is changing and developing so fast that this is one topic where it is essential to obtain up-to-date information.

Rapid review

1 List five kinds of record you would expect to be kept by most companies.
2 List the requirements for an efficient record system.
3 List four advantages of a paper-based record system.
4 What is microfilm and what are its advantages to a business firm?
5 What qualities would you expect from an 'integrated recording service'?
6 What is a microcomputer?
7 What is the difference between software and hardware in computing?
8 List seven advantages of a computer-based record system.
9 What is a 'back-up' computer disk?

Electronic publishing

Electronic publishing is a general term for a range of information services linking business and the consumer.

Teletext

The main teletext services in the United Kingdom are Ceefax for BBC 1 and 2 and Oracle for ITV and Channel 4. Teletext is defined as the transmission of pages of text and drawings alongside the normal television programmes. The service is free at the time of use but receivers have to be capable of receiving the transmissions. Users call up the information page desired by pressing the appropriate number on the remote-control keypad.

For the business organisation the teletext services provide a further means of transmitting information directly into the home. It supplements the other advertising and business communication media. It is also a means of ensuring that up-to-date information is transmitted on a whole range of subjects.

Prestel

This service is operated by British Telecom and makes use of the telephone network to provide what is claimed to be 'fast, low-cost and flexible two-way communication'. It can also be used as an internal communication system for a business organisation.

The user requests information through a telephone dialling link or by computer linked to the telephone and the information is relayed to a television screen or computer VDU.

Whereas the teletext services provide one-way information, Prestel enables the user to send messages and make use of many of the services on offer. For example, hotel rooms and air tickets may be booked and some areas are developing home shopping services. A limited form of electronic mail service is provided for private and business users.

For business firms Prestel can be more than yet another advertising and market-information link with potential consumers. Firms can use it as an information channel within the organisation and it may also be used as a means of linking company computers in different locations. Much of the published information available in local reference libraries can be obtained through Prestel at a saving in time and trouble.

This is another area of constant development and you should ensure that you have the latest available information on current services and ways in which the business firm can benefit from them.

Electronic shopping

A full electronic shopping service enables the householder to obtain details of goods and services on a television receiver or computer VDU and to order and pay for selected items by using a keyboard or computer. Such services are developing in some of the more populated areas of the country and a growing number of retailers are co-operating in their development. In most cases British Telecom's Prestel provides the essential two-way electronic communication channel required for the service. Future growth may be associated closely with extensions of cable TV services.

As with the other electronic services you need to find out and keep up to date with developments in your own area.

Rapid review

1 List the main teletext services available in the UK.
2 State one advantage of teletext for business marketing.
3 What is Prestel?

Exercises

1 Prepare a set of records for the members of your class showing their names, addresses, subjects being studied, sporting achievements and interests, and other achievements (e.g. Duke of Edinburgh Awards). In what order would you keep the records for ease of reference? How could you mark the records to locate, for example, those with similar sporting interests or those studying a particular subject? If possible, obtain details of a microcomputer software system that could be used to maintain records such as these.
2 Choose six text books currently used by your class and note their ISBN numbers. With the help of your school, college or a local library write a report explaining the ISBN number system and how it is used by libraries.
3 Some recording systems are alphabetical; some are based on numbers. Suggest two advantages and two disadvantages of each system.
4 Explain the use and benefits of microfilming to the modern office and describe the equipment likely to be involved in a modern office system.
5 Discuss as fully as possible the advantages and dangers of a computer-based record system in business.
6 Describe one teletext or one computer shopping system. Identify two groups of people for whom you think your chosen system is particularly useful.

17 Business in a changing world

Facing the inevitability of change

The certainty of change

The future will be different from today.

All of us, and all business enterprises, exist in a world of change and change that is uncertain. We cannot be sure of the way things will be in a year or in ten years' time. However, although we cannot be sure of the way things will be, there is one thing about which we can be sure – they will be different. This in itself can be a valuable piece of knowledge. Look at these two examples: In the early 1970s there was a 'property boom' in Britain. For many years 'bricks and mortar' have been regarded as a sound investment in the United Kingdom, more so than in many other countries, but in the early 1970s property prices began to rise very rapidly. In late 1973 the property 'bubble' burst. Prices stabilised and fell and many individuals and firms were ruined.

With the wisdom of hindsight it is obvious that property prices could not continue rising as they had been doing, otherwise everybody would have jumped on the speculation bandwagon. Everybody would have become rich and nobody would have had to work for a living ever again. Sooner or later prices had to level off. The shrewd saw this and took precautions even if they were unsure as to when the boom would break or why.

In the 1960s a major inquiry (the Roskill Commission) was held into the siting of a third airport for London. Among the evidence it commissioned was a forecast of demand for air transport in the future. By projecting the growth in air traffic then taking place, astonishing figures were obtained for the number of flights being undertaken by people in the twenty-first century. The Commission's researchers decided that these were absurd and introduced arbitrary limits into their forecasts. They were unsure what would cause the trend to change but they were fairly certain that the change would come. In the event air traffic was hit by the steep rises in the cost of aviation fuel in the 1970s.

In both these examples the important point was in seeing that something was going to happen even if it was unclear what or when. This can be a key element in a firm's corporate strategy and planning.

Strategies for change

There are two distinct ways a firm can prepare itself for coping with the uncertainty of the future. It can be:

Adaptable. This is a passive way of meeting change but it still requires careful planning. For example, the organisation should not be inflexible and rigidly bureaucratic. There may be an insistence on capital investment having a pay-back period of a very few years. Staff may be recruited as much for their personal attributes of adaptability as for their specialist expertise.

Itself the agent of change. This is an active response. Realising that change must come, the firm seeks to create this change, or at least shape it in a way favourable to itself. The firm emphasises research and development and extensive market research. Aggressive and sustained marketing campaigns are undertaken. There is likely to be a strong central planning team and an ambitious corporate plan with clear targets.

Rapid review

1 **Suggest two strategies for a firm facing a changing future.**

Types of change

The changes that a business will have to contend with can take a number of forms.

Market changes

The strength of demand is likely to change, as is the variety of goods and services demanded.

Some of these changes and their causes can be clearly foreseen. For example, the strength of demand for many goods is linked to customers' incomes. As incomes rise so more of most goods will be demanded. The increase in demand for some goods, e.g. consumer durable goods such as television, will be very rapid. For others, e.g. food, it will be slow – people are unlikely to eat twice as much bread if their incomes suddenly double. For most services, the demand is likely to rise rapidly as incomes rise. This is one reason why more and more people in developed countries are engaged in service trades.

For a few goods and services demand may actually fall as incomes rise. Economists call these 'inferior goods'. The demand for potatoes and for bus travel has behaved in this way in the past. Can you suggest why? Margarine used to be quoted as an example of an inferior good on the supposition that, as people's incomes rose, they would buy butter instead. However, skilful marketing strategies of the type mentioned earlier in the book, especially trading on images of health and slimness, have helped to create a market for 'high quality' margarine.

It can also be expected that demand will be affected by price and if you can predict price changes, then demand changes may also be predictable. For example, you may know that the cost of a raw material input such as oil is likely to rise in the long run. This will affect the price you will be able to charge, so, if customers are able to turn to lower-priced substitutes, demand is likely to level off or fall. The opposite, of course, may be true if advances in technology promise to make your product cheaper, although we have to bear in mind that technology may also be affecting the prices of substitutes.

When it comes to the variety of goods and services demanded, predictions of trends may appear more difficult. However, some analysis is possible. For example, there are now so many video machines in British homes that the scope for rapid expansion in this market is now over for the United Kingdom. Most of the demand in the future will be for new machines to replace existing ones, in contrast to earlier demand which was based on first-time buying. If improved machines are available, video owners and renters may be tempted to replace their video with a better quality product. This may be a more profitable product strategy than, for example, producing much the same machines as now but at a cheaper price, which would appeal to people without a video at present but would not appeal to the replacement market.

In addition it is possible, to some extent, to 'see the future today'. By this we mean the possibility that what is happening in one country, such as the USA, today, may be repeated in other countries in the future, especially as incomes rise there. This has fundamentally affected the corporate strategies of many firms. They may start by producing goods only for their home market, then begin to export in a small way to other countries. As the overseas market becomes established they may then aim for full multinational status with complete foreign production and marketing facilities.

Besides income and prices, the other major factor influencing demand is consumer taste. Changing tastes and fashions may completely alter a market and this may be thought of as one of the most unpredictable areas of change. Once again, however, a firm may adopt an active strategy to cope with this. Recognising that tastes are inevitably going to change the firm may, through its advertising and marketing, seek to influence the nature of the change in taste that is going to take place.

Changes in tastes may have far-reaching effects on the demand for apparently unrelated products. For example, the 'video boom' that we have mentioned has been suggested as a reason for the stagnation of the market for beer in the UK since about 1978. Customers appear to have expressed a preference for home entertainment to the public house. Remember, however, that in Chapter 1 we saw that it was sensible for a firm to ask itself the questions, 'What is our product? What are we really selling?' A firm in the 1970s which gave the answer 'leisure goods' rather than 'beer' would have been much more alert to the threats and opportunities offered by a major new competing substitute.

Changes in methods of production

As so many of the future changes in methods of production will be the result of new inventions and processes this may be thought of as an area which, by definition, is almost impossible to predict. If we knew what these processes and inventions were going to be they would no longer be innovations! However, we can, once more, make some fairly confident predictions about the nature and effects of these changes.

In the first place many of these innovations may already be in use in other countries or in other industries. We can already study the impact of the widespread application of robots in Japan. We remarked in an earlier chapter that the genius of Henry Ford lay not in the invention of a new technique, the assembly line, but in applying it to motor vehicle manufacture. A similar revolution at the time of writing is in the production of British national daily newspapers with the application of production methods already used elsewhere in printing and publishing.

Moreover, some fairly confident predictions can be made about the direction of change in various types of cost. For example, the long-term trend in the cost of energy and of raw materials appears likely to be upwards, as increasing demand interacts with limited supply. On the other hand, the whole point of innovation has been, and will continue to be, the reduction in other costs of production. The threat of possible scarcity in oil-based energy may well provoke innovations in other energy sources.

Finally, the trend in technology for at least a century or more has been to find ways of substituting capital for labour (replacing people with machines) and in so doing to make production more capital intensive, i.e. to increase the amount of machinery used in relation to the number of people employed. This has important implications for the amount of production that can be obtained for any given size of labour force and it also tends to make production methods rather more rigid as expensive machines are not always easy to adapt.

It is worth noting that technological advance need not always mean replacing people with machines. The reverse could also take place if cost conditions were to change so that production could be achieved at less cost if fewer machines and more people were employed. The Romans showed little interest in labour-saving devices, not because they were unimaginative but because slave labour was abundant and cheap.

Given the normal predictions, however, firms may well make plans on the basis that for years and decades to come they will be employing production methods that economise on raw materials and labour, are more automated, employ fewer but more highly skilled people than now, and which produce goods at lower costs and prices than they do today. Those plans will imply that *today* firms will be engaged in research and development orientated towards energy and material saving, automation and the recruitment and training of skilled workers.

It is worthwhile re-reading the last sentence and noticing the stress placed on what firms are likely to be doing *today*. The purpose of planning is often misunderstood. It should be emphasised again that when we plan it is not so that we can know exactly what we are going to be doing in the future. This is not only pointless, it is impossible, as none of us can predict or plan the future with any certainty. The object of planning is to alert us as to what we have to do *now* to be in a position to cope with the future. This applies to production planning, market planning, personnel planning and indeed any other form of planning.

In particular industries we can be more specific about the likely effects of technology. For example, in continuous process industries and bulk material production it is likely that the impact of technical economies of scale will continue to mean reorganisation into larger production units. Simple engineering effects point in this direction. In steel production for example, the replacement of the open hearth by the basic oxygen process increased the economic size of plant tenfold, in fact from an annual output of 300 000 tons to around 3 million tons. However, in many industries where past organisational economies of scale have produced large production organisations, the later electronic revolution of microcomputers and the like, have meant that smaller units have become feasible once more. The printing industry is an example. Another effect of microelectronics and robotics is the probable continuation of the rapid disappearance, not just of unskilled manual labour but also of some of the older established skills. The nature of the workforce is thus likely to change. We shall look at this trend again later in the chapter.

Change in social attitudes

Both demand and the methods of production can be affected by changes in social attitudes. For example, the market for some goods may be significantly affected by such changes. The sales of cigarettes have been reduced by adverse publicity concerning the health risks of smoking, by the anti-smoking campaigns and the restrictions on advertising and on smoking in public places that have followed. Changes in social attitudes resulting from a variety of causes have led to declining attendances at cinemas and at football matches.

Methods of production may have to change in response to social changes. For example, health and safety regulations may make it impossible to use some types of machinery or materials (e.g. asbestos, which was found to endanger health). Hours of work may have to change. There may be new requirements or regulations relating to the employment of women or young people. Worker participation may involve some degree of worker involvement in, or control over, decision making and this may extend to production methods and the products produced.

Social attitudes may appear to be among the most difficult things to predict but it is not impossible to make some forecasts nor to influence these to some extent.

Predictions can be made, once again, on the basis of what has happened elsewhere. For example, the interest in 'consumerism' in the UK followed in the wake of similar developments in the USA. At the time of writing, there are suggestions from Japan that traditional attitudes towards work and superiors may be changing. Since these attitudes have been the basis of so much Japanese management practice it is not difficult to imagine the implications for business organisation if this is true. Even if it is not we might forecast with some confidence that the exposure of Japanese young people to Western influences through television, radio and the press is likely to affect rather more than just taste in clothes and music.

Attempts to influence attitudes can take a number of forms. In the fashion industries, of course, strenuous efforts are made to create as well as to encourage trends. Other changes in social attitudes may be the result of pressure groups, e.g. the environmental or the consumerist groups. Firms put considerable expense and effort into either encouraging or resisting such groups, often with the use of pressure groups of their own. These groups can employ advertising campaigns, provide information and spokespeople for the media (press, television etc.) and can lobby politicians.

Changes in education

All of the previous sources of change might have their roots in educational changes. An increase in the general level of education of the public is likely to change attitudes, incomes and patterns of demand. People are likely to be capable of better standards of work but to be more demanding in terms of income and working conditions.

The effects of these changes are likely both to put more demands on firms and also to offer them more opportunities. All firms are affected by these changes whether they realise it or not. For example, educational opportunities for 16-year-olds are much greater than they were 25 years ago. A bright 16-year-old who would have left school at that age in 1960 is now much more likely to remain in full-time education for another two years, five years or even longer. Yet some firms complain that the standard of 16-year-olds they can recruit now is, on average, lower than that of two decades ago. Demands for educational standards for such people to be raised would simply backfire on firms such as these. Better educated 16-year-olds will either stay in education or make greater demands on the firms.

Rapid review

1 How might firms in the UK 'see the future today'?
2 List two influences on the demand for a consumer product that can be estimated for the future.
3 What kinds of future change in production methods can be predicted today?
4 State two ways in which changes in social attitudes can affect business firms.

The electronic revolution

One of the greatest sources of change lies in the micro-electronic revolution of the 1970s and 80s.

In the early 1960s computers were a rarity in business outside the very large companies. They cost many thousands of pounds, filled special air-conditioned rooms and were supported by expensive specialist staff. The first pocket calculators appeared around 1972 and cost around £100 (about £400 in 1985 values). If you ever see the 1966 futuristic science fiction film 'Fantastic Voyage' you can watch for the scene where a crucial calculation is worked out on a slide rule as though to emphasise the scientific nature of the proceedings.

Today, computers more powerful than the giants of the early 1960s sit on desk tops and cost a few hundred pounds. Computers, word processors and calculators are commonplace in factories, offices, schools, homes and among supermarket shoppers. This revolution has had several striking effects.

First, and most obviously, it has made it possible to do more work, or to do the same work *faster and more efficiently*. Computerised filing systems can hold much more information, be more accurate and up to date and be referred to much more quickly than conventional ones. Standard business letters can be prepared by word processors. There can be automated control of and feedback on, production processes.

Secondly and perhaps more significantly in the long run, there has been a complete *transformation of the production possibilities* in some industries. A large number of small printing firms, for instance, owe their existence to computerised methods. In retailing, bills can be accurately totalled by the automatic reading by laser of coded tags on goods (a long-run possibility is the automatic direct debiting of customers' bank accounts at the same time). In many industries old skills are being displaced by new ones. There is a personnel management problem here which is not simply a matter of coping with employees whose skills are no longer needed. Even those with the new skills can now appreciate that the pace of technological change is such that they might find themselves in a similar position in the future and consequently be concerned or even nervous about their own prospects.

Thirdly, complex *new industries and products* have come into existence. The obvious examples include the new hardware and software industries. Others include computer games, computerised electronic systems for cars, house security systems and specialised extensions of the telephone system. So far we can suspect that the long-term effects of such changes have hardly been felt. An example of what could happen can be seen in the experience of the toy industry in the 1970s. An enormous range of electronic toys entered the market and some major firms, which had continued to concentrate on traditional strong selling lines, experienced problems that, in some cases, led to their failure. Other firms in other industries may have much to learn from this warning.

Information overload

One effect of this revolution that can easily be overlooked is the danger of becoming overloaded with information. The capacity of management information systems for presenting data to decision makers is effectively infinite in comparison with the capacity of managers to absorb it. This situation was developing even before the electronic revolution. To understand the problem, imagine the dilemma facing a conscientious student who is given the task of preparing a project on a particular topic. In the reference library the student is confronted with a large number of books all related to the topic – too many for all to be read and understood. The information system is well thought out with careful cataloguing and reference numbering of the sources, but the more sources there are the more difficult the task becomes. In business the problem is even more complex because the information available for one decision might actually relate to another problem area not immediately under consideration but which will be affected by any decision taken.

Management scientists and software specialists, aware of these problems, have become conscious of the fact that management information systems are not sufficient on their own. In addition, there is a need for a **decision support system** which will automatically organise information, present it in usable form and alert decision makers to consequences elsewhere in the system.

This revolution also has its implications for the relationship between the head office and the branches of the business company or between the upper and the lower levels of management. Theoretically all information can be passed from lower to higher or more central parts of the organisation. It has been suggested in the recent past that the local management of branches of American multinationals in the United Kingdom have access to less information about what is going on in their own plants than is available to the central management in America. This is because information is channelled direct to the centre which can then decide how much to pass back to local managers.

This is certainly possible but is it desirable? In some cases, where decentralisation was thought to be a necessary evil existing solely to permit the processing of information, the official answer might be, 'Yes'. However, in Chapter 5, we noted that there were other advantages of decentralisation. For example, it may be better for business decisions to be made by the people responsible for carrying them out. If this is so the same technology which makes greater centralisation possible can assist decentralisation. Divisional managers can be allowed to have easy access to all the information stored in the headquarters data bank. Many firms now link microcomputers at branches with mainframe computers at head offices to make this possible. Of course, some managers may be reluctant to delegate this amount of responsibility to subordinates, an attitude that may communicate as much about the competence of the superior as of the subordinate.

Rapid review

1 **Outline three effects of the electronic revolution of the 1970s and 80s.**
2 **What is meant by information overload?**

Changing technology and the structure of business

We have just seen once again, as we noted in Chapter 5, that technology and the actual structure of business can be closely related. In the 1960s and 1970s this change in structure came to be associated with ever larger business units. This applied both at the plant level, with economies of scale appearing to lead to ever larger factories and administrative units and also at the company level where larger numbers of plants tended to be controlled within a single firm.

Small firms again

There are signs that this trend is being reversed. In the 1980s, in the UK, the number of plants employing more than 1000 people has been declining, though this may have much to do with the depressed economy at this time. There has also been an increase in the number of small firms that have started up. This, too, is probably due to the depressed state of the economy to some extent. When opportunities for employment are very small more people are tempted into self-employment as a better alternative to doing nothing. On the other hand we may be seeing the start of a trend towards greater decentralisation of business activity with firms finding that a smaller proportion of their needs have to be met by their own 'in-house' operations. A greater proportion can be sub-contracted out to smaller independent firms. Department of Employment statistics show that the greatest area of expansion of employment in recent years has been in 'business and professional services'.

The 'electronic cottage'

Even where activities actually remain within the organisation much greater geographical decentralisation is now possible. For example, with networked computers linked to central data bases there is no longer the need for management or any other decision maker to be physically close to information stores. The manager no longer needs to have all the files in a cupboard next door!

It has even been suggested that the need for large office complexes may soon pass. In theory, there is no reason why a great deal of today's office work could not equally well be carried out from home with people linked by telecommunications to one another and to computerised data stores. Such an arrangement would save real costs for the firm in terms of expensive office space, and for the worker in terms of travelling time.

However, such a change would not be without difficulties and drawbacks. It would require a mental revolution for many people to be able to work efficiently without the discipline of physically 'going to work'. Homes may not always be the most efficient places to work from, given the number of distractions and other demands upon workers' time they often present. You may have already discovered that it takes greater willpower to do homework than to work in the classroom – and it often takes longer. Nor should we lose sight of the human, psychological value of bringing people physically together to work in order to encourage teamwork and commitment which it may be more difficult to feel towards colleagues who communicate with each other only through data transmissions on a visual display screen. Some firms claim to have achieved considerable benefits from the encouragement of a more personal contact, e.g. by using telephones, and thereby tapping greater commitment towards the objectives of the business.

At the same time we should remember that the factory arose from the need to bring workers to a central place of work where they could be supervised and their products standardised and where they could use machines driven from a central source of power (originally a water wheel or a steam engine). Pre-factory manufacturing was based on 'outwork' carried out in people's own homes, using materials supplied by the manufacturer/wholesaler and producing goods which that same manufacturer undertook to market. This then was a system of centralised marketing, organisation and purchasing but with actual production decentralised throughout many separate independent units. One of the newest of modern industries, the production of computer software, is organised on very much the same lines. The programmer, working at home, produces software packages to specifications prepared by the central marketing organisation with materials supplied by that organisation.

Is it possible that we shall see at least a partial return to the pre-factory system of production? If this change is taking place the consequences for society, for family life and for the structure of communities will be immense. Truly there will have been an electronic revolution as momentous as the industrial revolution of the eighteenth and nineteenth centuries.

Rapid review

1   Suggest two reasons why the number of small firms has increased in the United Kingdom in the 1980s.
2   Give one advantage and one disadvantage of working from home instead of 'going to work'. Why is it now possible for an increasing number of people to work from home?

Exercises

1   You are a major supplier of goods used in the house building industry. Trends seem to indicate that housing costs are absorbing a greater proportion of people's income as the years go on. What account would you take of this in your long-term planning?
2   A campaign is started concerning the possible effects of artificial additives in foods. What is your response as a manufacturer of processed food?
3   As a solicitor, more than half your business is made up of house conveyancing. Government legislation has been passed to allow non-solicitors to undertake this work. How do you respond?
4   You are office manager of a traditionally run service engineering firm repairing domestic appliances. The firm employs three office staff and eight engineers. A computer salesman is trying to persuade you to invest in an office computer system. 'Everybody's getting them,' he says. What considerations will you bear in mind in deciding whether to buy? What further information would you seek?
5   You have just paid a considerable amount of money for the franchise to distribute an American toy called *Poltergeist People* in your country. You read in the press that the toy has been attacked in the USA by a fundamentalist religious sect. A colleague who has just returned from America tells you that its popularity has been swamped by a similar toy called *Fairy Folk* which is a tie-in to a film which is to be released in your country next year. What do you do?

Questions from examination papers

Short answer questions

1   Give *four* elements normally contained in a company's annual report. AEB 0(A) 1982
2   Outline *three* problems that might be encountered by a firm which decides to install a computer. AEB 0(A) 1983
3   Distinguish between capital expenditure and revenue expenditure, giving *one* example of each. AEB 0(A) 1983
4   Name *two* types of budget (other than departmental budgets) prepared by management accountants. AEB 0(A) 1984

5 Describe *two* advantages and *two* disadvantages of microfilm as a means of storing information. AEB 0(A) 1985

Essay questions

1 The credit controller of a large company manufacturing pharmaceutical products has noticed that there has been a significant increase in the time taken by many of its wholesale and retail customers to settle their accounts.
   a   Consider the effects this would have on the company if it continued.
   b   How might the problem be overcome (i) by the company itself and (ii) through an outside company? AEB 0(A) 1982
2   a   Why are large companies more likely to experience internal communication problems than smaller firms?
   b   What steps can be taken by the management of large companies to overcome these problems? AEB 0(A) 1984
3 Tom Lewis is considering setting up his own company to manufacture a product which he thinks has a great chance of success.
   a   State and comment upon *three* factors concerning the market which Tom will need to examine.
   b   Assume that Tom decides to go ahead. Explain, with the aid of a diagram, the advantages to be gained from undertaking break-even analysis. AEB 0(A) 1984
4   a   State and explain the stages involved in the recruitment and selection of personnel.
   b   What terms and conditions of employment must an employer communicate to his employees and how must this be done? AEB 0(A) 1984
5 Maxfashions is a small company manufacturing clothes for the teenage market.
   a   Describe *four* internal economies of scale that might be gained by this company if it expanded to increase its output.
   b   Assume that the company succeeded in increasing its size. Discuss *three* problems that it might now face. AEB 0(A) 1985
6 Comment on the view that better communication in business will be the inevitable result of improvements in communications technology. AEB A Level 1985

Role playing

Game 1 (suitable to follow Chapter 2)

Background

Joan and Anne trained together at the same hairdressing salon. They married and started families at around the same time. They kept in touch regularly and as their children grew up they both started to take on a few regular hairdressing customers.

They soon realised that by working together they could safely take on more work as they could arrange that one of them was available to look after the children while the other was working. With careful organisation their circle of customers grew but they needed more equipment and they also decided that they would cope better if they had their own vehicle kept chiefly for visiting customers.

They decide to approach Joan's bank manager to see if they would be able to borrow the additional money they needed.

Players

Joan is the businesswoman. She is keen to organise the business and hopes that it will expand as the children grow older.

Anne is more casual. She is a very good hairdresser but careless over accounts and is content to leave arrangements to Joan although she is a bit suspicious of banks and thinks they like to complicate everything in order to make more money for themselves.

The Bank Manager is under instruction from Head Office to encourage small businesses but is naturally cautious. He or she recognises Joan's business sense and has checked that she has always been a good customer of the bank. The bank is willing to lend the money they need but wants them to establish their business on a more formal basis, at least as a partnership but possibly as a small private company with Joan and Anne as the main shareholders and directors.

Task

The three players meet and discuss the position. The manager explains his willingness to lend the money but also explains the advantages of a more formal arrangement and describes the partnership and limited company. The two women ask questions. They must reach a decision as to what they are to do, the options being (a) to stay as they are, (b) to make a formal partnership agreement or (c) to form a private limited company.

Game 2 (suitable to follow Chapter 6)

Background

Rachel has steadily built up a successful dressmaking business over a number of years. She now rents a small workshop and employs 2 full-time and 6 part-time workers. She makes mostly individual garments, small runs of garments for definite orders. She sells through a range of local, independent shops and also does routine alterations for shops.

One of the shopkeepers is particularly impressed with her work and has had successful sales with one particular line in leisure wear. He believes that there is a wider market for this line.

He has access to money and he would like to start a joint venture with Rachel to go into mass production and distribution.

The players

Rachel is a very good dress designer and is able to obtain good work from her employees. She has never had any experience of large scale business and is very nervous of expanding the operation.

The shopkeeper was trained as a shop manager by one of the large multiples and has always had ambitions of building up his own large company. He is a good salesman and administrator.

Rachel's husband is the marketing manager for an engineering company and has a business studies degree. He is used to the problems of large scale production and distribution and is prepared to support and advise the venture.

Task

The three players meet and discuss the position. Rachel's husband explains the problems the venture is likely to face and the changes that will have to be made if they decide to proceed. They must make a decision whether or not to proceed and prepare a plan of action.

Game 3 (suitable to follow chapter 12)

Background

Stylex Limited is a private limited company engaged in light engineering. It is mostly owned by one family which also provides the senior managers of the company. It has been moderately profitable for many years but recently the 30-year-old son of the Managing Director has been playing a more important part in controlling affairs. He has been attending management courses and is clearly determined to modernise the company and make it more profitable. His most recent move has been to carry out a study of purchasing, stock control and office systems in the company and there are rumours that he intends to introduce computer systems that will destroy the jobs of three-quarters of the present clerical staff of sixteen.

Five of the staff, who previously worked in larger firms, are members of the Transport and General Workers Union and one of the purchasing clerks is generally recognised as the shop steward. She is now actively seeking to pursuade the others to join the union and has asked the full-time district officer to help.

Management has asked for the help of a consultant recommended by a large computer firm to help in persuading the employees to accept what it sees as inevitable and desirable changes.

Players

Bob is the Managing Director's son. He has a business studies degree and has attended short courses at the London Graduate Business School. He would have liked to have pursued a career in a large multinational company where in fact he had trained for some years as a company accountant but he had been persuaded to join the company by his parents. He is determined that it will become a large, modern, profitable company and is anxious to exert his authority and show his managerial ability.

Betty is the shop steward. She left school with just a few C.S.E.s and married young. Divorced two years ago she needs a job to keep herself and her seven-year-old daughter. She now regrets not having gained more qualifications and is beginning to realise that she has more intelligence and ability than had been recognised at school. She is enjoying her new union role and taking a real interest in it. Arguing with work mates and managers is giving her new confidence in herself.

Sarah is a computer systems consultant. Trained by one of the giant computer firms she now works for a growing firm of management consultants and believes strongly in the need to modernise office systems.

She has worked in the USA and cannot see any future for firms which refuse to modernise. On the other hand she believes that there is a bright future for small, dynamic firms which are prepared to use modern technology to the fullest possible extent. She has advised other firms in similar situations and sees no great problem in convincing this group of workers that change is necessary and desirable even if some have to lose their jobs. She has little sympathy for workers who are not prepared to accept new technology though she understands their fears.

Bob's father, the Managing Director, does not understand new technology. His main interest is in growing and showing roses. He has, however, always got on well with his workers and has been a popular boss. When younger he had been a good salesman and still has the loyalty of many of his long standing customers. He is anxious to retire to his roses but is afraid that his son may be too impatient and too demanding from the workers. He feels he should remain in charge until he is confident that his son really can run the company successfully.

Mr Denvers (no one seems to know his first name and would not dream of using it if they did) is the Purchasing and Office Manager. He is approaching retiring age and has been with the company since he left school. He has no paper qualifications but has an intimate knowledge of the product, the customers and the suppliers. He is anxious to retire before the arrival of computers but has a strong feeling of loyalty to Bob's father.

Task

The Managing Director has called a meeting. Present are himself, Bob, Sarah, Betty and Mr Denvers. They must reach a decision on how the new computer systems are to be introduced. The Managing Director wants the change to take place with the co-operation of the employees and without breaking the company's record of never having had a strike throughout its history. Betty wants to save as many jobs as possible and is prepared to go to considerable lengths to prove herself as a good trade unionist.

Game 4

Background

Whizkids Limited is a small private company employing around 100 workers of whom about 65 are machine operators in the production workshops where machine parts are manufactured for sale as components for the motor and aircraft industries.

Productivity per worker has been at a constant level for several years and is average for British standards but around 20 per cent lower than the levels believed to be achieved in West Germany and 30 per cent lower than those claimed in Japan.

The works trade union convener has lodged a wage claim in line with similar claims currently being negotiated within the framework of the Engineering Employers' Confederation.

The General Manager has proposed that the wages structure of all non-office manual workers be reorganised on the basis of a low minimum wage plus piece rates based on weekly production and a profit sharing scheme. He calculates that average earnings of skilled workers would rise by double the amount of the recent wage claim and that the cost would be more than covered by a substantial rise in productivity.

The players

The General Manager, Steve Rocket, is aged 31. Educated at the London School of Economics and the London Graduate Business School he has worked for several large multinational companies, most recently as assistant production manager for the British subsidiary of a large American multinational. He has been critical of the efficiency standards of Whizkids but gets on well with the Managing Director. He is ambitious to make the firm grow profitably – and to grow with it.

Bob Staple, aged 35, is the Personnel Manager and the son-in-law of the Managing Director. He feels his position is threatened by Steve's arrival. He has spent most of his working life at Whizkids. He dislikes payments by results schemes and believes they cause more trouble than benefits. He is a believer in the human relations approach to management.

Mr Whiz, the Managing Director, is aged 62 but has no intention of giving up control of the company which he founded and built up. He knows that he no longer has the technical and managerial knowledge to keep the company ahead of its competitors but hopes that these will be provided by Steve. He also hopes that Bob will provide a steadying influence.

Alan Bore, the works convener, is a skilled engineer aged 48. He has been secretary of the local branch of the engineering union for many years and is a local councillor and magistrate. He is active in the local Labour Party. He believes in a 'fair day's pay for a fair day's work' and also believes it is the 'boss's job to manage provided he respects the rights of the workers to be treated as dignified human beings'.

Peter Tiger is the union shop steward representing the unskilled workers who are members of one of the large general unions. He is aged 21 and has been with the company for two years. No one can fault his work and he has been largely responsible for organising and recruiting the unskilled workers for his union. He is also active in local politics and his ideas are well to the left of Alan's. He and Alan do not get on and he has been critical of Alan, accusing him on some occasions of having 'sold out to the bosses'.

Task

Meet and try to resolve the current wage negotiations seeking to achieve a settlement that is acceptable to management and the workers.

Comprehension exercises

(*Taken from examination papers*)

Question 1 AEB 0(A) 1982

Read the following extract and answer the questions which follow it.

ICE CREAM MEN PRAY FOR SUN
(Adapted from *Marketing* August 27, 1980)

Britain's ice cream men are furious about the weather. This is their fourth abysmal summer in a row and, however hard they try to 'deweatherise' the business, at the end of the day it is sunshine that makes the difference between good and bad sales performance.

Having resigned themselves to accepting this rather basic problem, the ice cream marketers have turned their attention to the challenge of making ice cream an all year round product. Helped by the massive growth in freezer ownership and the innovation of hand-held products such as 'Cornetto' and 'King Cone', this has proved highly successful. The price is a market worth £350 m this year, against £300 m in 1979. And a real dogfight is developing in the industry as the pace of change in the market place accelerates.

Walls, which reckons it has 39 per cent of the market against Lyons Maid's 31 per cent, is backing its hunches with an advertising budget of £2 m this year. Half of this will be put behind the 'Cornetto' brand and the 'Just one Cornetto' television campaign. Eric Walsh, general marketing manager at Walls, explained why the spend is three times more than that anticipated by their nearest rival, Lyons Maid.

'We are part of Unilever,' he says, 'and Unilever was built on good brands and putting in consumer investment over a period of time. This part of Unilever's philosophy has certainly rubbed off on us. We also have for the first time in many years, a new brand, 'Cornetto', which is very special. And when we see a campaign working we chase it with a lot of money. Lyons Maid is conservatively putting a £350 000 spend behind its 'King Cone' brand this year a similar hand-held product to the 'Cornetto'.'

A key development in the ice cream market was the decision in 1979 to increase VAT on ice cream sales to 15 per cent, a decision considered unfair because competitor products deemed to be 'food' escaped the new tax. 'It is also a difficult year because of the consumer recession,' argues Lyons Maid's marketing manager, David Brown. At the same time the industry is coming to terms with a massive change in the pattern of retailing in the UK. The emergence of freezer centres has been a great boon to ice cream manufacturers. 'Freezer owners buy twice as much ice cream as non freezer owners,' says Brown, who has repackaged the whole range of Lyons Maid dessert ice creams.

a What is meant by the phrases:
 i 'We are part of Unilever'
 ii advertising budget
 iii consumer recession
 iv increase VAT
b Why have Walls increased their advertising budget in 1980?
c From the information contained in the article, construct a pie chart to show the various shares of the ice cream manufacturers
d Explain how the increase in VAT to 15 per cent affects the purchasing decisions of ice cream customers.
e How could the Government prevent a merger between Walls and Lyons Maid, and why might it wish to do so?
f Give *two* examples of how repackaging can be used to increase sales of dessert ice cream to freezer owners.
g Name *two* economies of scale which it is evident that Walls possesses.

Question 2 AEB 0(A) 1982

Selmor is a firm which manufactures a single product. To expand its sales it engaged four new salesmen at the beginning of 1983. The quantities sold by each during the last six months are as follows:

	1983			1984		
Salesman	*December*	*January*	*February*	*March*	*April*	*May*
Adams	102	116	121	118	120	119
Blake	68	88	92	105	97	102
Collins	30	63	107	127	135	144
Davies	74	82	98	128	120	116

a Prepare a bar chart to illustrate the total sales for the six month period for each salesman.
b Calculate the average monthly sales of each salesman.
c Market forecasts suggest that the firm will now have to dismiss two of these newly appointed salesmen. Using the information available, write a report advising on the following:
 i which two salesmen should be **retained**;
 ii any legal duties arising in relation to the proposed dismissals.

Question 3 AEB 0(A) 1982

B. Smith opened a village general store on January 31st 1981. Examine the following summary of his Balance Sheets on the dates shown and answer the questions below.

Balance Sheet of B. Smith as at 31 January

Liabilities	1981	1982	Assets	1981	1982
Proprietor's Capital	42 000	42 000	Fixed Assets	50 750	55 900
Add Retained Profit		1 400			
		43 400	*Current Assets*		
Mortgage on Premises	12 000	12 000	Stock	6 000	4 800
Trade Creditors	3 000	6 000	Debtors	—	340
			Bank	200	300
			Cash	50	60
	57 000	61 400		57 000	61 400

a Give *two* examples of fixed assets which you would expect to find in this business.
b State whether it is possible to tell from the above figures the value of Smith's gross profit for the year ended January 31st 1982. Give a reason for your answer.
c Distinguish between long-term liabilities and current liabilities giving *one* example of each from the above balance sheet.
d Explain the term 'proprietor's capital' and state its amount after the first year of trading.
e During the year the total net profit was £2100
 i Calculate profit as a percentage return on the owner's initial capital invested.
 ii Calculate the current or working capital ratio at January 31st 1982.
f *i* Give *three* observations that an accountant might make when studying the return on capital invested and the working capital ratio of this firm.
ii What financial advice might be offered to B. Smith for the future of the business?

Question 4 AEB 0(A) 1983

Read the following extract and answer the questions which follow it.

Big Business backs the Tiny Computer
by Richard Brooks

The living-room invasion goes on. After a runaway success with video, the High Street shops have decided that the home computer is the latest piece of electronic gadgetry that's ripe to be plugged into the nation's tellies.

Until recently the microcomputer market has been confined to specialist shops, where buffs and the occasional small businessman pottered amongst the bits and bytes. But Sinclair's ZX81 changed all that by selling 120 000 in six months through mail order, and now the stores have decided that every home should have one.

W.H. Smith was first in last month with the ZX81, and has sold 10 000 in five weeks. Curry's, Rumbelows and Boots are set to follow. The BBC is launching a computer literacy series in January, and is marketing its own mini-computer to accompany it.

Most people now buying home computers say the main reason is to learn about computers and programming. Playing games takes second place, with use for work or home accounts a poor third. W.H. Smith's say most customers are men around 40 or young teenage boys. One microcomputer magazine estimated that the average age of microcomputer programmers is only 14.

Price and simplicity seem to have been the main factors behind the breakthrough to a wider market. Texas Instruments tried and failed to sell its 99/4 at more than £600 last year, and the feeling seems to be that computers must sell at below £350 to sit happily alongside other consumer electronic goods.

The ZX81 sells at £69.95, and requires no previous knowledge of computers. Its forerunner, the ZX80, retailed at £99.95 and led the way to the current drive on the High Streets.

Rumbelows is to sell the Commodore VIC, an American-owned product built in West Germany, for £190;

Boots is to sell the Texas Instruments 99/4 at a slimmed-down price of £299, and Rumbelows may also take this model;

Currys is to sell the Atari 400 at £345.

Rymans will also sell the 400, and the Tandy TRS 80, already sold in Tandy's own 200 shops.

The BBC is to sell its microcomputer at £235, and hopes to sell 60 000 in the first year. It will be made by Acorn, the Cambridge firm, who say that they could easily double production if the BBC has underestimated the public appetite for the computer age.

(Adapted from the *Sunday Times* 11 October 1981)

a   Assume that Sinclair and W.H. Smith continued selling the ZX81 microprocessor at the same rate throughout 1982. Assume also that the BBC achieved its expected sales target and that sales of all other microprocessors during 1982 were 20 000 per month.

Construct a bar chart to illustrate the total sales for 1982 of:

 i   the ZX81;

 ii   the BBC's Acorn;

 iii   all other microprocessors.

b   What is meant by 'breakthrough to a wider market'?

c   Outline *three* market considerations faced by any firm entering the micro-computer market.

d   As an organisation, in what way is the BBC significantly different from the other enterprises in the microcomputer market?

e   What major advantages does the BBC possess in marketing its own micro-computer?

f   Give *two* advantages and *two* disadvantages of mail order as a method of selling a microcomputer.

g   Why is it unlikely that the home computers mentioned in the article would be of much use to a large business?

Question 5 AEB 0(A) 1983

In 1982 Ray Wilson was made redundant. He invested his redundancy payment and his life savings in a village general store which he manages himself. After he had been in business for one year he prepared the following brief summary of his trading:

Trading and Profit and Loss Account of R. Wilson for the year ended 31 May 1983.

	£	£
Sales	65 000	
Less cost of goods sold	46 500	18 500
Assistant's wages	2 350	
Rent and rates	1 750	
Lighting and heating	350	
Insurance	175	
Total expenses		4 625
Net profit		13 875

a State Wilson's gross profit for his first year of business.

b From the above information calculate *two* percentages which would help Wilson to assess how successful he has been.

c Wilson would like to know whether his decision to invest in his own business had proved to be financially advantageous.

In order to answer this question, indicate

i what additional financial information, relating to the business, would be needed;

ii how this information could be used.

d A customer, V. Sharp, has noticed how the number of people using Wilson's shop has increased steadily during the year. He has seen the Trading and Profit and Loss Account and is thinking of asking Wilson whether he would sell the shop.

i What additional information would Sharp require before deciding how much the business was worth?

ii In which financial statement would this information be found?

e Wilson is not interested in selling his business and intends to increase his sales next year.

i Describe briefly *two* ways in which this might be achieved.

ii Assuming that sales increase by 30 per cent, that gross profit is one-quarter of the new sales figure and that total expenses increase by 20 per cent, calculate Wilson's expected net profit for the year to 31 May 1984.

iii What name is given to the kind of statement in which planned or expected profits are calculated?

Question 6 AEB 0(A) 1983

Botts Lake and Vean plc is a medium sized company which quarries gravel. During the last twelve years Tom Richards, the Personnel Manager, has seen his workload increase greatly. The Board has agreed that a Personnel Officer should be appointed to assist him.

a Draft an advertisement for this position suitable for inclusion in a national newspaper. The advertisement should indicate some examples of the type of work involved, the skills and qualities required as well as the general terms of employment.

You are expected to invent suitable relevant details.

b Outline *two* likely reasons why Tom's workload has increased so much.

Question 7 AEB 0(A) 1984

Read the following information and answer the questions which follow.

Early in 1982 Teignbridge councillors noticed the attention given by the media to the privatisation of refuse collection in Southend. They set up a working party to investigate the possibility of using private contractors in Teignbridge. The working party produced a report which contained the following information: 'Since 1974, the refuse collecting service in Teignbridge has been streamlined. The labour force has been gradually reduced from 71 to 43. At the same time the number of properties to deal with increased by around 2000. Comparative figures for 1981–1982 show that it cost Teignbridge £17.24 per tonne of refuse collected to Southend's £20.60. Southend has a higher population – 154 600 compared to Teignbridge's 95 400. Southend covers an area of 4161 hectares compared to Teignbridge's 67 610.'

Adapted from a report in *The Mid-Devon Advertiser* 2 April 1982

a Define 'privatisation' and explain why it is an issue which arouses considerable debate.

b Define 'productivity' and comment on the success or otherwise of Teignbridge refuse collectors since 1974.

c i Teignbridge council wishes to compare its refuse collection services with those of Southend. Draft a suitable table.

ii Calculate the population density of Southend and Teignbridge and comment on the significance of this calculation to a comparison of refuse collection in the two areas.

d On the basis of the evidence given in the report, would you recommend that Teignbridge council privatise their refuse service or not? Support your recommendation with comments on the productivity of the two areas mentioned.

e In which *two* major ways might a decisison to 'go private' affect Teignbridge businessmen?

Question 8 AEB 0(A) 1984

Read the following extract and answer the questions which follow.

Government will seek way to curb imports
by Robin Pauley

The Government is to consider ways of stemming the rising flood of imports of a wide range of products, particularly consumer goods from the Far East and cars from Spain.

A paper detailing selected items and countries of major concern has been prepared for Tuesday's Cabinet Economic (E) Committee, chaired by the Prime Minister.

It sets out action taken in the past and tries to explain why this has failed.

Proposals for controlling selected imports are put forward, though Ministers are understood to be anxious to avoid if possible overt tariffs and quotas because of the damage this would do to their reputation as defenders of free trade and market forces.

Measures involving 'voluntary restraint' could be one solution.

The Government has no intention of failing to observe existing General Agreement on Tariffs and Trade and Treaty of Rome agreements.

Recent evidence of a consumer led recovery through sharply rising volumes of retail sales has not been matched by rising orders for UK industry. Ministers are increasingly concerned that all the extra spending is going on imports.

Countries and regions which supply large amounts of consumer goods to Britain while operating very restrictive controls against British goods include Spain, South Korea, Japan, Brazil, and Eastern Europe.

Australia has also been a problem for UK exporters with both tariffs and quotas though there is no suggestion of retaliatory action. Canada has quotas of UK footwear and Brazil severe tariffs on the same items. Both are severe enough to exclude British footwear almost totally from both countries.

Cabinet Ministers are known to feel that Britain has been 'playing by the rules' while many other countries have not.

Frustration is heightened by the lack of success of attempts through political and diplomatic channels to persuade some countries, particularly Spain, to move more toward 'equitable access'.

Further evidence to reinforce Ministers' fears about imports is expected next week from the Confederation of British Industry's quarterly industrial trends survey, expected to show manufacturing activity remaining stagnant.

Its publication has been delayed while 40 major retailers are contacted to check the source of their improved sales.

Adapted from *The Financial Times* 23 October 1982

a In the context of the article, define the following terms. Make up an example of each one to illustrate your definition.
  i tariffs
  ii quotas
  iii 'voluntary restraint'
  iv retaliatory action
  v 'equitable access'
b Outline *two* separate reasons why the article suggests that the United Kingdom Government was considering the introduction of tariffs and quotas.
c Explain why 'overt tariffs and quotas' might endanger the United Kingdom Government's 'reputation as defenders of free trade and market forces'.
d Why would the United Kingdom Government have to take the Treaty of Rome into account before making a decision on import controls?
e Assume that the United Kingdom Government decided to introduce import

controls. State, with reasons, whether you would expect each of the following organisations to react favourably or unfavourably to such a decision.

  i a United Kingdom based car producer;
 ii the Trades Union Congress;
iii the Consumers' Association.

Question 9 AEB 0(A) 1985

Judy Daw owns and manages the Busy Bee Restaurant which operates an all-inclusive set price menu. At the start of 1984 she had the premises improved and extended at a cost of £50 000. Her aim was to increase trade and improve the profitability of the business. The following statement summarises the performance of the business before and after investing the £50 000.

Busy Bee Restaurant, Year ended 31 December

	1983		1984	
Number of meals served	25 000		50 000	
	£	£	£	£
Sales revenue		100 000		150 000
less: variable costs	35 000		75 000	
fixed costs	45 000		52 000	
		80 000		127 500
Net profit		20 000		22 500

a Draw separate pie charts for 1983 and for 1984, splitting the sales revenue into variable costs, fixed costs and net profit.
b *i* Define the term 'variable costs' and name *two* examples relevant to the above business.
ii Define the term 'fixed costs' and name *two* examples relevant to the above business.
c From the information given, explain how Judy has been able to double the number of meals sold.
d Using the above figures and any further calculations you find useful, comment on the profitability of the enterprise.

Question 10 AEB 0(A) 1985

Read the following extract and answer the questions which follow it.

The Unlisted Securities Market
In just over a month the Unlisted Securities Market will be celebrating its third birthday. Its proud parents, the Stock Exchange and the Wilson Inquiry into the City in the late seventies, have produced a robust and active toddler.

During its short life the USM has created more than a score of 'paper' millionaires overnight. Many investors have made small fortunes by investing in USM stocks, but some have had their fingers badly burned.

The idea behind the USM was to create an entirely new market in the shares of young, expanding companies which were either too new, too small or too speculative to comply with the tough standards laid down for a shares listing on the official Stock Exchange. So in essence a 'secondary' market was formed.

Before the USM came into existence, companies wanting a stock market quotation had to have minimum profits record of five years. Thus only the more established firms could obtain entry. For the USM, companies need not be more than three years old. This means that younger, smaller and more entrepreneural firms have a chance to raise money by offering some of their shares to the public. The USM provides a cheaper route for companies to trade their shares. It can cost anything up to £250 000 in brokers' and other professional fees for a firm to obtain a full listing on the Stock Exchange, but the expenses involved in a USM quotation are substantially lower – anything from £50 000 to £100 000.

One company that has benefited is the Strikes chain of hamburger restaurants. The business was built up from 1967 onwards with a number of Wimpy Bar franchises. Now it runs its own restaurants making around £2m profit each year. The company was floated on the Unlisted Securities Market in April this year with its parent company Comfort Hotels still retaining 90 per cent of the shares. The 600 000 shares originally offered at 43p each have since risen to a high of 75p.

The most celebrated debut on the Unlisted Securities Market has undoubtedly been that of Pineapple Dance Studios, whose Chairman and Managing Director is the former model Debbie Moore. She launched her company on the stock market last autumn by appearing in person on the Exchange 'floor', causing a near-sensation among the male stockbroking community. Both Moore and her husband, who is Finance Director, are now in the millionaire category. The 800 000 shares, originally offered at 52p each, have since reached a high of 153p. Recently, however, they fell to 115p.

(Adapted from *The Sunday Telegraph* 9 October 1983)

a What is meant by the following terms in the context of the article?
 i 'paper millionaires'
 ii speculative
 iii quotation
 iv more entrepreneural firms
 v parent company
b Give *two* advantages to a new company of a USM quotation compared with a full Stock Exchange quotation.
c The article states that 'Many investors have made small fortunes by investing in USM stocks, but some have had their fingers badly burned.'
 i Explain how this could happen, using an example from the article.
 ii Explain why this is perhaps more likely to happen with stocks quoted on the USM than with other stocks.
d *i* Define the term 'franchises'.
 ii State *two* advantages and *two* disadvantages, to someone setting up in business, of acquiring a franchise.
e Outline *two* likely uses for the finance that would be raised by a share issue.

Index

accounting ratios, 283–4
advertising, 79, 80, 101–3, 109, 110, 120–1
  media, 102–3
Advertising Standards Authority, 127
agents, 108
  buying, 111
annual percentage rate (APR), 123–4, 125,
  152
arithmetic mean, 266
articles of association, 24
assets, 281
  current, 242, 244, 245, 283, 284
  fixed, 242–5, 283
  tangible, 242–4
assisted areas, 59–60
attitudes and incentives, 225–7
average cost(s), 172–3, 176–7
  of stock (AVCO), 141–3
averages, 266–8, 279

balance of payments
  and business, 55
  difficulties, 55
  sheet, 283
bank(s), 158–9
  finance, 149, 150–1
  merchant, 159
Bank of England, 39, 55, 58
bar chart(s), 274–5, 279–81
batch production, 85
bills of exchange, 149, 165
body corporate, 22–3, 28
borrowed funds, 157
borrowings, 245
break even, 181
  analysis, 169
  point, 170
British,
  Overseas Trade Board (BOTB), 111
  Standards Institution (BSI), 118, 127
budget(s), 80, 180–2
budgeted accounts, 180–2

building societies, 38–9
bulk (breaking), 107
bureaucracy, 91–2
business,
  behaviour (constraints on), 68–9
  decisions, 9–13
  expansion scheme, 8
  firm and the consumer, 128
  functions, 73–82
  in the world economy, 63–5
  objectives, 9–10
  organisation of, 6–9
  organisations, 87–93
  social attitudes to, 68–71
  structure and changing technology,
    313–15

cancellable credit agreements, 124–5
capital, 11
  business, 155
  forms of, 155–8
  long-term and permanent, 153–8
  market, 158–64
    institutions of, 162
  need for, 153
  sources of, 155
  working, 245, 283
Carlill *v* Carbolic Smoke Ball Co 1893, 121
cash, 283
  at bank, 245
  discount, 150
  flow, 80, 82
  discounted, 154
centralisation (functional), 88
  and decentralisation (purchasing), 138–9
certificate of incorporation, 24
chambers of commerce, 209–10
change(s)
  certainty of, 304–5
  in education, 310–11
  in methods of production, 307–9
  in social attitudes, 309–10

change(s) *contd*
  market, 305–7
  strategies for, 305
  types of, 305–10
commercial bills, 165
Commission for Racial Equality, 186
Common Agricultural Policy (CAP), 61
communication(s), 237–64
  barriers to, 261–3
  electronic, 257
  formal and informal, 239
  in practice, 239–54
  need for, 237
  methods of, 254–7
  paper, 261
  threats from, 263
Companies Acts, 24, 25, 30
  Registry, 30
company(ies), 22–3
  accounts, 242–5
  and the public, 252
  associated, 31
  growth of, 31–3
  in practice, 27–31
  legal framework of, 22–7
  limitations of, 29–30
  limited by guarantee, 27
  limited by shares, 27
  limited liability, 22–33
  loans, 157
  setting up, 24
  subsidiary, 31
  types of, 24–7
  unlimited, 27
Competition Act 1980, 126, 127
computer systems
  and purchasing, 143–5
  business records, 297–301
Confederation of British Industry (CBI),
    208–9
conglomerate (merger), 32
consumer credit, 123–5
  law, principles of, 123–5
Consumer Credit Act, 120, 123, 124, 125,
    126
consumer protection, 114–128
  and the courts, 121–2
  institutions of, 126–8
  laws, 115–22, 128–30
  need for, 114–15
Consumer Protection Act 1961, 119
Consumer Safety Act, 119

consumerism, 309
Consumers' Association, 127
continuous process production, 85
Contracts of Employment Act, 185
control(s),
  and management, 231–3
  direct, 55–9
  on prices and incomes, 61
  on trade and exchange, 65
  problem of, 227–8
cooling-off period, 125
Co-operative Development Agency, 40
Co-operative Movement, 35–8
co-operative societies, 35–8
Co-operative Union, 36
  Wholesale Society, 35, 36, 37
co-ordinating activities (of management),
    82–3
corporate management, 87–8
cost(s), 11–12, 168–82
  and price
  average, 172–3
  control, 134–5
  direct, 170–1
  estimating, 179
  falling and rising, 174–5
  fixed, 168–9
  long-run, 169, 176–7
  marginal, 172–3, 175–7
  of credit, 180
  opportunity, 179–80
  overhead, 170–1
  relative, 11
  short-run, 169
  standard, 80, 171–2
  types of, 168–74
  variable, 168–9, 170
covariance, 289
credit
  card, 58
  control, 180
  sale, 149, 150
  trade, 149–50
creditors, trade and other, 245
currency values, changes in, 64–5, 136–7

Data Protection Act, 263
debentures, 155, 157
  unsecured, 157
debtors, 244
decentralisation, 88
decision support system, 312

delegating, 233
demand, reduction in total, 63
de-merger(s), 32
Department(s)
  of Education, 48
  of Trade and Industry, 47, 56, 209
depreciation, 169
design, 76–7
development areas, 59, 60
diminishing returns, 169
direct
  controls, 55–7
  sales, 105, 110
Director General of Fair Trading, 123, 127
director(s), 231–3
  board of, 231
  executive, 231
  non-executive, 231
  managing, 231
discount, cash, 180
  rate, 155
discounted cash flow, 154
diseconomies of scale, 175
  managerial, 175
dismissal, 188–9
dispersion, 269
distortion and bias (in communication),
  262–3
distribution, 79, 80, 105
  channels of, 105–9
  curve, 267–8
division of labour, 4–6
documentary credits, 165
Donoghue v Stevenson 1932, 121

economic growth, failure to achieve, 54
economies of scale, 7, 84, 175
  external, 175
  internal, 175
economy, mixed, 10
  problems of, 53–5
efficiency and objectives, 233–4
electronic
  communication, 257
  cottage, 313–4
  office, 257, 260
  publishing, 301–2
  revolution, 310–11
  shopping, 302–3
employees, and consumer law, 129–30
Employment Acts 1980 and 1982, 207
  Appeal Tribunal, 189–90

employment contract, 184–90
enterprise, 13
  zones, 59
Equal
  Opportunities Commission, 186
  Pay Act 1970, 187
European
  Community(ies), 39, 61, 66–8, 119, 126,
    187
  Regional Development Fund, 59
exhibitions, 103
expenditure, 282
export
  agents, 111
  associations, 111
  merchants, 111
Export Credits Guarantee Department
  (ECGD), 60, 112, 164, 166
exporters, government assistance for,
  111–12
exporting, 109–12
  problems in, 110

face to face meetings, 255
factoring, 149, 165
factors of production, 11–13, 169
  note on, 13
Fair Trading Act 1973, 126
filtering (in communications), 262
finance, 80–2, 107
  bank, 149
  need for, 148–9
  of overseas trade, 164–6
  sources of short-term, 149–53
  to obtain equipment, 151–3
firms, small, 5, 313
first in first out (FIFO), 141–3
forecasting, 6
forfaiting, 149, 165–6
forward (trading), 106, 136
franchising, 8, 108–9, 110
freeports, 59
frequency distribution, 276–7
functional (business organisation), 88, 89,
    90, 91
  authority, 91
futures, 106, 136

gearing ratio, 284
government(s)
  central, 46–8
  influence on business, 53–60

government(s) *contd*
  policies open to, 55–60
  services, 46–9
graphs, 277–8, 279
growth (of companies), 31–3
  internal, 31

Health and Safety at Work Act 1974,
    187–8, 249
Health and Safety Executives, 188
hedging, 136
hierarchies (management), 93
hire purchase, 149, 151
hiring, 149, 151
histogram(s), 276–7
horizontal, mergers/take-overs, 31–2

import
  duties, 65
  houses, 111
incentives, 58, 59–60, 62
income, 282
Independent Broadcasting Authority, 127
Industrial
  and Commercial Finance Corporation
    (ICFC), 158
  Training Act, 198
  Training Boards, 198
industrial development certificate (IDC),
    56
  tribunals, 186, 188, 189–90
inferior goods, 306
inflation, 54
information
  and management, 239–57
  and new workers, 251–2
  overload, 311–12
in-house journals, 250
insolvency, 29–30
Insolvency Bill, 29
inspection, 78
integration (by merger/take-over), 32
interest, 62, 155
intermediate areas, 59, 60
International Monetary Fund (IMF), 66
investment decision, 154–5
investments
  current, 244
  fixed, 242, 244–5
Investors in Industry plc (3i), 158
invoice discounting, 149, 165–6
issuing house, 159

job
  enlargement, 227
  enrichment, 227
  evaluation, 249
joint worker-management committee(s),
    211–12, 249

kitemark, 118

laboratory conditions (in market
    appraisal), 99
labour, 11
  division of, 4–6
land, 11
laser scanning, 144, 297, 311
last in first out (LIFO), 141–3
lateral merger/take-over, 31, 32
law(s)
  civil, 184
  criminal, 184
  and contract conditions (consumer
    protection), 115–17
lease back, 155, 156–7
leasing, 149, 151, 152–3
legal obligations (of the firm), 228
liability(ies), 282
  current, 245, 283–4
  limited, 19, 20, 22
  unlimited, 18
line (business organisation), 87, 89, 90, 91
linear progression line, 288–90
limited liability, 20, 22, 27–9, 30
  companies, 23–33
  partnerships, 19, 20, 22
Limited Partnerships Act 1907, 20, 22
local authorities, 48–9
location
  decision, 12–13
  industrial, 12–13
long-term capital, 153–8
  forms of, 156–8
  sources of, 155
loss, 283

maintenance, 78
management
  and shareholders, 241
  by objectives, 241
  corporate, 87–8
  of people, 210–14
  principles, 92–3
  span of, 92–3

styles of, 212–13
work of, 6–7
managing people, 225–8
market(s), 1, 2
  analysing, 104
  appraisal, methods of, 97–8
  assessing, 95–101
  organised, 105–7
  orientation, 79
  research, 79, 80, 95–104
  serving foreign, 110
  testing, 98–9
Market
  Third, 163
  Unlisted Securities (USM), 159, 162, 163, 164
marketing and sales, 78, 107
  mix, 109–10
mass production, 84
materials management, 139
matrix organisation, 89, 90
median, 266–7
memorandum of association, 24
merchandising, 103
merchant banks, 159
merchantable quality, 116
merger(s), 31–2
microcomputer(s), 296, 297–301
microfiche, 146
microfilm, 146, 296–7
misleading and deceptive presentation (of data), 278–81
Misrepresentation Act 1967, 121
mode, 267–8
money, 57–9, 62
monopoly(ies), 42
Monopolies and Mergers Commission, 48, 126
moral obligations (of the firm), 229
mortgages, 155, 157

nationalised industries, 10, 11, 40–6, 51
noise (in communication), 262
non-corporate organisations, 16–22

objectives
  and decision making, 234–6
  and efficiency, 233–4
  business, 9–10
  public sector, 10
Office of Fair Trading (OFT), 123, 125, 126, 127, 163, 209
organisation(s), 13

Over-the-Counter Market(s), 162, 163
overdraw, 58
overtrading, 284
overseas trade, 164–6
  finance of, 164–6

packaging (and display), 103, 109, 110
partnership(s), 19–20
  advantages of, 21
  features of, 19–20
  limitations of, 21–22
  in practice, 21
Partnerships Act 1890, 19, 20
pay, 186–7
payment(s) for work, 191–7
  by results, 191–4
  employers' problems, 192–4
  in kind, 196
  restrictions (foreign trade), 65
  stored, 196
  time, 191
  workers' attitudes to, 194
percentages, 271–2, 279
permanent capital, 155, 156
personnel
  of the modern firm, 228–30
  department, 210–11
photocopiers, 146
pie graphs (charts), 273–4, 279–81
piece rates, 191, 193
planning, 6, 234
policy changes, effect on business, 60–2
practical considerations (of the firm), 229–30
pressure groups, 62, 70
Prestel, 302, 303
price, 177–8
Prices Act 1974, 120
pricing, 109, 110
  cost plus, 178
  incremental, 178
primary (activities and production), 3, 5
private
  limited company(ies), 30
  sector, 10, 11
    interdependence with public sector, 49–51
privatisation
  case against, 44–6
  case for, 44
  issue, 43–6
product life cycle, 98

production, 1–4, 75–6
  basis of, 3–4
  batch, 85
  choices in, 10–13
  continuous process, 85
  engineering, 77
  factors of, 11–12
  mass, 84
  systems, 82–7
  and specialisation, 85–7
  unit, 83–4
profit(s), 9, 242, 286–7
  gross, 242, 286–7
  net, 286–7
  operating, 242
  sharing in, 194–5
promoting sales, 101–4
protection (trade), 65
Public Sector Borrowing Requirement
  (PSBR), 44, 45
public
  corporation, 41–3
    objectives of, 42–3
    problems of, 41–2
  limited company(ies), 30
  relations (PR), 104
  sector, interdependence with private
    sector, 49–51
published data (in market research),
  100–1
purchasing, 74, 75
  and modern technology, 143
  and uncertainty, 135
  centralised, 138–9
  decentralised, 138–9
  functions, 132–7
  importance of, 133
  objectives of, 133–5
  organisation and procedures, 137–9

quality and safety (consumer protection),
  188–9
Quasi Autonomous National Government
  Organisations, 48
questionnaires, 99–100
quotas, 65

random sample, 100
range, 269–70
ratio(s), 271–2, 279
recruitment and opportunities at work,
  185–6, 190

record(s), 293–301
  computer systems, 287–301
  film based, 296–7
  need for (business), 293–4
  paper, 295–6
  systems, requirements for, 294–5
redundancy, 188–9
research and development, 76–7
regional
  assistance, 56, 58, 59
  policies, 56
Registrar of Companies, 23, 24, 27
registration (of companies), 23–4
regulated agreement (consumer credit),
  123
Restrictive Practices Court, 163
retained profit, 155, 156
robotics, 86
robots, 86
Rochdale Pioneers, 35
  principles, 36

Sale of Goods Acts, 17, 116
sale(s) activities, 79, 80
  promotion (other forms of), 103, 109, 110
scale of operations, 82–3
scatter diagram, 285
secondary (activities, production), 3, 5
service(s), 3–5, 117
  industries, 83
  provided by borough council, 50
shares, 26, 155, 156–7
  ordinary, 155
  preference, 155
Sex Discrimination Act, 186
shop stewards, 205–6, 212
short-term finance
  need for, 148–9
  sources of, 149–53
small
  claims, 122
  firms, 5, 313
    problems of, 7–8
    survival of, 8
social attitudes
  and business, 68–71
  and business management, 70–1
  and the law, 69–70
software (computer), 297–9
sole proprietors, 16–19
  advantages of, 18
  features of, 17–18

sole proprietors *contd*
  limitations of, 18–19
specialisation, 4–6
  and production systems, 85–7
speculation, 163–4
specialist advisory and service
    departments, 74
sponsorship, 103
staff (organisation), 89–90, 138
standard costs, 80
  deviation, 270–1
statement of directors, 24
statutory declaration, 24
stock(s), 244–5
  control, 139–43
    methods of, 140–1
  valuation of, 141–3
Stock Exchange, 159–64
structure and management of the firm,
    231–3
suggestion schemes, 250
Supply of Goods and Services Act 1982, 17,
    117

take-over(s), 31–3
tariffs, 65
taxation, 57, 58, 153
  direct, 57
  indirect, 57, 62
telephone, 255–6
teleprinter, 256–7, 258
teletext, 301–2
tenders, 135
tertiary (activities, production), 3, 5
theory X and theory y, 213
Third Market (Stock Exchange), 163
trade
  associations, 209
  credit, 149–50
  fairs, 103
  union(s), 201–8
    bargaining, 203–4
    in the workplace, 204–6
    need for, 201

membership, 202, 203
power of, 206–8
structure of, 204
types of, 201–2
Trade Descriptions Acts, 17, 120, 229
  Union Act 1984, 207–8
  and Labour Relations Act 1974, 201
Trades Union Congress, 202–3
trading and profit and loss account, 282–3
training for work, 197–200
transport, 79, 107
trends, calculating, 285–90

undertrading, 284
unemployment, 54
  regional, 54–5
Unfair Contract Terms Act 1971, 116
unit production, 83–4
unity of command, 90–1
Unlisted Securities Market (USM), 159,
    162, 163, 164
utmost goods faith, 128

variables, 277
variance, 270–1
vertical merger/take-over, 31, 32
voluntary chain, 8

Wages Councils, 185, 186, 190
weights and measures, 119–120
Weights and Measures Acts, 119
Which? (magazine), 127
wholesale, 106
wholesalers, 106
wholesaling, 107–8
  functions of, 108
word processors, 145–6
work, need to, 213–14
worker co-operatives, 40
working
  capital, 245, 283
  conditions, 187
workplace representatives, 206–7, 212,
    249